Critical Muslim 17

Extreme

Editor: Ziauddin Sardar

Deputy Editors: Hassan Mahamdallie, Samia Rahman, Shanon Shah

Senior Editors: Aamer Hussein, Ehsan Masood, Ebrahim Moosa

Publisher: Michael Dwyer

Managing Editor (Hurst Publishers): Daisy Leitch

Cover Design: Fatima Jamadar

Associate Editors: Tahir Abbas, Alev Adil, Nazry Bahrawi, Merryl Wyn Davies, Abdulwahhab El-Affendi, Marilyn Hacker, Nader Hashemi, Jeremy Henzell-Thomas, Vinay Lal, Iftikhar Malik, Boyd Tonkin

International Advisory Board: Karen Armstrong, William Dalrymple, Anwar Ibrahim, Robert Irwin, Bruce Lawrence, Ashis Nandy, Ruth Padel, Bhikhu Parekh, Barnaby Rogerson, Malise Ruthven

Critical Muslim is published quarterly by C. Hurst & Co. (Publishers) Ltd. on behalf of and in conjunction with Critical Muslim Ltd. and the Muslim Institute, London.

All correspondence to Muslim Institute, CAN Mezzanine, 49-51 East Road, London N1 6AH, United Kingdom

e-mail for editorial: editorial@criticalmuslim.com

The editors do not necessarily agree with the opinions expressed by the contributors. We reserve the right to make such editorial changes as may be necessary to make submissions to Critical Muslim suitable for publication.

C. Hurst & Co. (Publishers) Ltd., 41 Great Russell Street, London WC1B 3PL

ISBN: 978-1-84904-625-1 ISSN: 2048-8475

To subscribe or place an order by credit/debit card or cheque (pound sterling only) please contact Kathleen May at the Hurst address above or e-mail kathleen@hurstpub.co.uk

Tel: 020 7255 2201

A one year subscription, inclusive of postage (four issues), costs £50 (UK), £65 (Europe) and £75 (rest of the world).

The right of Ziauddin Sardar and the Contributors to be identified as the authors of this publication is asserted by them in accordance with the Copyright, Designs and Patents Act, 1988.

A Cataloguing-in-Publication data record for this book is available from the British Library.

IIT PUBLICATIONS

APOSTASY in ISLAM

A Historical &
Scriptural Analysis

TAHA JABIR ALALWANI

APOSTASY IN ISLAM: A HISTORICAL AND SCRIPTURAL ANALYSIS • Taha J. Alalwani

Pb: ISBN 978-1-56564-363-5 Hb: ISBN 978-1-56564-364-2
• September 2011

The Qur'an and the Sunnah promote freedom of belief. The author shows there is no evidence whatsoever for the death or any penalty in Islam for exiting the Faith.

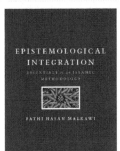

EPISTEMOLOGICAL
INTEGRATION
ESSENTIALS OF AN ISLAMIC METHODOLOGY

FATHI HASAN MALKAWI

EPISTEMOLOGICAL INTEGRATION: ESSENTIALS OF AN ISLAMIC METHODOLOGY
Fathi H. Malkawi

The work makes the case that fundamental to any Muslim recovery is laying the foundations of sound thinking and values that integrate the two main sources of knowledge: Revelation and Reality under the umbrella of Tawhid.

ISBN 978-1-56564-557-8 pb
ISBN 978-1-56564-569-1 hb
2014

Marketing Manager, IIIT (USA)
Tel: 703 471 1133 ext. 108 | Fax: 703 471 3922
E-mail: sales@iiit.org | Website: www.iiit.org

Kube Publishing Ltd, United Kingdom
Tel: 01530 249 230 | Fax: 01530 249 656
E-mail: info@kubepublishing.com | Website: www.kubepublishing.com

HALAL FOOD FOUNDATION

Halal Is Much More Than Food

The Halal Food Foundation (HFF) is a registered charity that aims to make the concept of halal more accessible and mainstream. We want people to know that halal does not just pertain to food – halal is a lifestyle.

The Foundation pursues its goals through downloadable resources, events, social networking, school visits, pursuing and funding scientific research on issues of food and health, and its monthly newsletter. We work for the community and aim at the gradual formation of a consumer association. We aim to educate and inform; and are fast becoming the first port of call on queries about halal issues. We do not talk at people, we listen to them.

If you have any queries, comments, ideas, or would just like to voice your opinion - please get in contact with us.

Halal Food Foundation
109 Fulham Palace Road,
Hammersmith, London, W6 8JA
Charity number: 1139457
Website: www.halalfoodfoundation.co.uk
E-mail: info@halalfoodfoundation.co.uk

 @HFF_UK

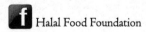 Halal Food Foundation

The Barbary Figs

by

Rashid Boudjedra

Translated by
André Naffis-Sahely

Buy a copy of Rashid Boudjedra's *The Barbary Figs* at
www.hauspublishing.com or by calling +44(0)20 7838 9055
and a recieve a copy of Khaled al-Berry's memoir
Life is More Beautiful than Paradise free.

RASHID AND OMAR are cousins who find themselves side by side on a flight from Algiers to Constantine. During the hour-long journey, the pair will exhume their past, their boyhood in French Algeria during the 1940s and their teenage years fighting in the bush during the revolution. Rashid, the narrator, has always resented Omar, who despite all his worldly successes, has been on the run from the ghosts of his past, ghosts that Rashid has set himself the task of exorcising. Rashid peppers his account with chilling episodes from Algerian history, from the savageries of the French invasion in the 1830s, to the repressive regime that is in place today.

RASHID BOUDJEDRA has routinely been called one of North Africa's leading writers since his debut, *La Répudiation*, was published in 1969, earning the author the first of many fatwas. While he wrote his first six novels in French, Boudjedra switched to Arabic in 1982 and wrote another six novels in the language before returning to French in 1994. *The Barbary Figs* was awarded the Prix du Roman Arabe 2010.

CM17

January–March 2016

CONTENTS

EXTREME

VIIRS 2013-11-07 16:16:31 GMT...

REVIEWS

ET CETERA

CRITICAL MUSLIM

Subscribe to Critical Muslim

Now in its fourth year, *Critical Muslim* is the only publication of its kind, giving voice to the diversity and plurality of Muslim reporting, creative writing, poetry and scholarship.

Subscribe now to receive each issue of Critical Muslim direct to your door and save money on the cover price of each issue.

Subscriptions are available at the following prices, inclusive of postage. Subscribe for two years and save 10%!

	ONE YEAR (4 Issues)	TWO YEARS (8 Issues)
UK	£50	£90
Europe	£65	£117
Rest of World	£75	£135

TO SUBSCRIBE:

CRITICALMUSLIM.HURSTPUBLISHERS.COM

41 GREAT RUSSELL ST, LONDON WC1B 3P
WWW.HURSTPUBLISHERS.COM
WWW.FBOOK.COM/HURSTPUBLISHERS
020 7255 2201

EXTREME

INTRODUCTION
POSTNORMAL BLUES

Ziauddin Sardar and Samia Rahman

Superpowers. Of all the possible superpowers in this best of all possible worlds, which one would you most like to possess? We sought the counsel of a four-year old girl. Without hesitation she replied that she wished she could 'make everything pink'. An extreme desire from a tender, innocent mind. Much like Greek Mythology's King Midas, described by Aristotle as having starved to death after his superpower wish that all he touches should turn to gold is granted, the realisation of extreme fantasy often belies an ugly reality. A world devoid of all colour except pink would rapidly lose its appeal even for little girls yet to shake off cultural norms that seek to shape their colour preferences. Extremism is, after all, in the eye of the beholder. Of course, the prism through which a four-year-old views the world can be rather black and white (or pink!) and in an attempt to negotiate and reconcile themselves to the intricacies of the culture into which they have been born, the behaviour of young children – for example going into melt-down because they don't want to eat their peas – can seem a little extreme. Yet this is their context and no amount of cajoling or consoling can divert from their reality as they perceive it at that particular moment. This is obviously a disposition the British government takes very seriously, promptly enrolling a three-year-old Muslim child from London's Tower Hamlets onto its de-radicalisation programme amid fears the child was vulnerable to extremist influence. British prime minister David Cameron is particularly consumed by the issue, describing the fight against (Islamic) extremism as the 'struggle of our generation', ignoring the multitude of other ills that would benefit from a bit of superhero attention. Government guidance on counter-extremism has suggested that school teachers look out for tell-tale signs of radicalisation, such as expressing disapproval of gay marriage. Considering 128 Conservative MPs voted against the same-sex marriage bill, it would appear the PM needs to look a little closer to home. Hyperbole and hysteria resonate in these contemporary, chaotic and unfathomable times, yet it cannot be denied that in the popular imagination extremism has become synonymous with Islam. Or has Islam become synonymous with the extreme?

Extremism is both: a prized human attribute and the most despised proclivity of human nature. On the one hand, it is the propensity to endure, to strive, to achieve new heights, to go beyond what is thought possible, to break records or new ground or old fears to open new horizons of human possibilities. On the other hand, extremism can manifest itself as the depths of human depravity, the motive force of brutality, sadism, oppression, deliberate barbarism visited on designated dehumanised victims that defies the norms of what we fondly term as humanity. In either case, for good or ill, extremism is us. Extremism is a quintessential human trait. In one form it is applauded, rewarded and envied; its other negative expression occasions horror and incomprehension. And there lies the rub.

It is easy to marvel at and endorse the extreme single-minded determination that characterises the positive uses of human capabilities. History is replete with examples of how athletes, explorers, inventors, entrepreneurs, writers, artists or philosophers have been and are honoured, held up as the finest examples of human potential because they dare to go to extremes. In the extremes of their endeavour such groundbreakers give us intimations of the perfectibility of humankind. And yet we recoil from and seek to disown the innumerable instances history affords where unwavering determination has and does drive individuals and groups to extremes in pursuit of their vision of perfection because it usually embraces a virulent, deliberate violence bent on the eradication of anything or more significantly anyone that fails to conform to or comply with their ideals.

Wonder at the achievements garnered by the extremes of positive genius belonging to all of humankind, they exemplify 'us' at our best. Somehow this ready pride does not equate with the incomprehension we reserve for the destructive potency of evil genius. The positive is human, the negative we would rather term inhuman. We are unwilling to say the evil of such extremism is of us and within us, a common shared human capacity though history argues no age or society is immune. Virulent extremism with all its brutal absolutist horrors always occasions simplistic explanations that sidestep, deny or obscure acceptance of a human component that has anything to do with normality. In short we search for scapegoats – forces over and beyond that make people do inhuman things. The focus is drawn to religion and ideology as forces that make people act as brutes to their fellow human beings; forces that define and divide 'in' groups and 'out' groups and order their relationships and thereby explain what makes bad things happen.

Bad things happened in Paris in January and again in November 2015. The horrific attacks on the satirical magazine *Charlie Hebdo*, and coordinated terrorist attacks throughout the city that killed 130 people, prompted endless discussion on 'Islamic extremism'. It was, with few exceptions, one-dimensional and simplistic; and it reflected the worldview of the extremists themselves. In his book *Understanding Comics*, which is drawn in the form of a comic and features the author as one of the cartoon characters, American cartoonist and comics theorist Scott McCloud argues that the essence of comics is iconic abstraction. He explains how this medium boils everything down to its icon image. The result is that a lamp looks like a lamp and is not ornate or embellished. A jaw is chiselled, colours are bright, and there is no need for detail or delineation. It could be argued that this is how both those who occupy extreme fringes perceive the world and those who are horrified by their actions see the world. Their understanding of everything around them is condensed into iconic abstractions.

Iconic individuals often become the personification of good and evil. Consider, for example, the saintly Aung San Suu Kyi. Here is a democrat standing up to military dictators, a fighter for human rights who has suffered fifteen years of house arrest. For her troubles, she has garnered numerous honours and prizes, including in 1991, the Nobel Prize for Peace. She has even been lionised in a feature film – *The Lady* (2011). This woman can do no wrong. Yet, if she is not advocating she is at least complicit by her active silence in the perpetuation of a stark evil: the brutal oppression of the Rohingya people in Myanmar, whose only crime is that they are in a minority. She does not regard them as citizens of Myanmar despite the fact that they have been living in the Rakhine State of Burma (as it was then known) since the sixteenth century. She refused to say anything when the Rohingya were being burnt alive and driven from their homes by Buddhist fanatics even cautioning journalists not to 'exaggerate' the plight of these wretched people. Her party actively discourages Muslim candidates. Still, the honours and garlands continue.

Suu Kyi is a Theravada Buddhist. It is worth noting how the contemporary West has iconised Buddhism as a superhuman religion of peace and natural harmony. Yet authoritarianism, violence and xenophobia is as evident in Buddhism as any other religion. The Zen Masters carried a samurai sword for good reasons. The founding principles of Taoism require that healing energies necessary to remedy the problems of the world be allowed to balance themselves and not be set off-kilter by human interference. The belief is that it is better to live in unquestioning harmony with the existing natural order, however difficult this may make life. But we are all too aware of what happens when an unquestioning worldview comes face to face with human nature. That's what extremists are made of.

Religion and ideology, however reified as inflexible absolute law that must be operated, enforced and obeyed in purist perfection, nevertheless exist in history only as human interpretations, in the forms and understandings that human minds and natures conceive for them. To blame religion or ideology as the cause of extremism is to exonerate individuals and communities who implement and enact barbaric brutality in the name of God. Religion or ideology is no simple lever. They are not implacable imperatives driving groups or entire populations to unconscionable actions. How religion or ideology come to be used as rationale and justification for extremism and all the horrors people can commit in their name is far from simple and caught in the complex circumstances of time and place.

A superhero is a simple, reduced figure that becomes a symbol. And comics are the ideal medium for linear superhero narratives. Traditionally, comics were never intended to be life-like as this would require such a huge effort of artwork so as to render the task almost impossible. Many artists do not aspire to this anyway as they are more interested in the full extent of aesthetic possibilities available to them within the definitions of the genre they have chosen. From this emerges an interesting parallel between extreme political views and the iconography of comics. They are both abstracts. Comics are iconic abstractions that were never meant to be realistic, and extremists occupy a space that must never be allowed to dominate reality. The dominant narrative surrounding Islam and Muslims is preoccupied with extremes, but surely that is not the entire picture? Ivan Carromero Manzano agrees. In 'Long Way Home' he subverts the comic book genre by using pixel art superimposed on photography in his visual exposition of extremism as more than just polarised ends of a spectrum. He employs the small but growing trend of drawing over photographs, which has become popular as superhero comic fans increasingly favour similitude. His comic strip retains the iconic abstraction that symbolises the simplification of narrative and his characters remain abstract and indistinguishable from each other. Yet, in a deconstruction of the notion of 'othering', by placing the story within a context that invokes realism, Manzano's artwork engages with the complexity of the real.

Extremists eschew complexity and insist on living a life dominated by black and white, minus all the colours of the universe. But complex reality is impossible to ignore. As both John Sweeney and Scott Jordan point out, we are living in a specific period that has been characterised as 'postnormal times'. Our epoch, writes Jordan, is 'characterised by 3Cs: complexity, chaos and contradictions. We live in a world where complexity is the norm, characterised by a plethora of independent parts interacting with each other in a great many ways. Everything is connected to everything else in networks upon networks that generate positive feedback that amplify things in geometric proportions leading to chaos. We thus end up with many positions that are logically inconsistent and contradictory'. In postnormal times, notes Sweeney, 'things we take for granted become uncertain, our understanding of things can become a form of ignorance, and longstanding norms, if not the very idea of normalcy itself, break down before our very eyes'. In a globalised, highly networked, complex, contradictory and chaotic world, where uncertainty and ignorance are the dominant themes, all varieties of extremes take the central stage. Sweeney explores extreme climate change and highlights emerging terms that are being used to describe the interconnected complex phenomenon. 'Anthropocene' is used to emphasise the central role of humanity in shaping the geology and ecology of earth. Anthrobscene marks the 'various violations of environmental and human life in corporate practices and technological culture that are ensuring that there won't be much of humans in the future scene of life.' And technopocene highlights 'a new level of mindfulness on the part of humans for themselves and their technological offspring'. The pendulum swings from one extreme to another: so the solutions proposed for this 'age of extreme weirding', are themselves absurdly extreme. Geoengineering is suggested to change the climate and geology of the entire planet. Biological engineering is proposed so we have shorter, more adaptable and smarter people who can cope with the drastic changes that lie ahead.

Notice how many extremes have now become dominant themes, each containing an inherent contradiction that is not easy to resolve. Refugees, driven from wars in Syria, Iraq and Afghanistan, are risking their lives to get into Europe in unprecedented numbers. In certain countries, such as Hungry and Slovakia, the champions of 'European values' are beating, tear-gassing, and humiliating them. A video that went viral showed a female Hungarian television reporter tripping an old man who was carrying his young son in his arms and kicking a child. India, the 'biggest democracy in the world', is ruled by an extremist party, BJP, enthralled to a segment of society that has fascistic tendencies – the RSS. Half the population of America – mostly Republican supporters – believe that it is their fundamental right to carry guns and the only way to reduce gun crimes and mass killings is to increase the circulation of guns. 'The 80 richest people in the world hold as much wealth as the bottom 3.5 billion, moreover, on current trends by 2016 the top one per cent of the population will hold more than half of the world's wealth', Benedikt Koehler points out. Corruption is not just part of the global system, it is the system itself! As Jerry Ravetz notes, 'corruption is everywhere' driving fantasy and greed, 'fuelled by computers and rationalised by junk mathematics'. Indeed, Ravetz suggests, 'the corruption of some key element of our civilisation could cause its downfall'. Western governments see terrorists everywhere, introduce draconian laws to restrict the freedoms of their own citizens, but then protect, encourage and pay homage to the incubator of extremism – Saudi Arabia. It is a country where ordinary poor Muslim workers are treated with contempt, barbaric inhumanity and exploited at every opportunity, as we discover from Rahul Jayaram's moving story of the Indian labourer, Humsari Hussain.

Only one thing is certain in this world of rampant extremism. 'Postnormal times (PNT) cannot be saved by Superman flying faster than the bullet or by The Matrix's Neo accepting his being the chosen one and defeating the Agents', writes Jordan. 'The hero of postnormal times cannot simply defeat the bad guy or defuse the bomb, for PNT cannot be managed toward resolution. The postnormal hero is a navigator above all. This hero is challenged by the complexity of the world and our multiple selves, he is at the mercy of utter chaos, and subdued by countless contradictions. The postnormal hero is faced with taking our old conceptions, putting them to the test, and demanding that we re-educate ourselves or be doomed to fall at the hands of the true enemy – ourselves'. Which is precisely what happens to the hero of American Sniper. Our hero is Chris Kyle, the late Navy SEAL, who became iconic for killing people, 'the most lethal sniper in American history'. His 'higher calling' is to kill the enemy threatening America; and his exploits make him a legend as 'Americans long to have a symbol to stand behind like Captain America'. But the new enemy Kyle encounters is not easily identified. 'The Communist, The Japanese, The German, all with distinguishable characteristics easily caricatured, now are usurped by a shadow. The enemy is no longer a human who can be diminished through multiple rinses of nationalism and racism. The enemy is a spectre, almost inhuman. Thus, America must also lose its humanity'. This is not an ordinary war – but an extreme one: it is not about 'men against men, good versus evil, it is what remains of the sacred human versus Lucifer himself'. As the enemy is no longer human, 'much like aliens in sci-fi flicks, they are simply beasts and killing them is no big deal. The other soldiers around him echo the themes of American exceptionalism, racism against the people of the Middle East, and an overall blood lust surrounds questions of good and evil, the nature of God, and the sanctity of life. All of this is a haze of white noise surrounding the cold omniscient scope's eye that Kyle becomes'. Both in reality and in the film, Kyle loses his mind; in reality, he 'meets his end at the hands of another twisted mental product of contemporary America'.

The deaths and destruction that western foreign polices have created in the Middle East, Afghanistan and Pakistan, are a product of the 'twisted mental product' that cannot cope with complexity. Indeed, defining 'the enemy' itself becomes a complexity problem. Just who is a 'terrorist' is not easy to pin down, as Gordon Steffey shows in his examination of official documents that attempt to produce a 'Terminology to Define the Terrorists'. Is the enemy 'Islamic' extremism or 'Islamist' extremism, or '*takfiri* death cult', or is it simply 'violent extremism'? How does one discriminate between groups 'claiming' Islam and 'extremist groups' that use Islam for nefarious ends? How Islamic do you have to be – Islamic, very Islamic or very, very Islamic – before you become a security threat to the US of A and Europe? And how do you treat the right-wing indigenous extremists that define all of Islam as evil?

In the haze that surrounds postnormal times, 'our' extremists are not easy to see. Consider *Charlie Hebdo*. Now here is a publication that, by its own admission, practices extreme prejudice. It wallows in its particularly virulent brand of French racism and xenophobia. It goes out of its way to humiliate the powerless. It demeans immigrants. Even the iconic image of a little boy who died crossing the sea was not spared. Women kidnapped by Boko Haram to sell as sex slaves are derided. In *Charlie Hebdo* cartoons Jews have hooked noses, blacks have thick lips and Arabs and Muslims are always ugly, deranged, homicidal maniacs. And yet, in a display of extreme iconic abstraction the world jumped onto the 'Je Suis Charlie' bandwagon. It is one thing to condemn a brutal atrocity; quite another to side with racist extremists in the name of freedom of expression. Heads of state, including Israel's Benjamin Netanyahu (who is keeping the entire nation of Palestine locked up in a cage and does not hesitate to bomb them at every opportunity; and who now alleges that the Mufti of Jerusalem inspired Hitler to commit the Holocaust, thus painting the entire Muslim community as Nazi sympathisers – what could be more hideously extreme than that!), headed a march of solidarity for the victims through the streets of Paris. The *Charlie Hebdo* affair was stripped of any complexity. Hardly anyone looked at just how privileged this magazine is. It is published in a country where the logo of freedom of expression adorns T-shirts but where Muslim women are not free to choose what they wear. It is a country where a quarter of the population supports the extremist National Front Party.

Like much else in postnormal times, satire too is becoming extreme. Or as Samir Younés puts it, it has become mean. 'Meanness can be developed into an art and can become accepted as an art by artists who gratify their adulating public with their personal opinions. Meanness becomes a form of entertainment that operates on the principle of the emotional elimination of the other. An increase in artistic meanness is also accompanied with an increase in the demand for such meanness. The more humour is allied with insolence, irreverence, irony, cynicism, sarcasm, mockery, sadism, and above all, iconoclasm, the more of it is needed. Intellectual meanness reaches particular effectiveness once the visual and verbal arts combine as they do in paintings and their titles, in caricatures and their captions, and especially in the ever-present empire of television'. The economy of the media, particularly 24-hour television channels, perpetuate and multiply stereotypes at accelerating pace. Extremists always make better (blood curdling) television. In contrast, the voices of rationality appear too calm, too ordinary, too boring – not very good for the ratings. The liberals and moderates thus have little room to shape the dominant narrative that speaks for them and about them. For many years in Britain, Anjem Choudary, leader of Al-Muhajiroun, was presented as the voice of British Muslims despite being an extreme figure and far from representative of the majority voice. Yet his radical views were allowed to shape the perception of Muslims in wider British society. In the US, the Fox Network specialises in airing extreme views and thus has the highest ratings. In postnormal times, extremism has a natural tendency to attract attention and perpetuate itself.

This is why hatred of Muslims has now become the new normal. Islamophobia is now the prerogative of all. It is not unusual for Muslims to be abused on buses, tubes and on the streets of Britain. In October 2015, a video went viral showing the abusive, expletive-ridden and Islamophobic tirade of a black British woman against a pregnant hijab-wearing woman on a London bus. As Joseph Harker noted in *The Guardian*, 'when a black woman can stand in a bus and tell someone, without irony, to "go back to their own country" it shows how deeply embedded the hatred of Muslims has become in our society. The media, and everyone else, have a duty to do everything they can to counter it'. Yet it is exactly the media that stokes extreme reactions to Muslims, compounding a multitude of negative messages in popular culture. The award-winning US series *Homeland*, now in its fifth series, has long been accused of stereotyping Muslims either as terrorists or potential terrorists and employing simplistic conflations in its portrayal of complex conflicts within the Muslim world that would be laughable if they weren't so dangerous. They are insidious because, for many viewers, this is not pure drama, it is the medium through which their attitudes towards Muslims are informed. In an attempt to make *Homeland's* Berlin set mirror a Syrian refugee camp, the show's producers asked Arab street artists to scrawl Arabic slogans on the wall. Knowing full well that no one on the set cared a jot for complexity and substance, as long as it all looked superficially plausible, they produced graffiti that translated as 'Homeland is racist' '#Blacklivesmatter' and 'Homeland is a joke and it didn't make us laugh'. It was a brazen and ingenious act of political photobombing subversion. Heba Amin, one of the street artists, wrote in her blog that for *Homeland's* producers, 'Arabic script is merely a supplementary visual that completes the horror-fantasy of the Middle East, a poster image dehumanising an entire region to human-less figures in black burkas and moreover, this season, to refugees. The show has thus created a chain of causality with Arabs at its beginning and as its outcome - their own victims and executioners at the same time'.

So while we condemn the bloodthirsty rampage of the Kouachi brothers, we should comprehend what drove them to such extreme actions. French citizens of Algerian descent, their marginalised, gruelling lives of economic malaise and disaffection had barely been touched by Islamism while growing up in the secular French care system. They burst out of the *Charlie Hebdo* office declaring 'the Prophet is avenged'. Yet, they hardly knew anything about the Prophet; their actions would have made him weep bitterly. For the vast majority of sensible, rational Muslims watching the unfolding horror on the television and social media, such reactionary violence carried out in the name of love was unfathomable.

Yet, the love of the Prophet has itself become a complex issue, taking on an extreme dimension. It is, as Raza Ali says, a strange kind of love. The Prophet, who is described in the Qur'an as 'but a mortal' and 'a human being as a messenger' (17:93-94), and who himself insisted that as a human being he could not perform superhuman miracles, is elevated to unimaginable horizons – his name is said to have been written on the Throne of God, his light was created even before the universe, and he is above all other Prophets. His physical appearance, his dress, his habits, his everyday behaviour in seventh century Arabia, is to be imitated, even the length of his beard has to be matched exactly. Ali argues that the mythology surrounding the Prophet has existed for centuries. But its extreme manifestations began after 9/11. It is a love that makes people judgemental, inflexible, irrational and even drives them to murder other people. But it is a love that 'directly contradicts the many documented examples of the Prophet's humanity, forgiveness and humility. The kindness, patience, humility, forgiveness, and affection for others and nature, he reportedly exemplified, is not part of this love'. It is a love that ultimately deprives the lovers of their own humanity. It may be love 'of' the Prophet but it is not the love that he radiated.

Love of any kind is also absent amongst Muslims in their propensity to rush to judgement. Extremists perpetually judge other Muslims: they seem to have an inbuilt imanometer that measures people's faith (iman). Everyone's iman is found wanting, it just does not reach the level required on the imanometer. Either their dogmas (aquida) are wrong, or their ritual practices are not correct, or their attire (in the case of women) or facial furniture (in the case of men) is not suitable. If they are unable to find any other shortcoming, then the fact that they have a smile on their face or are a bit happy is enough to deride them. At least that is what Samia Rahman discovered when she examined the furore surrounding the 'Happy Muslims' video. It was made by a group called The Honesty Policy and uploaded on YouTube in April 2014. It upset many Muslims to see other Muslims, men and women, dancing happily to a pop tune. 'An unhappy theme of many discussions' on the video, Rahman notes, 'was the disproportionate scrutiny directed at the female participants', which degenerated into gross misogyny. The participants were accused by some of being reactive and apologetic. Anti-Muslim segments of the social media accused the participants of being sympathetic to extremism and radicalisation. That the makers of the Happy video chose to remain anonymous became an unwelcome sideshow. It fed into an unease, writes Rahman, that has 'rendered activists from all denominations and those with even a whiff of a public profile hyper-paranoid about a hidden agenda of those they may be seen with, share a platform with, and even happen to be photographed walking past. Among Muslim groups there is the indelible taint that comes with becoming involved, even fleetingly or tenuously, with an organisation that is suspected, never mind proven, to be funded by the government or some other objectionable entity. The polarisation between those for and against the counter-terrorism machine has created a groundswell of conspiracy theories buzzing around any and every new initiative. The consequence is a scramble to ensure one is hermetically sealed from possible exposure to designated toxic individuals that reputations could not possibly survive association'.

The extremes that even an innocuous attempt to portray Muslims in a humorous and joyful light can generate is an indication that we are never more than a hair's breath from extremism becoming normal in postnormal times. In any complex, interconnected situation, positive feedback ensures that extreme positions multiply geometrically and take off exponentially. To really understand such situations, we need to appreciate their complex contexts – not just the complex present, but also the historic trends, the impact of geopolitical actors then and now, and the composite reality on the ground. This is what Anne Alexander attempts in her analysis of ISIS – the mythical movement that has moved with the speed of Superman to occupy great swathes of the Levant as well as the darkest recesses of our imaginations. The question on everyone's lips is who are ISIS, how have they come to dominate the political landscape of the Middle East, and what can be done about this unstoppable powerhouse of nightmares. Alexander takes us back to the 2003 Iraq War, which greatly amplified the sense of injustice, particularly at the hands of the West, that must be acknowledged for its role in destabilising an entire region and providing seemingly just cause for extremists. The inability of the allies to comprehend the complex sectarian make-up of Iraq and the provocation of Shia-Sunni tensions by their favoured Prime Minister, Nouri al-Maliki, laid the foundations for the birth of ISIS. It is not just the failure to acknowledge the legitimacy of grievance, Alexander makes clear, but the suppression of such sentiment alongside the promotion of the narrative that grievance is a mere vehicle for terrorism, that has brought us to this cataclysm. ISIS turns out to be a useful iconic abstraction that serves the purpose of Western powers in the war against terror: 'both Western leaders and their local allies in the Middle East present the struggle with ISIS as an existential battle for survival in which there are only two sides. Stripped of their rhetoric invoking the defence of Western civilisation, or appeals to national unity, their message boils down to a simple ultimatum: "It is either them or us". For Cameron, Hollande and Merkel as for Sisi, the only alternative to ISIS is the strong state: in Europe this means sharpening legal instruments for the surveillance and coercion of not only Muslim citizens, but potentially anyone who dares to depart from the prepared narrative of fighting "extremism" and "radicalisation"'. In his review of Arun Kundnani's astute book *The Muslims are Coming*, Talat Ahmed reinforces Alexander's assertion that experience of the war on terror has been significant in the rise and rise of extremist ideology. The normalisation of anti-Muslim discourse along with entrenchment of Islamophobia has further accelerated the spread of extremism.

There is, of course, the other side of the equation. Muslims themselves, and how they interpret Islam, are also responsible for perpetuating extremism. It is not enough for Muslims to blithely repeat that Islam is a religion of peace and hope that all the problems will just go away. We need to question the dogma that serves as a springboard for extremist thought and action; and tackle the historical precedents for extremism in Islamic tradition. By denying the existence of dogma you remove the ability to challenge it from within the historical traditions it claims to originate. The urgent task that faces all Muslims is to root out the extremist ideology within Islam that presents Islam as unchanging and static and threatens to become the norm. Farouk Peru describes this extremist ideology as 'Islamofascism'. A consequence of the supremacy of absolutist dogma in Islamic discourse, he writes, 'Islamofascism is not essentially Islamic but rather an interpretation by the Islamofascists themselves. There are elements within the Islamic tradition which this group choose to ignore or downplay ostensibly because of their potential to undo the system of teachings they promote'. Peru argues that the social construction of the Sharia or the subjectivity of hadith literature is not adequately acknowledged, and has become entrenched in the teaching and practise of Islam today. The Sharia supports 'Islamofascism by legislating against any kind of activity which would undermine their integrity. The system deters Muslims and non-Muslims from disturbing the status quo of the power structure, denying everyone under its influence the basic freedom of thought'. The hadith literature was written retroactively and the events it describes 'did not actually occur as the hadith literature tells us but rather reflected the political tendencies of the Muslim community of later periods, which needed the legitimacy of the companions in order to validate their particular dogma'. A great deal of hadith was manufactured to justify a particular dogma or political position. Together the hadith and Sharia have created 'a framework of doctrines' to which all must adhere; this body of sacred knowledge, 'contained within the corpus of Islamic tradition', 'strikes awe in the typical Muslim mind. The power of the monopoly on the only acceptable truth dissuades, even intimidates, believers from thinking for themselves and challenging prevailing opinion'. Only by dismantling this framework, and the power of the theological elite and challenging their 'knowledge fascism', Peru suggests, can extremist ideology be confounded.

One particular characteristic of extremists is their belief that history begins and ends with the arrival of the Prophet Muhammad. Nothing that happened before – the period of ignorance (*jihaliya*) – or since is of much significance. Hence, their propensity to destroy archaeological sites, cultural property and anything else that they deem as representative of unbelief – including the history and cultural property of the sacred city of Mecca itself. Hence the destruction of the Bamiyan Buddhas by the Taliban, the ransack of Timbuktu by Al-Qaeda in the Islamic Maghreb (AQIM), and the massive destruction of heritage and cultural property, including Palmyra, by ISIS. But, once again, this is not a perversion that is simply limited to Muslims. In 'Statues of Identity', Elma Berisha contemplates the significance of religious artefacts and the intrinsic relationship between cultural heritage and the affirmation of identity. As she tours the symbolic temples and statues of South East Asia she is reminded of the single-minded effort to destroy archaeological and cultural artefacts by Serbian militants as they sought to eradicate non-Serbian iconography from Bosnia and Albania. While hiking to the top of the central highest temple in Angkor Wat, Berisha is intrigued to discover that she is roaming what was originally a Hindu temple before the region was conquered by Buddhists: 'I pondered the irony of our guide explaining the presence of the eight-armed Vishnu statue at the apex temple, albeit, with a forcefully replaced, still intact, Buddha head.' (Buddha himself experimented with extreme behaviour. It was his belief that all human action tarnishes the soul with a negative dust weighing a person down to the extent that they are caught in a cycle of repeated rebirth. Renouncers would endure extreme conditions such as abstinence from food and drink or standing exposed under the midday sun in an attempt to burn off their past activities. Only then will they be able to create space for the permanent soul to expand to the size of the universe, eventually liberating them from *samsara*). The Hindu extremists destroyed the ancient Babri Mosque in Ayodhya, India, in the belief that it was built on the temple of Ram. In Cambodia, as Bashira notes, the Khmer Rouge freely plundered ancient sites to finance their wars; and André Malraux, French novelist, theorist and Minister of Cultural Affairs, 'removed nearly a tonne of stones from Angkor Wat in 1924' to decorate the Museums of France. The British Museum is full of looted artefacts and cultural property. The destruction of cultural property, Berisha concludes, is a product of 'modern hatreds and fictional totalitarian extremisms turning against historical realities of multicultural ethos and coexistence'.

In the final analysis, extremism is really about the fear of 'multicultural ethos and coexistence'. It is anchored on the belief that one's own community has the monopoly on truth, there are no other notions of truths, and other claims to truth cannot be tolerated. And it is a belief that is gaining common currency in postnormal times, when pluralism and diversity come knocking on every door, everyone is connected to everyone else, everything is enveloped by contradictions and complexity, and we are perpetually at the edge of chaos. Like monopoly capital, monopolistic truth is evident everywhere – in religious communities as well as those who claim to be secular and atheists.

Take, for example, the Sikh community, seen by the British media as a model of moderation and virtue. But, as Sunny Hundal informs us, extremism is rampant amongst Sikhs who are experiencing a growing puritanical movement. Amongst all the ethnic communities in Britain, Sikhs are most eager to join such extremist groups as the British National Party (BNP) and the English Defence League (EDL). Hundal suggests that Sikh extremism manifests in two ways: 'open xenophobia that can fuel hate-crimes; and attempts by some to impose their views on others under the guise of religious puritanism'. Any form of criticism or self-reflection is seen as an insult to the community. In 2005, the play *Behzti*, which makes reference to the rape of a woman in a Sikh Gurdwara, was met with protests and vandalism. Such was the strength of emotion that the play was eventually shut down after the police advised that they could not guarantee security. 'The furore shocked many in the mainstream media who had earlier assumed Sikhs wouldn't do anything like the events around *Satanic Verses*. But the parallels were there. Some wanted to sue the writer, herself a Sikh, for incitement of hatred against Sikhs; others started spreading baseless rumours about the play and the writer; there was the inevitable cry that people shouldn't be allowed to insult Sikhism (the play didn't). Of course, she got death threats too, but since the notion of Sikh extremism doesn't fit the media narrative there was little focus on that'. Fundamentalists wish to impose 'strict interpretation of the *Rehat Maryada* (a set of codes set out by scholars in 1950), which prohibits marriage between Sikhs and non-Sikhs at a religious ceremony'. Thus, inter-religious weddings are regularly disrupted, the parties involved threatened, and are not allowed to take place. Various segments of the community are constantly declaring that Sikh girls are being lured by Muslim men who aim to convert them. Honour killings are not unusual. Liberals and moderates are regularly ex-communicated from the community.

The 'New Atheists', analysed by Andrew Brown, are just as extreme. Indeed, the parallel with religious fundamentalism is stark. Brown argues that the New Atheist movement 'was a social rather than an intellectual development' with 'two intellectual novelties' which have been forgotten. 'The first was the doctrine that moderate religious believers are actually more wicked and dangerous than the ones who burn witches or blow up children. The second, of course, was the nonsense of "memes", which speaks to a deeper or at least more imaginative longing: that the world works according to a few lovely simple and comprehensive explanations – in this case, something supposedly Darwinian'. Brown finds the 'exuberant nastiness' of New Atheism and their projection of Islam as evil 'disgusting'. He links their contempt for religious communities to the rise of neo-conservatives in the US. The rapid emergence of disbelief in America, he argues, is 'a response to the destruction of the old, valued and valuable role for a particular sort of labour: in this case, the labour of the intelligentsia'. New Atheism is little more than extreme fundamentalism of the college educated.

Undeniably, the neo-conservatives have a great deal to answer for. The extremes of poverty and wealth, a product of neo-conservative extreme economics, are irrefutable factors in the growth of extremism. In his sobering documentary *Bitter Lake*, Adam Curtis parallels the confounding chimera of Islamic extremism with the rise of neoliberal economics in the West. Social injustice and economic malaise combine to create a vacuum that all variety of absolute truths have been quick to fill – including the absolute truth of neo-cons themselves that climate change is not a product of extreme human activities. In fact, a major factor behind the wars in the Middle East, and subsequent arrival of refugees on the borders of Europe, as Sweeney points out, was a severe drought that began in 2006 and lasted until 2011. It led to the displacement of people from rural areas to the cities and subsequent competition for diminishing resources causing strain and political tension. Despair is an ideal state of mind for extremism to flourish.

To understand the causes of extremism, and its rapid expansion, we need to appreciate the complexity of our times. Complexity cannot be tackled by simple, one dimensional solutions – a quick war, a new foreign policy initiative, supporting our dictators against their dictators. Moreover, in postnormal times, there is no 'us' and 'them'. There is only all of us – together; and every component of us is connected to all other components that make us a human community. So the truths of others are as important to them as are our own truths are to us. Security of others matters as much as our own security. For freedom to be meaningful it should be equally available to all. Our collective contradictory demands and desires cannot be resolved but only transcended. Everyone must have an equal voice in a polylogue of interplay of cultural ideas and perspectives. These are not mere aspirations, but the demands of postnormal times where contradictions, complexity and chaos are glaring realities. Unless we learn to engage with the complexity of the real world, everything may end up painted with a single colour of chaos – pink or otherwise.

ISIS

Anne Alexander

The slick violence of the propaganda of the deed which ISIS has made its trademark continues to mesmerise. The threat appears to be everywhere: in British teenagers' bedrooms, whispering and calling through Kik and WhatsApp. Killing diners and concert-goers in Paris. On the beaches of Tunisia, slaughtering sunbathers. In the ruins of Palmyra. Overrunning Yarmouk refugee camp near Damascus. Making alliances with Boko Haram in Nigeria and temporarily raising its black flag over Derna and Sirte in Libya. Losing Tikrit but taking Ramadi. Camped at the gates of Baghdad.

Most news coverage of ISIS oscillates between the extremes of overconfident predictions of the organisation's imminent demise and exaggerated depictions of its prowess, reflecting the difficulties which the rise of this 'state' has caused the global powers and their local allies. I believe that the rise of ISIS needs to be understood as a partial expression of the group's leaders' ability to build a political and military organisation aided by the interaction of three interrelated historical processes.

The first is the catastrophe which engulfed America's imperial dreams of remaking Iraq in a neoliberal image after 2003. However, rather than remake Iraq, US policy has played a central role in unmaking Iraqi society (even if the name of the state survives). US politicians divided a country they could not otherwise rule, triggering ethno-sectarian war between Kurds and Sunni Arabs in Northern Iraq and between Sunni and Shi'a Arabs in the centre of the country and in particular around the capital, Baghdad. The geo-political realignments at a global and regional level as a result of the US defeat in Iraq have been equally significant, taking the outward form of sectarian polarisation at a regional level between camps of allies associated with the competing ambitions of Tehran and Riyadh, and these in turn have fed into and intensified sectarian polarisation at a local level, particularly in Iraq and Syria. ISIS has proved adept at turning these realignments to its leaders' advantage: feeding off the atmosphere of poisonous sectarianism encouraged by the Saudi rulers as they sought to contain and defeat popular mobilisations in the Gulf and posing as the sectarian defender of Sunni interests against Iranian encroachment in Iraq and the wider region.

The catastrophic defeat of the Syrian revolution is the second process which has played a central role in the rise of ISIS. It is intimately linked to the overall defeat of the revolutionary wave of 2011, which shook the region from Morocco to Bahrain, but contributed its own dynamics and created specific opportunities for ISIS's leaders at critical moments in the group's recent evolution. The collapse of the revolutionary hopes of 2011, combined with vicious counter-revolutionary violence directed at the region's most important reformist current within the Islamist movement – Egypt's Muslim Brotherhood – was always highly likely to set the scene for the revival of terrorism as a political tactic. ISIS benefited from the tide of despair flowing across the region, offering a flag of convenience for some whose hopes of achieving social and political change by other means were dashed.

These two processes have interacted with a third: the development of what could be loosely termed a 'jihadi international', connecting armed Salafist groups engaged in separate struggles through the exchange of fighters and the alignment of political and military actions. Over the last three decades this has allowed some military leaders to gain experience in different countries and groups to experiment with different forms of cooperation. It has created a pool of experienced fighters and well-established transnational methods of recruitment, financing and communication. This network is a site of competition and rivalry as much as cooperation however, as the shift in allegiances from Al-Qaeda to ISIS over the past year demonstrates. It exists in a state of tense symbiosis with the governments of Western Europe and the US: functioning simultaneously as their necessary 'enemy within' and 'enemy without', legitimising at a single stroke both anti-Muslim racism at home and imperialist wars abroad.

Imperial disaster in Iraq

The most important process which underlies ISIS's emergence as a significant military force in 2014–5 is the entrenching of sectarian competition in both state and society in Iraq as a result of the US invasion and occupation. US intervention followed more than ten years of a sanctions regime which had hollowed out the state and plunged Iraqi society into poverty. It then turned both state and society over to the unstable control of competing sectarian forces. The rise of ISIS is a direct outcome of strategies adopted by US officials, and the continuing intervention of US and other imperialist forces in Iraq only makes escape from the vicious logic of sectarianism more difficult.

The US has played a fundamental role in the sectarianisation of Iraq. Firstly, the occupying power created a system of political representation on a 'consociational' model based on the pre-conception of Iraqi society made up of mutually hostile, religious and ethnic communities. This approach interacted with the dismembering of Iraq's national institutions through plunder and privatisation, leading to the cannibalisation of the state by competing sectarian and ethnic parties. These groups allocated resources and jobs to their supporters through the practice of *al-muhasasa*, a sectarian quota system. Finally the US counter-insurgency strategy was crucial to the emergence of ISIS as one sectarian military formation among many (albeit one of the most vicious and effective).

Faced with a popular insurgency involving both Arab Sunni and Arab Shi'a Islamist and nationalist armed groups, the US sought to make political and military alignment between the resistance fighters impossible by using Shi'a religious leaders to win the support of anti-occupation Shi'a factions for confessional unity behind a political settlement which guaranteed Shi'a parties the lion's share of state power for the first time. In the meantime, US forces carried out a vicious campaign of military repression in Sunni majority areas: including the bombardment of towns such as Fallujah into submission, mass arrests, torture and humiliation of detainees.

Many groups involved in the early stages of the armed struggle against US occupation used nationalist rhetoric to justify their actions and primarily targeted US troops. A prominent exception was a small Islamist group founded by Abu-Musa'b al-Zarqawi. Al-Qaeda in Iraq (AQI) concentrated its efforts on igniting a sectarian civil war through bombings of Shi'a mosques and pilgrimage sites in a campaign which reached its height during 2006–7. Meanwhile sectarian Shi'a militias, such as the Badr Brigade and the Mahdi Army worked as anti-Sunni death squads in the police, killing and torturing hundreds of Iraqis every month. Just under three years previously, the Mahdi Army had been the leading armed Shi'a force in the military resistance to US occupation, but its leader Muqtada al-Sadr had heeded the call by Shi'a religious leaders such as Ali al-Sistani, to leave fighters in largely Sunni areas to battle on alone and instead to mobilise a 'Shi'a' vote to justify parcelling out the state between the Shi'a parties allied to the US. AQI's brutal sectarianism repulsed many Iraqis in Sunni-majority areas. US commanders seized the opportunity to successfully mobilise Iraqi Sunni tribal forces against AQI in the 'Awakening' movement and 'Sons of Iraq' programme. The 'Awakening' made important concessions by allowing enrolled Sunni fighters to bear arms provided they used them under the direction of US commanders, who also provided food and employment in an effort to win 'hearts and minds'. Meanwhile the numbers of US troops in Iraq surged to 166,000 by the end of 2007, aiming to reconquer the country they had invaded four years previously. Zarqawi was killed by US troops, attacks on the occupying troops from other groups reduced and levels of violence dropped back.

However, this proved to be a temporary respite for the US. The 'surge' of troops which underpinned the new tactics was unsustainable, particularly after the global financial crisis of 2008. The US shift towards a military 're-balancing' between Sunni and Shi'a armed groups through the creation of 'Sons of Iraq' had created yet another body of armed men recruited on a sectarian basis. They were then transferred to the command of sectarian Shi'a politicians, who viewed them not as potential partners but as a threat to be eradicated.

The final tragic instalment in the story of the resurrection of ISIS from the ashes of AQI took place in 2010-2013. Elections in 2010 looked temporarily to have opened up opportunities for Sunni politicians to carve out a space for their parties within the state: the Al-Iraqiyya electoral list took first place beating incumbent prime minister Nouri al-Maliki's State of Law list. Al-Maliki refused to accept the results, using a series of judicial manoeuvres to block the formation of an al-Iraqiyya government. From December 2012 a string of senior Sunni politicians were arrested or charged with organising sectarian attacks, and when Western Iraq erupted in mass protests, al-Maliki crushed the demonstrations by force. Sectarian violence escalated, fighters from AQI (now rebranded as Islamic State of

Iraq) returned to the streets of Ramadi and Fallujah and political groups in Sunni majority areas who had argued for reforms within the existing state structures of Iraq were marginalised.

All of these elements can be seen at work in the events leading up to the collapse of the Iraqi army in Mosul and ISIS's seizure of the city in June 2014. Sectarian competition over the fabric of the Iraqi state fuelled by privatisation and the divide and rule tactics of the occupying power channelled resources and influence towards sectarian parties and their militias. Shi'a militias working in the Interior Ministry, or with the support of Iraqi Armed Forces and their commander-in-chief Nouri al-Maliki, did not just target Zarqawi and his partisans. They killed, tortured or forced from their homes thousands of Sunni citizens, while systematically excluding Sunni politicians from the higher levels of the state. The hollowness of the Iraqi army, with its thousands of 'ghost soldiers' who drew their pay but never materialised on the battlefield, was not the mere product of cronyism but also reflected the calculations of Al-Maliki and his kind that it was an insufficiently sectarian instrument for their purposes.

Faced with the onset of the global economic crisis in 2008 and with a majority of Americans now opposed to expensive foreign wars, President Obama's policymakers turned to regional partners to manage the conflict, who in turn grew in stature and influence. Three of these powers are long-standing partners of the US: Turkey, Israel and Saudi Arabia. The fourth, Iran, is an old antagonist. Iran is now slowly being integrated into the new regional balance of power following the best part of a decade of arms-length engagement with the US through its Iraqi Shi'a Islamist allies and latterly the conclusion of a deal to lift sanctions in return for Iranian concessions over its nuclear programme. The creation of an enlarged space into which regional powers are able to project their ambitions has accelerated sectarian polarisation both in specific conflicts, such as Iraq and Syria, and at a regional level. This is because the relative weakening of US domination has intensified competition between those powers capable of filling the gap.

Arab revolutions defeated

While the history behind ISIS's emergence in Iraq goes back to 2003, the group's rise in Syria took place over a much shorter timescale. The brutal counter-revolution launched by the Assad regime against the uprising of 2011 set in motion the process leading to ISIS's formation in April 2013, through a merger of an Al-Qaeda affiliate in Syria, Jabhat al-Nusra with the Islamic State of Iraq (formerly AQI). Although this union proved short-lived, with JN commanders repudiating the transborder ambitions of ISIS's Iraqi leadership, ISIS continued to grow in strength, making a breakthrough by seizing the Syrian provincial capital of Raqqa from other Islamist opposition forces in January 2014.

ISIS's emergence at a late stage in the revolutionary process in Syria, in the context of the utter physical destruction of large areas of the country and the impoverishment and displacement of most of the population, underscores the point that such an outcome was not an inevitable consequence of the 2011 uprising. On the contrary, the slogans adopted by protesters during the first stage of the Syrian revolution were strongly anti-sectarian. This was a genuine revolution from below, which threw up new forms of popular governance in areas where the state was forced to retreat. In the flowering of political activism, which accompanied the popular mobilisation against the regime, a constant theme was the danger that sectarianism posed to grassroots unity, crucial to the revolution's ultimate success. The forms of struggle adopted by revolutionary activists at the beginning of the uprising were mass protests, civil disobedience and local strikes, all of which became platforms for the projection of anti-sectarian slogans. However, the popular uprising mutated into a military struggle in which the key protagonists were the regime's forces and armed Islamist groups. There is not space here to fully explore the reasons for this transformation and its consequences, but we can outline the main problems confronting Syria's revolutionaries. The first of these was that the uprising began in the marginalised cities of the country's periphery, and although it quickly reached the suburbs of the capital, the mass protests and strikes did not achieve an early breakthrough in either Damascus or Syria's second city of Aleppo. Secondly, the extreme brutality of the war for survival launched by the regime prompted the rapid militarisation of the struggle as revolutionary activists attempted to defend themselves and their communities from the relentless onslaught of Assad's forces. A third factor was the deliberate efforts by the regime to turn the conflict into a sectarian civil war: it deployed paramilitaries and death squads drawn from the Alawi regions and mobilised regional military allies on a sectarian basis, such as Iranian special forces, Hezbollah and Iraqi sectarian Shi'a militias.

The sectarian strategy of the Assad regime was mirrored by the intervention of the Gulf States, which poured arms and funding into Syria for the use of Sunni Islamist armed groups, helping to propel them into the military leadership of the anti-Assad forces. It was in this context that ISIS appeared first in Syria, arriving late on the scene. Syria provided a crucial hinterland for the revival of ISIS in Iraq, and was the site of the movement's first important territorial breakthrough. Following a common pattern this was not the result of ISIS forces capturing territory, but through ISIS securing political and military hegemony over the armed Islamist groups that had already captured Raqqa. ISIS followed in an even more extreme and brutal manner the pattern set by the rise of other armed Islamist groups: these groups were not only able to push aside other political currents and popular institutions which had emerged in the leadership of the early stages of the revolution. Rather they worked to repress and break such organisations, impose conservative moral codes on public behaviour and set up their own governing institutions in areas under their control.

The impact of counter-revolution in Syria on the development of ISIS needs to be set in the wider context of the defeat of revolution in other countries in the region, particularly Egypt and Tunisia. The rolling back of the wave of popular uprisings coincided with the acute crisis of reformist Islamist organisations such as the Egyptian Muslim Brotherhood and the Tunisian Ennahda movement, which were propelled into office through elections during the first phase of the revolutions. The catastrophe which engulfed the Muslim Brotherhood in Egypt was double-faced, spanning disillusion and frustration among large sections of the organisation's electorate and supporters (one sign of which was its sharply falling share of the popular vote and declining voter turnout during the elections and referenda which took place in 2011 and 2012). Combined with the steadily rising tide of social protests over living costs, wages and conditions at work, some of which was mobilised by workplace activists who identified politically with the Islamist movement, the Brotherhood's wilting electoral performance could be read as a sign of disappointment among sections of the movement's popular base that its claim to provide a parliamentary route to genuine political and social change had proved to be hollow.

The other factor precipitating the Brotherhood's crisis was the implacable hostility of the old regime to even the most modest political reforms, and its capacity to first stall and then reverse the democratic gains achieved thanks to the popular uprising in 2011. It was the counter-revolutionary offensive led by the core institutions of Egypt's old regime – the armed forces, interior ministry, judiciary and media – which was decisive in ejecting the Brotherhood from office in the coup of 3 July 2013. Mohamed Morsi spent the second anniversary of his overthrow in jail, under sentence of death along with the majority of the Brotherhood's senior leaders. Tens of thousands of the organisation's cadres and members have been jailed, and hundreds condemned to execution by the military regime's hanging judges. Outside the jail walls, the Brotherhood was wracked by internal struggles over the question of whether to continue with the organisation's long-standing commitment to non-violent political struggle or launch armed resistance. Meanwhile armed Islamist groups claiming to represent ISIS's 'Province of Sinai' stepped up attacks on military installations near the border with Gaza.

The tensions within the Brotherhood over the question of violence should not obscure the fundamental differences between Islamist mass movements and military formations of the Jihadist tendency. If sections of the Brotherhood's membership or activists are pushed into arguing for an armed struggle, this reflects despair that Egypt's ruling class has decisively shut the door on the Brotherhood's attempts to change the political system electorally from the inside. ISIS's leaders have only ever sought to conquer the state militarily from outside. ISIS is not, and never has been a mass movement. Nor was it incubated in the ferment of mass social and political struggles. It is a military organisation which emerged as one of the actors in an insurgency which it sought from the beginning to transform into armed sectarian conflict. Its existence is born out of defeat and its growth predicated on the continuation of those conditions.

Nevertheless, the current triumph of the military and security apparatus of the old regime in Egypt over the Brotherhood will make ISIS's political and military strategies appear more attractive to some. Where the Brotherhood seems weak and on the defensive, ISIS appears strong.

ISIS vs Al-Qaeda?

How are we to understand the transnational dimensions of ISIS's activities? From one perspective, ISIS's emergence as a serious challenger to Al-Qaeda for leadership of the major international networks of jihadi armed groups can be understood as simply the latest chapter in a much longer history, which goes back to the decision by the US to facilitate globalisation of the armed struggle against the Soviet-backed Afghan government in the 1980s. This was the conflict which pulled in Saudi and Egyptian Islamists escaping disillusion and repression at home in order to fight the US proxy war alongside the Afghan mujahideen. The story of how Al-Qaeda arose out of the reconstitution of some of the networks which had channelled fighters and funding towards Afghanistan, but later switched their efforts towards attacking the US and its allies, is well-known. As Al-Qaeda's star waned, the rise of ISIS can be seen as partly an inter-generational struggle over strategy and tactics where the most recent and spectacular military victories exert a centrifugal pull on international jihadi networks.

ISIS has attracted jihadi fighters from outside Iraq and Syria but its core leadership appear to be Iraqi and to have been largely schooled in war within Iraq. Their experience differs from that of the group's founder figure Abu Musa'b al-Zarqawi who left Jordan for the Afghan jihad, returned and then made Iraq his theatre of operations after the US invasion of 2003. Abu-Bakr al-Baghdadi, otherwise known as Caliph Ibrahim, appears to have been born, raised, politicised and trained as a fighter in Iraq (passing through US custody in Camp Bucca on the way). So the rise of ISIS reflects an additional dynamic: the way in which the strategies and tactics adopted by a particular group of jihadi commanders have intersected with specific conditions in the region and beyond, producing military and political successes which in turn have shifted the international jihadi networks' centre of gravity, attracting fighters, funding and media attention. In other words, ISIS's elevation as competitor to AQ is intimately connected with its military success in Iraq and Syria. It is the group's seizure of Raqqa and defeat of the Iraqi army in Mosul which have pushed other armed groups to look towards it, and attempt to emulate.

Of course there are other expressions of the intergenerational divide between AQ and ISIS, such as ISIS's adoption of a communications strategy well-suited to the social media age. Communication is important: it brings in recruits, funding and notoriety. 'Propaganda of the deed' is all the more effective if the camerawork is professional and the accompanying music chosen to resonate at the appropriate emotional register.

ISIS skilfully utilises a violent cinematic style which needs to be set in a wider context, enabling us to understand it not as something exceptional, but rather as an extreme example of general trends. While there is no space to explore these themes properly here, they could include the creation of new markets and mechanisms for the circulation of hyper-violent, voyeuristic video content, the wide-scale appropriation of social media tools and spaces by both state and non-state combatants, and the shift towards image-based rather than text-based communication online. ISIS's decision to show, rather than simply tell, audiences in the West about their cruel methods of execution, created a dilemma for news organisations: should they relay the content, or edit it? If they edited it, would that undermine or amplify the message that ISIS wanted to get across? However, versions of this dilemma are played out regularly in newsrooms as journalists and producers decide whether to trade off the expected surge in traffic to their website against complaints by viewers or regulators if they republish or link to graphic content which is already circulating online in other fora.

Should we see ISIS's media practices as stylistic expressions of the logic of asymmetrical warfare, using video cameras, low cost weapons and an internet connection to create psychological effects of 'shock and awe' among the group's Western adversaries? We can certainly question the assumption that because video footage of drone or missile strikes released by Western militaries or their Israeli allies doesn't show burnt flesh and human pain in close up, that somehow the act itself is less morally repugnant. In the first case the point is to overwhelm the viewer with the graphic representation of violence, in the second, the point is to disassociate the act from its consequences: the physical impact on the 'targets' is the same. All of this is separate from questions of guilt or innocence or whether the dead and injured were 'worthy' or 'unworthy' victims of violence.

There may also be another dynamic at work: Aaron Zelin argues that ISIS's model for relations between its central command and outlying affiliates differs from AQ's in a number of important ways. AQ focussed on winning groups to a strategy of concentrating attacks on Western targets, often retrospectively taking the credit for military actions. One of the problems with this approach was the 'franchises' often became a drain on the overall resources of the group (becoming political, military and financial liabilities), as groups tended to affiliate to AQ once they got into difficulties. AQ's leaders also struggled to win local groups to stick to their strategy of concentrating military operations on the US and its allies, rather than local regime. AQ's emphasis on clandestine military operations, rather than local 'state-building' activities has also been hard to win consistent support for.

By contrast, Zelin argues, ISIS's approach has been to insist that groups wanting to affiliate must undergo a process of internal consolidation first (sorting out their political and military differences and choosing a single leadership) rather than selecting groups after the fact based on their success in carrying out a spectacular operation. Moreover, ISIS has prioritised winning military, political and social hegemony within a given territory rather than exclusively focussing on US-linked targets.

A key reason why the international jihadi networks which ISIS aspires to lead have proved so resilient (or more accurately why they have been able to revive themselves multiple times) is because of the enduring role of Muslims as the most important 'Other' for the Western imperialist powers in the neoliberal era. In Europe the shift from racism based on differences in colour to supposed differences in culture has been particularly noticeable: the barrage of anti-Muslim sentiment in the mainstream media increasing in intensity and scope in tandem with assaults by the state on Muslim citizens' civil and democratic rights through 'anti-terror' legislation, ritualised 'loyalty tests' and discrimination against Muslim religious practices.

At the same time as proclaiming that Muslims in general are blameworthy for the atrocities of whichever international jihadi bogeyman happens to be ascendant, the governments of Western Europe and the US have of course a long history of complicity with the noxious dictators of the Middle East (whether of the republican or royalist variety). The institutions of torture and humiliation at the heart of the US imperial project, such as Guantanamo Bay would have had far fewer inmates were it not for the systematic collaboration between the US and the regimes of the Middle East that handed over their own citizens through the rendition programme. Western governments and corporations have also provided most of the states in the region with all the ammunition they need in their wars against their own people for decades, and despite a brief lull in 2011–2, arms sales have skyrocketed again in the shadow of the gathering counter-revolution.

Remaining and expanding

The sketch outlined above goes some way to explaining why ISIS exists – but does not explain what ISIS is. In particular, what are we to make of Al-Baghdadi's claim to be the leader of a state? In this regard even the use of the group's name by mainstream news organisations and governments spurs controversy: David Cameron criticised the BBC for using the title 'Islamic State' in July 2015 after over 100 MPs signed a letter calling on the corporation to adopt the label 'Daesh' instead. According to Jessica Lewis of the US military think tank, the Institute for the Study of War (ISW), ISIS's emergence is a threat not only to the existing states of the region, but to the entire modern political order, as it aims to 'wreck rather than join the modern state system.' Beyond the hyperbole of casting ISIS as an existential threat to the global capitalist order (no doubt intended to bolster ISW's advocacy for the renewal of US military intervention in Iraq and Syria by committing ground troops to the fight against ISIS) Lewis's designation of ISIS as both a state and 'counter-state' is a useful insight. As a 'counter-state', its political and military strategy drives towards the goals of making Iraq and Syria, the two states whose lands form the core of its territorial project, not merely ungovernable but unviable in their current form. There are important differences between ISIS strategy in relation to the regimes in Baghdad and Damascus, of course. In the military arena, the Iraqi regime and its partners, including the Kurdistan Regional Government and the US, is ISIS's principal adversary. Until October 2015, ISIS's main adversaries on the ground in Syria were other Islamist forces, while the Assad regime had reportedly been able to come to pragmatic arrangements with the group over fuel supplies and trade. Russian officials claimed that their backing for the offensive by Syrian government forces was aimed at ISIS, although this was met by counter-claims from NATO members that the primary targets were Assad's other Islamist foes. The aftermath of the Paris bombings in November also saw the dramatic escalation of French bombing raids against ISIS, which began in September 2014 with attacks on ISIS positions in Iraq.

Conceptualising ISIS's military and political goals in relation to Baghdad as the actions of a counter-state help to explain why progress toward preparations for an offensive to recapture Mosul was so slow during 2014-2015. In these terms, military success can be measured by ISIS's ability to pin down Iraqi armed forces around the capital, while processes of sectarian 'cleansing' accelerated the 'unmixing' not only of Baghdad itself, but of the provinces of Salah-al-Din and Kirkuk to the north. And it is not only ISIS which is responsible for sectarian 'cleansing' operations in these areas: Shi'a Islamist militias such as the Badr Brigade, the Promised Day and the Asa'ib Ahl al-Haq have forced thousands of Sunni families from their homes and businesses around Amerli in Salah-al-Din province.

Yet, reducing ISIS merely to a 'counter-state' misses a key point. ISIS's claim to be a state is crucial to the group's ideology and practice in several different arenas. Within the areas under its dominion ISIS has staked its authority not simply on military victories, but on the creation of executive institutions which claim to provide some basic services, including health care and education, take responsibility for public infrastructure and the provision of fuel and food, regulate public and private morality and even stop shopkeepers from selling rotten tomatoes and counterfeit medicines. Not only is this a project which has set itself the challenge to build a 'real state', the kind of institutions it appears to want to build seem to have more in common with the Ba'athist state of the twentieth century than some re-imagined Medieval polity where Caliphal authority is simply inscribed on the coinage and intoned in Friday sermons.

The degree to which ISIS claims to have realised a new state also distinguishes the group from rivals such as Al-Qaeda within transnational jihadi networks. Al-Qaeda never claimed to be more than a 'base', alternately a hinterland retreat where fighters could gather before a new offensive and a distributed network of cells operating as 'safe houses' in enemy territory. Despite Bin Laden or Zawahiri's critique of the 'idolatrous' regimes they fought against, the idea that they or their lieutenants might constitute the executive of a new ruling order was put off until some far-distant victory.

ISIS's political and military methods aim at establishing spaces where the authority of the group's leadership is unchallenged. In some cases this process has flowed from ISIS success in winning political hegemony among existing armed factions or persuading other groups' fighters to desert for ISIS. It was by a combination of these methods that ISIS made its first major advance in Syria with the capture of Raqqa. In other cases, ISIS troops have won territory in battle first and claimed political authority over it afterwards. Once military and political hegemony has been established, ISIS has usually quickly moved to assert social control over the population, while claiming to set up various institutions of government. Thus, according to purported ISIS documents published online, following a period of re-education and 'repentance' teachers and other state employees are offered the 'choice' of returning to their former jobs. (Those who refuse to 'repent' are warned they will be declared apostates).

Patrols ostentatiously checking whether private and public observance of religious ritual conform to ISIS's definitions have been reported in numerous locations under ISIS control. The brutal and spectacular punishment of those deemed to have broken ISIS's moral codes or challenged the group's political authority has become a notorious hallmark of ISIS rule. Reports from Raqqa and Mosul during the year since the cities fell under ISIS control regularly speak of crucifixions, beheadings and amputations for a wide variety of 'crimes'.

Besides the regular use of extreme violence, the other hallmark of ISIS's methods has been the group's systematic sectarianism. The two have often gone together, with the victims of violence being selected on no other grounds than their religious faith. Shi'a Muslims and Yazidis in Iraq and Coptic and Ethiopian Christians in Libya are among the groups to have been targeted in this way by ISIS. These are not random acts of violence, but a carefully considered tactic. ISIS's leaders have long held the strategic goal of literally unmaking Iraq, that is to say accelerating the sectarian disintegration of the country to a point where the confessionally and ethnically mixed society, which spanned the last eighty years of the twentieth century, no longer exists. Sectarian violence serves ISIS at a number of different levels: it may be calculated to provoke Western military intervention or to trigger revenge attacks by other sectarian groups or to terrify populations into fleeing ISIS's advancing troops. It also seeks to implicate Sunni residents in areas which ISIS controls in the group's atrocities and bar them from reintegrating into any post-ISIS society.

The military balance sheet on ISIS's first year as rulers of Mosul and Raqqa makes grim reading for the group's opponents. RAND Corporation analyst Linda Robinson summed up the key issues in testimony to the US Congress in June 2015, concluding that ISIS has proved to be 'resilient, adaptive and agile' despite losing around half of its fighting force since August 2014.

ISIS's developing capacity for 'hybridised warfare' has been an element in its success. The group has proved adept at switching between guerrilla tactics and the manoeuvres of conventional warfare, possibly as a result of recruiting a number of former Ba'athist officers to senior command positions. ISIS's commanders have made costly errors, such as losing large numbers of troops in the attempt to take Kobane after the odds shifted dramatically against them as a consequence of US-led air strikes. Yet a year after the fall of Mosul they were still capable of deploying troops to defend frontlines hundreds of miles long. Nor had political or social crisis in the major urban centres under their control undermined ISIS military performance during that time. On the contrary, ISIS's political and military structures appeared to be still functioning brutally and relatively efficiently. According to Patrick Cockburn by May 2015 the group was even successfully conscripting men in some areas to replenish its fighting forces.

ISIS's military resilience over the past year is thus linked in numerous ways to the group's ability to wage war in the way that states do: not only by deploying fighters and resources but also by enforcing the military mobilisation of the population in territories under its control. It is the context for this 'stateness' which is crucial. In order to appear as a viable state (at least temporarily) ISIS does not need to compare itself to the government of the USA, the UK or even the Iraq of Saddam Hussein. Rather it needs to appear more like a state than the immediate competition. If the immediate competition is another armed group, then ISIS's military successes – boosted by the presence of experienced fighters and captured military hardware – are a key element in its claimed 'stateness'. If the competition is no state at all and people are tired of surviving the jealousies of competing petty warlords then the attraction of

ISIS's brutal version of 'law and order' is at least partly explicable. Can ISIS's repression ensure that farmers are able to get their goods to market without fear of being waylaid on the highway? If the competition is a state which delivers services and enforces laws, but only for the benefit of citizens of a particular creed, then ISIS's apparent offer of state-like 'protection' and 'retribution' for those wrongs may appear appealing.

Yet although all these factors are important to understanding ISIS's resilience, they are still largely related to the weaknesses and failings of the group's nearest adversaries and competitors. A state whose leaders set themselves the task of compelling Iraq, Syria and the regional and global powers to accept their existence by force of arms would face enormous challenges. Could they transform the 'warlord economy' which has underpinned much of their military expansion into a war economy: mobilising not just fighters but production and distribution once the looted plunder runs out? Could they align themselves with the economic and political interests of merchants, farmers or industrialists prepared to put a portion of their investments into the service of the state and its war machine? Do some of those in Mosul who have aligned themselves with ISIS fantasise about restoring the city's pre-Iraqi economic hinterland, stretching into the fertile Jazira region which spans the border between Iraq and Syria? Or are they remembering the convergence of interests between major Mosul landowners, the Ba'th Party and pan-Arab nationalist army officers which triggered the attempt to ignite a revolt against the regime of Abdel-Karim Qassem from the city in March 1959?

There are formidable obstacles which lie in the way of melding together long term economic processes, historical memories and newly-hardened sectarian identities into the basis for a viable state. In the case of ISIS there is also an obvious contradiction between the dynamics of state formation as they appear to be playing out in the specific context of the Jazira region and ISIS's claim not to be a state of 'the Sunnis of the Jazira' but the eternal, universal state of Muslims everywhere. The narrow definition of who is 'a Muslim' according to ISIS's leaders is not the issue at stake here: rather it is the tension between the specific conditions in Iraq and Syria which underpin ISIS's current territorial status and the grandiose claims to universal statehood which resonate with ISIS's role as a transnational network of armed fighters.

Conclusion

Both Western leaders and their local allies in the Middle East present the struggle with ISIS as an existential battle for survival in which there are only two sides. Stripped of their rhetoric invoking the defence of Western civilisation, or appeals to national unity, their message boils down to a simple ultimatum: 'It is either them or us'. For Cameron, Hollande and Merkel as for Sisi, the only alternative to ISIS is the strong state: in Europe this means sharpening legal instruments for the surveillance and coercion of not only Muslim citizens, but potentially anyone who dares to depart from the prepared narrative of fighting 'extremism' and 'radicalisation'. In Sisi's Egypt, the strong state doesn't bother with any of the niceties of democratic process: the spectre of ISIS is invoked to justify extrajudicial executions, disappearances, torture and mass death sentences. Meanwhile, ISIS's leaders call for Muslims to take sides in an apocalyptic battle against the 'Crusader' states, pointing to rising Islamophobia and repression to convince the waverers: 'It is either them or us'.

Yet the question remains: where does the real alternative lie? In 2011, the popular uprisings across the region appeared to offer an escape route from an earlier cycle of imperial aggression, repression and jihadi counter-violence. Yet the nagging doubts remain: did the revolt from below precipitate an even deeper social and political crisis? Would it have been better if the millions who took to the streets in Tunisia, Egypt, Bahrain, Libya, Syria and Yemen had remained at home, voiceless and passive but at least spared the horrors of terrorism, civil war and emboldened authoritarianism which stalk the region today? Was rebellion really 'worth it', as the opinion writers of the Western media condescendingly ask those who risked everything for 'bread, freedom and social justice'?

This too is a false choice. The social processes behind the rise of ISIS and its' kind are deeply embedded in the economic and political system we live in today. This is true at a local level in many individual countries across the Middle East and beyond and at a global level where rivalry over control of the strategic resources of the region drives imperialist competition to dominate its territories, its oil and gas and its markets. This is not to say that the emergence of movements promising to build a reactionary, sectarian utopia through transnational violence is inevitable under neoliberal imperialism, but that only by uncovering the workings of this system can we explain their rise. The corollary of this argument is that it is building resistance to neoliberal imperialism from below that offers a genuine alternative to a society which produces such horrors.

It is important to get the emphasis right here: it is tempting to elevate the horrible crimes of the jihadi movements to parity with the barbarism of those who rule the global system. To do this is both factually wrong and politically paralysing. Abu-Bakr al-Baghdadi is a vicious sectarian thug, who has set up a brutal regime which is responsible for the murder of thousands and the displacement of hundreds of thousands. However, even if he continued in power for decades, the magnitude of these crimes would not begin to approach the scale of destruction wreaked on Iraqi society by the elected leaders of the Western world over a quarter century of sanctions, occupation and war. Likewise, the brutality of ISIS towards the Syrian people should not be allowed to obscure the fact that the primary responsibility for the catastrophe which has engulfed the country, including the exile of over half its population, lies with the Assad regime. In both of these cases, it was in the debris of a ruined society that ISIS was able to flourish. The upshot is that more of the 'War on Terror', whether in the form of Western bombing in Syria and military advisers in Iraq, or Assad's barrel bombs, or Sisi's scorched-earth policies in Sinai's poorest districts, is no answer to ISIS and their like. Nor, of course is Cameron's systematic scapegoating and demonisation of Muslims in Britain through forcing nursery-school teachers and social workers to spy on them.

It is movements organised around the struggles against poverty, neoliberalism and dictatorship which provide the best starting point for constructing an alternative future where the voices parroting ISIS's hateful politics are drowned out, not by the scream of industrialised warfare from the West, but by mobilisations for social justice and democracy uniting ordinary people of all religions and none against their real enemies. Nor do we need to play out fantasy politics in order to imagine what such a movement could look like in large parts of the Middle East. The mass mobilisations of 2011 in Egypt and Syria had precisely this character. At the time, not only did ISIS barely exist, but other jihadi groups were equally marginalised, including Al-Qaeda, its terrorist strategies for the overthrow of *al-Taghut* (the tyrants) temporarily consigned to complete irrelevance.

EXTREME WEIRDING

John A. Sweeney

'When the going gets weird, the weird turn pro.'
Hunter S. Thompson

Bandar Mahshahr is no stranger to heat. It is not uncommon for this northern Iranian hamlet to experience consistent highs above 45 degrees Celsius during the summer. But, when the heat index topped 74 degrees Celsius (165 degrees Fahrenheit), which was the second highest heat index ever recorded globally, the world took notice. Bandar Mahshahr is now inextricably linked to the extreme impacts of global warming. For years, reports have warned that extremes would overtake the global climate system, and this inhospitable 'normal' ripe with 'heatwaves, floods, droughts and wildfires' would become 'the new reality of an ever warming world.' However, just because we have been told to expect more extremes does not mean that we have, or will gain, the capacity to forecast and/or mitigate them. Indeed, the causal relations underlying the global climate system are decidedly complex, and climate change is complicating things further. As noted in *Nature*:

> Extreme weather and changing weather patterns – the obvious manifestations of global climate change – do not simply reflect easily identifiable changes in Earth's energy balance such as a rise in atmospheric temperature. They usually have complex causes, involving anomalies in atmospheric circulation, levels of soil moisture and the like. Solid understanding of these factors is crucial if researchers are to improve the performance of, and confidence in, the climate models on which event attribution and longer-term climate projections depend.

While the extreme heat of Bandar Mahshahr was short-lived, the prospects for limited certainty, if not absolute ignorance, concerning the global climate system are all-too-long-term in scope and scale. In short, the climate system as we know it and have flourished and adapted to it – is going postnormal, and attempts to map the territory ahead are appearing increasingly Sisyphean. Such is life in the Anthropocene – an epoch of extreme weirding. How weird are things going to get? This might be the defining question of the twenty-first century.

The Mauna Loa Observatory reported in May 2013 that atmospheric carbon dioxide reached 400 parts-per-million for the first time in 'more than 2.5 million years.' Putting this disturbingly symbolic, and extreme, milestone into perspective, scientists note that the last time atmospheric carbon levels were this high 'the globe's temperature averaged about 3 degrees C warmer, and sea level lapped coasts 5 metres or more higher,' which is to say that the world was a radically different place – one, as it were, absent of humanity. Although there continues to be debate about the diffuse effects of increasing atmospheric CO_2 levels, there is little debate about the cause: human activity, particularly the energy-intensive mechanisms of industrial and post-industrial capitalism. In short, we have weirded the global climate system, and as this process is ongoing, we live in a world subject to extreme weirding.

Global Weirding, rather than global warming, is more than just a play on words – it is a prognosis. As I have argued elsewhere, global weirding 'is a fitting moniker for the emerging meshwork of (1) increasing technological advancement, dependence, and ubiquity, (2) impending ecological catastrophe(s), and (3) the transnational drive and reach of postnormal actants.' By postnormal actants, I am referring explicitly to the networked relations underlying and surrounding us all, which becomes especially apparent in what Ziauddin Sardar has called Postnormal Times (hereafter PNT). In PNT, things we take for granted become uncertain, our understanding of things can become a form of ignorance, and longstanding norms, if not the very idea of normalcy itself, break down before our very eyes. This, if anything, is what is meant by global weirding, and extreme weirding points toward the increasing power of severe phenomena to mutate our sense of being in the world. In the parlance of PNT, the convergence of 'complexity, chaos, and contradictions' is already and will continue to result in systemic disruptions, which can and might begin with actors of various scope and scale.

When a street cart vendor immolated himself in Tunisia in December 2010, few, if any, could forecast the impacts to come. In a time of extreme weirding, Mohamed Bouazizi is a quintessential example of a postnormal actant. However, it is only when we understand his selfless act of protest in light of the networks – many of which used online platforms to organise – formed around political critique in the region that the weird dynamics of PNT become most apparent. Thanks, at least in part, to networked media, the uprisings across the Middle East and North Africa spread like wildfire. Such metaphors are more than fitting, especially as some point toward the extreme impacts of climate change as a factor in the spread of protests throughout the region. As a report on the systemic disruptions underlying the protests in Egypt notes, 'a once-in-a-century winter drought in China reduced global wheat supply and contributed to global wheat shortages and skyrocketing bread prices in Egypt, the world's largest wheat importer. Government legitimacy and civil society in Egypt were upset by protests that focused on poverty, bread, and political discontent.'

Although political discontent was certainly present during Mubarak's despotic rule, an extreme rise in the price of bread was a unifying force that brought together various interests – it literally weirded the Egyptian political landscape. It is certainly the case that humanity has always been susceptible to extreme events, but it would be foolish to assume that history holds the key to understanding and navigating PNT. How can we think through such changes? What conceptual lenses might aid in making sense of the seemingly implausible? How weird are things going to get? To account for and ordain humanity's extreme impacts on the global climate system, two internationally renowned scientists, Paul Crutzen and Eugene Stoermer, coined the term Anthropocene 'to emphasise the central role of mankind in geology and ecology.' Given the extreme weirding to come, it might be of use to employ a long view – both backward and forward – to understand what the Anthropocene might portend.

In 1873, an Italian geologist, Antonio Stoppani, used the phrase 'Anthropozoic era' to conceptualise the geologic-scale impact of human activity. Although noted by Crutzen as an intellectual forebear, the extent of Stoppani's insight has only recently emerged, at least for an English-speaking and reading audience. Expressing his wonder at advent of the Anthropozoic epoch, Stoppani exclaims, 'We are only at the beginning of this new era; still, how deep is man's footprint on earth already! Man has been in possession of it for only a short time; yet, how many geological phenomena may we inquire regarding their causes not in telluric agents, atmosphere, waters, animals, but instead in man's intellect, in his intruding and powerful will.' As one of, if not, the earliest scientific voices to note the abiding, which is also to say extreme, impact of human activity, Stoppani's prescient pronouncement was rare for its time, if only for its attentiveness to scale, but such sentiments would soon become commonplace among those within the emerging discipline of ecology.

While this nascent scientific area of inquiry developed in the latter half of the nineteenth century, the critical concept of an ecosystem did not become widely accepted until the release of Arthur Tansley's *The Use and Abuse of Vegetational Terms and Concepts* in 1935. The advent of the ecosystem concept did much to further the systemic analyses of human activities on the biosphere, but a host of thinkers around the turn of the century were already making grander claims about the role and possible outcomes of human-driven changes to the planet's operations, which is to say that some had theorised the world as a single, unified system – one, as it were, increasingly coming to grips with the extremes of human control.

Less than a century later, however, notions of command and control, if not stability, concerning the global climate system were being called into question. In 1988, James E. Hansen from NASA provided testimony at a Congressional hearing on climate and specifically used the term 'global warming' to describe 'a cause and effect relationship between the greenhouse effect and the observed warming.' With the publication of Bill McKibben's *The End of Nature* (1989), which many consider 'one of the first books for a general audience about global warming,' the stage for the Anthropocene was set. Many were keen to find a way to conceptualise the extremes of life in 'the Anthrocene,' which is the proto-term used by Andrew Revkin, an author and journalist writing for the *New York Times*, in *Global Warming: Understanding the Forecast* (1992) to denote 'a geological age of our own making.' By the time Crutzen 'made up the word on the spur of the moment,' which is perhaps a bit of an embellishment given the term's rich conceptual history, not to mention Stoppani's Anthropozoic and Revkin's Anthrocene, the idea emerged that human activity was having extreme impacts on the planet's biosphere. It was well-established in the scientific community, but the existential implications of the term, which suggests that nature no longer exists, continues to be a point of contention for many.

So many things we take for granted as 'normal' have now become extreme that it is not easy to have all extreme behaviour encapsulated in a single term. Our technology has become extreme, modernity has acquired extreme connotations, our economic system is extreme, corporate behaviour is extreme, almost every ideology has gone extreme. Not surprisingly, some experts are trying to coin terms that focus on particular aspect of our extreme epoch.

In light of the role of technological advancements, from the advent of the steam engine to the apotheosis of algorithms, in precipitating and, assuaging the extremes of the Anthropocene, Pierre Berthon and Brian Donnellan, two ecologists from Bentley University, Boston and National University of Ireland respectively, suggest that a more fitting moniker might be the Technopocene. This, they argue, promotes 'a new level of mindfulness on the part of humans for themselves and their technological offspring.' Humanity has never limited itself to natural processes, although it remains intimately interconnected and intertwined to the workings of the world. As such, the Technopocene provides a more acute diagnosis, and, perhaps, prognosis of/ for the challenges of the Anthropocene, especially as many feel that the only way to avert crisis may be to double-down, so to speak, by engineering the planet's complex adaptive life systems. The Technopocene, then, should not be understood as an extreme version of the Anthropocene but rather be seen as its conceptual antecedent as there have never been humans devoid of technology, which continues, for better or worse, to define us as a species. While the Technopocene lacks the lustre and shine of the Anthropocene, there is much to be said for selecting an appropriate designation for what humans have done and are continuing to do to the planet.

As a means to capture the extreme human impact on the planet, Jussi Parikka, a Finnish academic focusing on media studies, coined the term 'Anthrobscene' to mark the 'various violations of environmental and human life in corporate practices and technological culture that are ensuring that there won't be much of humans in the future scene of life.' Arguing that the only means to make sense of contemporary techno-culture is through the lens of geography, Parikka emphasises the immense materiality of our all-too-modern lives and, as it were, futures. As with atmospheric carbon levels, which will continue to increase for fifty years even if all emissions ceased tomorrow, there is no way to undo the structural changes that techno-culture has had on the planet. This extreme is easy to see when one looks at aerial images of the mines used to harvest the precious minerals and metals necessary to the devices all around us, and the Anthrobscene forces us to confront how 'media feeds back to earth history and future fossil times.' In short, Parikka reminds us that the tenets of modernity are all too contemporary.

In *We Have Never Been Modern*, Bruno Latour, the French philosophr and sociologist of science, poses an incisive critique of the causes and effects of modernity's enduring, albeit affectively performative, legacy: humanity's separation from nature. From the modernist purview, the task of the sciences, especially physics, was to examine nature as object and report back accordingly. In separating politics and physics into two different worlds, modernity was trenchantly Newtonian in its perspective of the natural and, by extension, the social. In affirming the discreetness of natural objects, modernity inculcated a pathological fixation on progress and growth that drove the greatest expansion, and by extension concentration, of wealth in human history, but this story, as it were, may not have a happy ending. As Latour notes, 'So long as Nature was remote and under control, it still vaguely resembled the constitutional pole of tradition, and science could still be seen as a mere intermediary to uncover it. Nature seemed to be held in reserve, transcendent, inexhaustible, distant enough. But where are we to classify the ozone hole story, or global warming or deforestation?' In calling into question the limits and destructiveness of the modernity's false notion of nature, Latour argues that global warming was always-already human and natural, which is to say that we have never been modern, or separate from nature. This, if anything, is what the Anthropocene, and its many variants, are meant to convey. But can this idea truly prepare us for what might lie ahead?

Although many are struggling to see an end to the bloody conflict in Syria, some have sought to understand its origins, and climate change is a key suspect. According to a study published in the *Proceedings of the National Academy of Sciences of the United States of America*, 'the conflict in Syria shows an impact of an extreme climate event in the context of government failure, exacerbated by the singular circumstance of the large influx of Iraqi refugees. Multiyear droughts occur periodically in the [Fertile Crescent] due to natural causes, but it is unlikely that the recent drought would have been as extreme absent the century-long drying trend.' Although some, notably Canadian journalist Gwynne Dyer, believe that climate wars are likely in the years ahead, the recent escalation of refugees into Europe, primarily from Syria and Libya, signals that extreme weirding is having and will continue to have mortal consequences. While there is plenty to be concerned about now, many think the worst is yet to come, although it is hard to ignore the extreme weirding happening all around us.

Ground zero for extreme weirding in the United States is California. The state's motto is Eureka, which harkens back to its gold rush days. This exclamatory phrase translates as 'I have found it!' and is linked to the Greek inventor, Archimedes, who is said to have uttered the phrase upon making a great discovery. Unfortunately, all that California has discovered is how extremely weird the world has become. At present, 97 per cent of the state 'is experiencing some degree of drought', and the area has seen such little precipitation that the Sierra Nevada snowpack is at its lowest point in '500 years'. Conditions are perfect for forest fires, and the state's governor recently declared a state of emergency after a mega-fire burned '50,000 acres' in the northern part of the state. While many residents might welcome a record storm, scientists predict that the beleaguered state will face one of the strongest El Nino events on record. Driven by warm ocean temperatures, which are a direct consequence of climate change, the impact of a 'Godzilla El Nino' might be nothing short of catastrophic as flooding and landslides are certain to wreak havoc on already stressed response systems. As California's GDP is over $2 trillion, which puts it just ahead of Brazil, the effects of a massive El Nino event are sure to have global consequences.

The extreme weirding brought about by climate change has led some to consider radical 'solutions,' which remain speculative and host a range of uncertainties. While some believe that the only way humanity might abate extreme weirding is through climate modification initiatives, others have turned to consider more confined, yet equally contentious, 'remedies.' In 2012, Mathew Liao et al, a group of scientists from Oxford and New York Universities, published an article, 'Human Engineering and Climate Change,' in *Ethics, Policy, & Environment* to much fanfare. Arguing that 'the biomedical modification of humans' should be on the table in the light of the extreme weirding to come, the authors suggest that enhancing empathy, fostering a pharmacological intolerance to carbon-intensive products like red meat, and engineering shorter people are reasonable and, perhaps, less risky than large-scale climate engineering initiatives. Although Liao and his colleagues make it clear that they do not advocate involuntary human engineering as a course of action, they are firm in their conviction that wilful bioengineering initiatives should be 'considered and explored further,' especially as this course of action 'could make behavioural and market solutions more likely to succeed.' While humans have always experimented upon themselves, if only as a result of technological innovation, intentional biophysical modification as a means to mitigate climate change represents an extremely weird response to a daunting challenge. Extreme leading to more extreme!

In a world overcome by extreme weirding, humans might not only have to worry about novel threats but also dangers from the past that are expected to resurface as the global climate system goes postnormal. This dynamic is most apparent in the tundra region where permafrost traps the things of nightmares. The 2003 discovery of a giant virus, which is still microscopic, startled the scientific community, and while scientists are confident that none of what has been found so far poses any 'threat to humans or animals,' the same scientists concede the possibility that 'dangerous viruses do lurk in suspended animation deep below ground' as the prehistoric permafrost creates conditions whereby infectivity endures. Although such a scenario comes off sounding like science fiction, the effects of extreme weirding cannot be underestimated or resigned to whimsy. This, if anything, is what the Anthropocene – as an epoch of extreme weirding – can and might teach us: the unthinkable is increasingly becoming the unavoidable.

THE LIGHT OF MUHAMMAD

Raza Ali

As a child in Karachi, I remember my father used to take us to see the procession of *Youm-e-Ashour*. I belonged to a Sunni family. The main participants of the procession were Shi'a, but on this day our love of the Prophet and his family brought all Muslims together. Among the cries of 'Ya Hussain! Ya Hussain!', a shirtless group of mourners would beat their chests red in rhythm; some would whip themselves, while others used more dangerous and sharper instruments that led them to bleed as a result of the injuries they sustained. Then there was always at least one group that struck their heads with their hands. The rest, making less extreme gestures, slapped their chests gently with one hand in sync with the crowd.

As I have observed that the ritual was a means of catharsis, of dissipating the unbearable pain felt by the Shi'a community as they remembered the tragic death of Imam Hussain and his supporters. Everyone wore black. At every corner a *sabeel* was set up to distribute cold sherbet to those present, whether they were there to mourn or not, or even if they were not thirsty or were only hanging around in the hope of receiving a free cold drink. We watched the lavishly decorated horse called *zuljanah* striding through the centre of the procession, called the *tazia*, alluding to the agonising final journey of Imam Hussain. After, the spectacle moved off the streets, our families would sit in front of the TV, gathered together to watch elegies sung in melancholy lament, railing against the cruel events that define the Shi'a experience. Finally, the gathering of *Shaam-e-Ghareeban* (eve of the strangers) would bring this sombre spectacle to a climax by meticulously recounting the final hours of Imam Hussain and his family's travails through the eyes of various narrators. This was a ritual that took place every year. It was a fixture in our lives, played out in innocence amid an atmosphere of cultural cohesion, respect and tolerance. Not for a moment did we ever consider it to be anything other than a fascinating family day out and a reflection of the diversity of the Pakistan in which we lived.

What for me was a fun annual experience to look forward to was in fact a powerful display of veneration of the Prophet. But it also symbolised the way in which extreme love for the Prophet can prove divisive. On the 10th of the Islamic month of Muharram Muslims worldwide, particularly Shi'a Muslims, mourn the martyrdom of Imam Hussain, grandson of Muhammad. Hussain entered the grounds of Karbala on 2nd Muharram 680 with his family. His intention was to challenge the caliphate of Yazid, son of Muawiya. His brother Hasan had chosen to revoke any claim in favour of Muawiya – a senior companion of the Prophet – in order to bring peace amongst Muslims who had been fighting for many years on the issue of 'right to rule', which was the main reason for the split between Sunni and Shi'a Muslims. After a long siege by Yazid's army, Hussain was finally martyred on the 10th. It was a defining moment in Islamic history that made the Shi'a-Sunni fault-line a permanent one.

Both the Shi'a and Sunni communities ostensibly demonstrate their love of the Prophet and his family. The Shi'as insist on the primacy of the Prophet's family far more than Sunnis and regard only members of his family as legitimate rulers of the Muslim community. Sunnis, however, defend Abu Bakr, who succeeded the Prophet, championing his love and loyal companionship of the Prophet. For Sunnis, the Prophet died with his head on the lap of his wife, Abu Bakr's daughter, Aisha. The Shi'a claim he died with his head on the shoulders of his cousin Ali. But both sects agree that the Prophet loved his grandsons Hasan and Hussain. He is reported to have said: 'O Allah, I love them, so love them.' Just as he loved his family and companions, his followers of both the Shi'a and Sunni tradition loved them, passionately, extremely, as they loved him.

But it is a strange kind of love. During my adolescence, I frequently heard the words '*Kaafir Kaafir, Shi'a Kaafir. Jo Na Maanay Woh Bhi Kaafir*' (Disbeliever, disbeliever, Shi'as are disbelievers. Whosoever doesn't accept that is also a disbeliever). So one group that claimed to love the Prophet was denouncing another group that also loved the Prophet in the harshest terms. Not only a whole community labelled *Kaafir* but also the non-Shi'as who joined the throng at the Shi'a processions of *Youm-e-Ashour* were denounced as infidels. Suddenly, it was unacceptable to share the grief of my Shi'a brothers and sisters. These hard-line sentiments, with no time for compassion or empathy, were gaining currency throughout Pakistan.

It is not just the Sunni and Shi'a schism that illustrates extreme love for the Prophet. I have always found the inner mystical connection with the divine love that Sufism strives for fascinating. The source of their love is, of course, the Prophet Muhammad. Could it have an intricate link with the Shi'a-Sunni conflict? Three out of four popular Sufi orders start their chain from Ali and one from Abu Bakr. They are Sunni but take the Shi'a Imams as their leaders. For example, Abdul Qadir Gilani was a Hanbali scholar as well as the founder of the Qadiriyya order. It seems to me that Sufis created a middle-ground between the bitter divide of Sunnis and Shi'as by taking from both and extending the ideas to include various practices, grades and honours. However, in certain Sufi groups the love of the Prophet is taken to an extreme dimension. The Prophet becomes the centre of elaborate narratives of creation, which are popular amongst sects with mystical leanings. These stories put the Prophet not just at the centre of the formation of the universe but even before creation. One particular narrative I have heard quite often, said to be based on hadith, echoes the design of the universe in the following words:

> It is related that Jābir ibn 'Abd Allāh (r) said to the Prophet (s), 'O Messenger of Allāh, may my father and mother be sacrificed for you, tell me of the first thing Allāh created before all things.' He said: O Jābir, the first thing Allāh created was the light of your Prophet from His light, and that light remained in the midst of His Power for as long as He wished, and there was not, at that time, a Tablet or a Pen or a Paradise or a Fire or an angel or a heaven or an earth. And when Allāh wished to create creation, he divided that Light into four parts and from the first made the Pen, from the second the Tablet, from the third the Throne, then He divided the fourth into four parts (and from them created everything else)

This account has absolutely no support in the Qur'an. The hadith refers to a concept called Mohammadan reality or light. The Qur'an contains the words 'there has come to you from Allah a light and a clear Book' (5.15), which is used as proof that the word light refers to the Prophet. The famous 'verse of the light' is also interpreted in the same vein to mean that 'light upon light' refers to the Prophet:

Allah is the Light of the heavens and the earth. The example of His light is like a niche within which is a lamp, the lamp is within glass, the glass as if it were a pearly [white] star lit from [the oil of] a blessed olive tree, neither of the east nor of the west, whose oil would almost glow even if untouched by fire. Light upon light. (24.35)

But in the Qur'an the use of the word light is much broader than the hadith. We can possibly draw a parallel with the Christian trinity where the father and the son are essentially of the same substance. It is possible that in an effort to raise the Prophet's stature in competition with Christian beliefs the idea of Muhammadan Light was invented. In the Qur'an, initially the word light refers to previous scriptures in the same way it refers to the Qur'an. So, we read, 'indeed, We sent down the Torah, in which was guidance and light' (5.44) and 'We gave him the Gospel, in which was guidance and light' (5.46). Light and darkness become themes in the Qur'an symbolising the dichotomy of being guided or lost: the role of the prophets is to bring people from darkness to light. Of the Prophet himself it is pronounced: 'this is a Book which We have revealed to you, [O Muhammad], that you might bring mankind out of darkness into the light by permission of their Lord' (14.1); and the same for Moses, 'We certainly sent Moses with Our signs, [saying], "bring out your people from darkness into the light and remind them of the days of Allah"' (14.5). The individual who accepts the guidance is the 'one whose breast Allah has expanded to [accept] Islam and he is upon a light from his Lord' (39.22). The individual 'did not know what is the Book or [what is] faith, but We have made it a light by which We guide whom We will of Our servants' (42.52). Thus, those who have accepted the guidance then also possess the light, which suggests that it is about goodness and truth.

Another popular narration that gives the Prophet an entirely different status with regard to order and purpose of creation reports that after Adam had made his mistake and wanted to ask for forgiveness he said, 'O my Lord, I am asking you to forgive me for the sake of Muhammad.' To which Allah replies how did you know? Adam said that he saw the name of Prophet Muhammad written on his throne, so he knew Allah loved him. Allah said, 'O Adam, I have forgiven you, and were it not for Muhammad I would not have created you.'

Once again, there is no evidence of this in the Qur'an. The words used by Adam to ask for forgiveness are mentioned in the Qur'an but there is no suggestion that Adam knew of Muhammad. Sufi theology relies heavily on such weak narrations to build up the idea that the universe culminated in the love of the Prophet. What could be more extreme than to suggest that were it not for the Prophet, God would not have created anything?

I am reminded of the story of al-Busiri, whose poem I used to hear frequently in my childhood. Born in the thirteenth century, al-Busiri was a Sufi poet of the Shadili order, and lived in Egypt. He suffered paralysis on one side of his body. In this time of darkness and despair he wept and prayed and composed a poem in praise of the Prophet. He prayed for the Prophet to intercede on his behalf and ask Allah to relieve his suffering. He repeatedly sang this poem until he went to sleep. That night, we are told, the Prophet appeared in his dream, wiped his face and put his own mantle (*burdah*) over Busiri's paralysed body.

When he awoke he found his paralysis was cured and he could walk again. He left his house to go out and came across another Sufi. The Sufi asked him about the poem he had written about the Prophet during his sickness, which surprised him because he had not yet told anyone about it. The Sufi told him that in his dream he saw him recite that poem to the Prophet, who was pleased with it and wrapped his mantle around him curing his sickness. So Busiri gave him the poem and the events were related to others. The poem reached Bahauddin, vizier of King Tahir. His viceroy, Saaduddin was going blind and he came to hear of this poem. When he placed it on his eyes it cured his blindness.

The poem is appropriately called Qasida Burda or the 'Poem of the mantle'. It is well-known across the Muslim world and has been translated from Persian to Chinese. I grew up listening to different versions and developed a fond affection for the composition. I was captivated by the many virtues and benefits attributed to the poem. Recitation of the poem promised to bestow long life or wealth or a much-coveted male child. It is believed to alleviate droughts and hardships. It can protect from calamities, disease, possession and robbery. Success is promised in whatever heart's desire it is recited. The words are beautiful and it is mesmerisingly sung in all its versions and manifestations. It begins with salutation to the Prophet:

MawlaYa SalliWa Sallam Daiiman Abadan. This excerpt is a good illustration of its flavour:

> For had it not been for him this world would not have come out of non-existence. Muhammad is the leader of both worlds and both creations (man and jinn).
>
> And of both groups, Arabs and non Arabs.
>
> Our Prophet, the one who commands good, forbids evil.
>
> There is none More truthful than him in saying 'No' or 'Yes'.
>
> He is (Allah's) most beloved, whose intercession is hoped for.
>
> For every fear (and distress) that is going to come (on the day) of agony (and fears).
>
> He called (people) towards Allah, so those who cling to him.
>
> Cling to a rope which will never snap.
>
> He transcends all the Prophets, physically and in (noble) character.
>
> And (the other Prophets) cannot come near his in knowledge and noble nature kindness.
>
> They all obtained from Rasulullah (Muhammad) (Like a) handful (of water) from the ocean or (a few) sips from continuous rains.

Sufism intrigued me, but during my university days I had an opportunity to spend some time with a quite different Islamic movement – Tablighi Jamat. The Jamat was created over a hundred years ago and has become a global organisation, now boasting millions of followers around the world. It started in the area of Mewat in India and was called the 'Kalima' party because member became known for teaching people the basic declaration of Islamic faith. The story goes that the founder, Maulana Ilyas despaired of his neighbours. He noticed that although they were Muslim by faith, their cultural practises betrayed a strong Hindu influence. He would cry and pray to God for guidance on how to make them better Muslims. It was this desire to save their souls that inspired him to set up Tablighi Jamat.

My over-riding memory of the Jamat is their preponderance of the beard. The most conspicuous and identifying symbol of a Muslim man is particularly close to Tablighi Jamat's heart. The Tablighis are strict in following the Sunnah, a word interchangeably used with the word hadith in traditional Sunni schools. Sunnah is defined as everything that the Prophet said, did or approved of. The Tablighis argue that the Sunnah provides a lived example of the revelation of the Qur'an. Thus, it too is revelation of a different type and is equally obligatory as the Qur'anic injunctions. The beard is considered a Sunnah purely because the Prophet had it and he is believed to have said, 'trim your moustaches and let your beards grow'. In their gatherings I observed them obsessing over the minutiae of beard etiquette. Each of my friends who had become committed to the Jamat began by growing their beard long. They urge you to grow it to what they consider to be the proper Sharia length. I have witnessed grown men cry because a Muslim brother had shaved his beard. They say that the Sunnah of the Prophet is being flushed down the drain and it pains them immensely because they love him so utterly.

The Sunnah of the beard has always confused me. According to hadith, the Prophet was known to dye his beard. This is a popular practice among the Barelvi sect, particularly in the Indian sub-continent where men will use henna to dye their (often greying) beard. In another hadith it is said that he warned, 'Jews and Christians do not dye', and asked Muslims to 'act differently from them'. In a number of narrations mention of trimming the moustache and leaving the beard has been listed as an element of *fitrah* or nature. It seems to me that this is not an obligation but an attempt by a budding community to differentiate itself from those who are already established. To identify themselves clearly so that others would know their numbers and in a confrontation, of which there were many, their unique appearance may serve a purpose.

There was a major transformation amongst my peers after 9/11. There was an upsurge in the inclination towards religiosity and it was expressed primarily through the Sunnah of the beard as an expression of love for and emulation of the Prophet. A community under stress almost naturally and predictably reverts to symbolism and self-identification as an act of defiance, solidarity and preservation.

Extreme love for the Prophet extends beyond the beard and is disproportionately concerned with what one must not do. During Friday prayers, I have often heard these words in the sermon: 'the worst of things are those that are newly invented; every newly-invented thing is an innovation and every innovation is going astray, and every going astray is in the Fire'. One might say that those who hold views closer to the Salafi point of view assert such statements in an attempt to remind those who they consider to have invented unacceptable methods of showing love for the Prophet, such as celebrating his birth. The concept of innovation in Islam is labelled *bid'a*. This stick is often used to beat those who may be of Sufi or unorthodox inclination as there are multiple practices – such as pleading for intercession, visiting graves, performing *dhikr* (remembrance) in solitary or at gatherings whether this involves sitting silently to singing and dancing – that characterise these communities and which the Salafis find insufferable.

I was still young when I became aware of these oppositional ways of expressing love for the Prophet. My father had put me in a madrasa to learn the Qur'an. It was located in a busy market street and every afternoon, after school, I walked from the building where I lived through this road. It was crowded with shops on the sides and shacks and stalls that encroached on the road. There was no space for cars to pass so mostly it was used by people walking or motorcycles weaving their way through the pedestrians. This madrasa was part of a Barelvi mosque, known for their Sufi inclinations. Almost immediately opposite was a Salafi mosque.

Friday afternoons would turn into a sermon match on loudspeakers. The targets of both were the sellers and buyers on the street. The Barelvi mosque would blast invocations and praises of the Prophet as justifications for all their 'innovative' practices. It would decry the Salafis for being devoid of love for the Prophet. The Salafi mosque on the other hand would roundly condemn them for *bid'a*. They would reel off a list of all the practices they considered un-Islamic and attack them. Their favourite retort was to remind their rivals across the street and anyone else within earshot of the Prophet's words 'the worst of things are those that are newly invented'. All kinds of accusations would fly back and forth.

I usually prayed at the mosque where I studied. When I walked in I would be met with large and looming framed posters telling me the reasoning behind practices such as keeping the hands at waist level during prayers and kissing the backs of both thumbs and wiping them over one's eyes, as a sign of respect, whenever the name of the Prophet was spoken during the call of the *muezzin*. I also had the opportunity to pray at the Salafi mosque across the road and they too had corresponding posters, which asked the worshippers to keep their hands at chest level while praying and raising the hands to their ears every time the words *Allahu*

Akbar were said during prayers. Their timing for the late afternoon prayer was also slightly different, which I found occasionally convenient. It would be difficult to say who loved the Prophet more but both claimed to display the greater devotion to him. I don't doubt the sincerity of either but I do wonder whether the Prophet would be happy to see his followers competing over his love like this.

The Salafis and the Sufis are a stark example of the ways in which ardent love for the Prophet can be so contradictory. But there are others. In the Qur'an the words '*khatamun nabiyyin*' are usually understood to mean the 'last of prophets'. It forms the foundation of the belief held by the majority of Muslims. That is, except for the Ahmadis, who believe that these words do not represent the closing of the door of prophet-hood but its pinnacle. According to this interpretation the words are taken to mean 'seal of prophets'. Ahmadis are followers of Mirza Ghulam Ahmad who was born in India in 1835. He was a scholar of Islam and was renowned for his debates with Christian missionaries on theological matters. The issue of interpretation in the Qur'an would have remained academic until it was claimed that he was the promised Messiah and Mahdi and a non-law bearing prophet. Such an idea challenged the 'finality of prophet-hood' of the Prophet Muhammad and exploded into accusations of apostasy, blasphemy and subsequent threats and acts of violence.

Pakistan is perhaps the only country to have declared the Ahmadi to be non-Muslim on the basis of this. Although there are irrevocable differences between Sunni and Shi'a and Salafi and Sufi sects of Islam, and they routinely brand each other as disbelievers, but there has been no successful attempt to declare them non-Muslim at an official or constitutional level. The Ahmadis were, however, considered beyond the pale and in 1974, an amendment to the Pakistani constitution declared them to be non-Muslim, thanks to the pressure from conservative religious groups. What inevitably followed was an environment of persecution where Ahmadis were not permitted to self-identify as Muslims. They were barred from building mosques and, if they persevered, were told that their place of worship should not have any outward resemblance to a 'typical' mosque. They were forbidden to 'pose' as Muslims and official documentation such as ID Card or Passport required either the endorsement of the 'finality of prophet-hood' or declaring oneself as a non-Muslim. Non-Muslims are also not allowed to enter the two holy sites, Mecca and Medina, hence an Ahmadi holding a Pakistani passport would be unable to perform the pilgrimage, Hajj. Over the years, Ahmadi mosques have been burnt, and thousands of them have been killed and persecuted – not just in Pakistan, but also in Bangladesh and Indonesia.

A childhood friend of mine is an Ahmadi. It had never occurred to me to screen people according to their religious persuasion or sectarian beliefs before deciding whether or not I got along with them, which is why I have friends who are Sunni and Shi'a, Salafi and Sufi, Muslim and non-Muslim, believer and atheist. I have never been of the disposition that their beliefs or lack thereof are any threat to my own. We vigorously debate issues, get worked up and frustrated but, after all that, go back to being friends because we enjoy each other's company. Through this particular friend, I came to understand the difficulty of being an Ahmadi in Pakistan. But I only fully realised the intensity of prejudice harboured by others first-hand when another ex-classmate made a veiled threat against his life on an alumni mailing list. I had studied with these people and I did not know them to be this extreme. In fact, I had travelled with the one who actually made the threat and he seemed to be an ordinary young man whose interests included video games and girls. His conversion to this level of vitriol was eye-opening. This too is a post 9/11 incident and all these instances of extremism make me wonder how the psyche of the average Muslim has been altered by that atrocity.

I feel certain that 9/11 was a watershed moment for Muslims, but there have been others. During the Danish cartoons debacle I heard the story of Ilam Din on a local Pakistani television channel. Ilam Din was born in Lahore before the partition of India under British rule. In 1923 a pamphlet called *Rangila Rasul* (roughly translated as Colourful Prophet) was published by Mahashe Rajpal. It contained a salacious poem about the Prophet and referred to his many wives and his private life, contrasting this with Hindu saints who led more hermetic lives. There was uproar amongst the Muslim community. According to the legend, Ilam Din was passing by the Wazir Khan mosque and saw a crowd raising slogans against the publisher. He decided to kill Rajpal for his blasphemy. He obtained a dagger, entered his shop and stabbed him to death. He was arrested, put on trial and sentenced to death. In the Pakistani context this story has become the stuff of folklore as the defendant's lawyer was none other than Muhammad Ali Jinnah, the founder of the nation. (Although I learned later that he was not the original lawyer but was brought in for the appeal.) He claimed that Ilam Din was overcome by feelings of veneration of the Prophet and reacted emotionally. This same defence was used during the trail of the horrific murder of Farkhanda in March 2015. A conservative Muslim sympathetic to the Salafi version of Islam, she was lynched and set on fire by a mob in the centre of Kabul after an argument with a Sufi mystic, or *pir*, escalated into baseless accusations that she had burned a copy of the Qur'an. In Ilam Din's case, Jinnah could not save him and he was later sentenced to death but he acquired the status of a martyr for having given his life to protect the honour of the Prophet. But the atrocity committed against Farkhanda is not an isolated example. From the Rushdie to *Charlie Hebdo* affairs people have been killed for the love of the Prophet. Extreme love of the Prophet leads Muslims to become irrational and paranoid.

Indeed, the very idea that you can blaspheme the Prophet seems rather absurd. Those who do not believe in Islam have no reason to be sensitive about the honour of Islamic personalities, particularly when, it seems to me, the same courtesy is not always extended to figures revered by other faiths. I had a similar conversation with a few friends on Facebook where I raised the proposition that blasphemy cannot make sense because every emerging religion is inevitably seen by the adherents of the established ones as blasphemous. All new religions rely on denying the validity of the beliefs of previous religions and demoting their sacred personalities from whatever elevated position they occupy. The reaction of my friends was of denial. They claimed they did not blaspheme against the Jews or Christians and respect all their 'prophets'. But that was the point, they were still looking at them through the lens of Islam and whatever personalities and history we shared was the criteria for respecting 'their religion'. I felt compelled to raise the case of gods and idols in Hinduism. In my experience there is little respect for those who are dismissed as 'idol-worshippers', denounced for their misled beliefs as *kuffar* (infidels) and *mushrikeen* (those who associate, idolators). We even have names for them. The tags may just mean deniers of Islam and polytheists but the feeling that they evoke in the mind of a Muslim is not neutral by any means.

The Quran's advice on the issue is 'do not insult those they invoke other than Allah, lest they insult Allah in enmity without knowledge'. The verse continues to clarify the issue of difference between religions by saying, 'we have made pleasing to every community their deeds. Then to their Lord is their return and He will inform them of what they used to do' (6.108). Followers of Islam seem to have dispensed with this advice. The burning alive of a Christian couple in Pakistan, who were accused of blasphemy, is symbolic. If one believes that God has reserved the right to punish or reward, how can impatient Muslims appoint themselves the arbiters of justice? They encroach on not only God's rights but also assume, while on earth, the role of God on the day of judgement. I asked my friends, 'Isn't that blasphemy in itself?'

The extreme love for the Prophet that renders some followers of Islam judgemental and inflexible directly contradicts the many documented examples of the Prophet's humanity, forgiveness and humility. The kindness, patience, humility, forgiveness, and affection for others and nature, he reportedly exemplified, is not part of this love. Indeed, the art of being human personified by the Prophet has been forgotten by many Muslims. As they clamour to profess ever louder their extreme love for the Prophet, they are busy calling each other out, thrashing each other with absurd books of theology, and even killing those who dishonour their Prophet. This is extremism in love 'of' the Prophet. But also complete absence of the love that he radiated. This extreme love, instead of facilitating empowerment and generosity of spirit, has bred insecurity, belligerence and paranoia. It is akin to growing a tree in a glass box. There is insufficient room to grow. The tree starts to bend and twist in an effort to find space. It ends up distorted and ugly instead of an example of the beauty of nature. More importantly, it is unable to serve as shade or shelter for anyone. It needs to be brought out of its box.

THE ENEMY WITHIN

Farouk Peru

Conventional wisdom tells us that Muslims who commit acts of violence are acting on their own impulses and for their own complex and misguided reasons. Yet I don't think this is the whole story. What is missing from the complete picture is the inconvenient truth that by waging jihad and murdering civilians, as occurred in the attacks in Paris and on the beaches of Tunisia, these individuals are not actually operating outside the boundaries of Islamic tradition. Muslims who commit acts of violence in the name of Islam are seeking to dominate Islamic discourse. Those unfamiliar with the Islamic tradition and its teachings, including Muslims themselves, the barrage of images depicting inhumanity at the hands of extremists of ISIS, Boko Haram et al could unsurprisingly lead them to conclude Islam does indeed promote violent teachings. However, Islam is not a single set of ideas. Rather, there is an ideological stream within the Islamic tradition that has been exploited to justify violent acts of extremism. In order to understand where this thinking came from, we must go back to the origins of Islam itself.

Islam is a human tradition which began with Prophet Muhammad. The human-ness of this heritage does not preclude the belief that the Prophet Muhammad experienced revelation from Allah. This revelation, which is in a textual form that we know today as the Qur'an, was initially verbal (even the word 'qur'an' means 'recitation' or 'reading'). The process which culminated in the text was entirely human, even by admission of the Qur'an itself (80: 11-16). Furthermore, what we now know as 'Islamic' literature, also includes the extensive hadith collections (sayings and actions of Prophet Muhammad), *tafsir* (exegetical writings on the Qur'an), *seerah* (biographical literature of the Prophet), *fiqh* (jurisprudence literature) and other classical texts. Islam is a rich doctrine spanning centuries of conversation and research.

It should thus come as no surprise that there are deep divergences within the Islamic fold. These differences of opinion, initially found among the companions of the Prophet, gradually became reified as schools of law. The question that arises is: if the companions of the Prophet did have disputes — and hadith literature itself testifies to the fact — then why did they not simply iron out those differences when the Prophet was alive?

There are two possible answers. First, the information regarding the companions was written retroactively. That is, these events did not actually occur as the hadith literature tells us but rather reflected the political tendencies of the Muslim community of later periods, which needed the legitimacy of the companions in order to validate their particular dogma. Second, the Prophet wanted the companions to think for themselves and did not want to interfere with that dynamic. In this scenario, the Prophet would have foreseen that plurality of thought was in fact a matter of course and there was no reason to quell it.

In any case, over time various trajectories in Islamic thought emerged. Perhaps the most obvious divergence is that between the Sunnis and Shi'a. Although this difference first arose out of a dispute regarding the leadership of the community, it gradually developed into a theology itself. It reflected itself in hadith literature as well as exegetical materials. As if this was not a big enough rift, further avenues of thought developed within each tradition of Sunni and Shi'a. The strands within the Sunni tradition were not exactly harmonious with each other even though they did originate from the same belief system.

The most outstanding path was of course orthodox practice or what one would describe as the contemporary dominant view of Islam. This is a core Islamic identity in which a Muslim recognises the fundamental principles — the five pillars — and strives to practise them. It is not an overtly political identity. Muslims may choose to accentuate the focus of their faith to the liberal end of the spectrum or the extremes of mysticism (*tasawwuf* or Sufism). In between there are practices ranging from ultra-orthodoxy to moderate tendencies, which have emerged over time in response to an array of social and political circumstances.

The theoretical tradition that we refer to as 'violent extremism' resides under this wide umbrella of Islam. I prefer to call it Islamofascism. It is not essentially Islamic but rather an extreme interpretation. There are elements within the Islamic tradition which this group chooses to ignore or downplay ostensibly because of the potential to undo the system of teachings they promote. Even though the term is controversial, specifically amongst Muslims, Islamofascism is apt because it epitomises the overall characteristic of the system it labels. It is usually used pejoratively but I utilised the moniker merely to theorise what is a comprehensive network of belief. It is Islamic in the sense that it originates from the Islamic tradition that Muslims vocalise in their discourse and uses terms which exist within the Islamic framework, the most obvious one being jihad. The word 'fascism' was grafted on because it connotes oppression. This oppression may manifest itself in a plethora of ways and affect miscellaneous parties but its salient symbolism is the eradication of an individual's freedom, in this case to determine his or her understanding of Islam. Islamofascism mediates between the individual's relationship with Allah.

The system of Islamofascism first emerged at the point in Islamic history when the authority of the Prophet was elevated to the status of an unparalleled figure in human history. This claim was made by religious scholars, the ulama, who purported to be inheritors of the Prophet and therefore qualified to control the oligopoly of knowledge, which would psychologically coerce Muslims into obedience on pain of blasphemy. Using this authority, the ulama created the concept of a community that was exclusive in its integrity and named it the 'ummah'. The ummah would be bound to a comprehensive legal system (the so-called divinely mandated Sharia) and the enforcement of Sharia would be by a state instrument of expansive and imperialist proportions. This would be known as the so-called *ad-dawlah al-islamiyyah* (Islamic State) led by a *khilafah* (successor to the Prophet).

Anyone who has read the *Seerah* (lit. 'journey'), which is a genre of literature and refers to the biography and history of the Prophet Muhammad, would be aware of the two broad stages of his life as a prophet. The first spans the period of his initial preaching of Islam in Mecca, which lasted thirteen years, and the second his subsequent emigration to Medina along with his companions. In the latter stage, he effectively founded a city state in Medina, ratified in the Constitution of Medina. In this document, an agreement was made between the Muslims led by the Prophet and the converted tribes of Medina along with the Jews and Christians, which stated that they would live as a single community in the sacred space of the city.

This contract, it is argued by the ulama, brought into existence the very first 'Islamic state', ruled by the Prophet Muhammad for the next ten years until his death at which point the first caliph Abu Bakr was named successor and thus began the caliphate, perhaps retrospectively named. History tells us that even at this time, Abu Bakr did not have unanimous support from the nascent Muslim empire as some factions preferred Ali ibn Abi Talib, the cousin of the Prophet to be their leader, which he eventually became as the fourth caliph nearly twenty years later. This institution of caliphate also did not seem to bode well for the early caliphs as only Abu Bakr died of natural causes. His successors, Umar ibn Al-Khattab, Uthman ibn Affan and Ali ibn Abi Talib himself were all assassinated. These were the first and last of the democratically elected caliphs and subsequent to that, invariably, monarchies ruled. This is where fascism began.

The first of the monarchies, the Umayyads, with one exception, were said to be worldly kings who expanded their empire for the sake of filling their coffers. Muawiyah ibn Abu Sufyan who founded this dynasty was said to have died as the richest monarch in the world. There was simply no suggestion of democratically elected caliphs (after the initial four) during this or any other period in the history of the caliphate. Instead, the faction who supported Ali, the Shia, were denounced as traitors and heretics. These denouncements were even traditionalised as part of the ritual of Friday prayers. The oppression required to uphold the power of the caliphate monarchy cannot be underestimated.

The Umayyads were overthrown in a bloody coup a century later by the Abbasids whose dynasty ruled as caliphs for the next 500 years or so. Although there was a flourishing of Islamic culture during this time, they were also a brutal regime that even stifled Muslim scholars. The most famous victim of this regime was probably Ahmad ibn Hanbal whose uncritical literalism was not appreciated by the officialdom until his demise. It is indeed ironic that ibn Hanbal's thinking is now the basis of the extremist Wahhabi sect.

Possibly the most salient element of fascism practised by the caliphates is the notion of 'offensive jihad' (appropriately termed as this jihad does indeed offend our ethical sensibilities). This form of jihad went on to legislate that the Islamic state should not have stagnant borders. Once the state is established, it should approach its neighbours and offer them three options: acceptance of Islam (meaning the Islamic state's form of Islam and their control of the neighbouring state); acceptance of the hegemony of the Islamic state and thus the neighbouring state's acceptance of the *dhimmi* or protected status, and finally, war. It is this very same ideology that inspires movements such as Hizb ut-Tahrir and Al-Muhajiroun and is the blueprint for their Islamic State. Another feature of the caliphate is cultural colonisation whereby any colony that comes under its influence would be subsumed and unable to retain any vestiges of 'native' culture as this would be 'unIslamic'. The caliphate is essentially an Arabic institution based on ancient customs of warring tribes.

So, what does an Islamofascist need to govern an Islamic State? Sharia law of course, which turns out to be possibly the most famous face of Muslim extremism in the world today. This is due in no small part to the media attention lavished on it. Its barbarism is lapped up by news providers and social media and the horrors of ISIS compounds this global focus on the Muslim other. Although Sharia law is infinitely more complex than the simplistic interpretations of ISIS and other extremist groups, one can legitimately ask: to what extent do the heinous practices associated with violent extremists come from the Islamic corpus of law?

Sharia law is an intricate legal system which is understood by Islamists to be divine and thus unalterable. Enthusiasts of ISIS see Sharia as the ideal system to govern mankind and strive to institutionalise even its partial features in secular spaces. However, far from being a unified set of information with unanimously confirmed laws, Sharia is highly contested. There are thought to have been more than five hundred schools of law in the early period of Islam, emphasising the extent of independent reasoning that was prevalent at the time. However, as the imperialist caliphs increasingly drew strength from legal backing, these schools were whittled down to around twenty and eventually reduced to the four schools now in existence.

The components of Sharia law are said to be the Qur'an, the Hadith literature, *Qiyas* (analogical reasoning) and *Ijma* (consensus) but there is no agreement on the sources that constitute Sharia law even amongst the four schools of law. The Shafie school accepts all four sources but their *ijma* component requires agreement from every single Muslim, something totally impossible to achieve. The Hanafi school places extraordinary emphasis on *Qiyas* and thus its founder, Abu Hanifah, was seen to be anti-hadith. The Maliki school prioritises the *ijma* of Medina because it was the birthplace of Islamic governance and would thus contain the correct rulings believed to be verified by the Prophet himself. Finally the Hanbali school was much more partial to literalism and only gave authority to the Qur'an and hadith. All of which illustrates that Sharia law, far from being unambiguous and unalterable, does not even find agreement on the fundamental sources upon which it is supposed to be based.

As a system, Sharia supports Islamofascism by legislating against four kinds of fundamental freedoms. It outlaws any activity which would undermine is dominance. The system deters Muslims and non-Muslims from disturbing the status quo of the power structure, denying everyone under its influence the basic freedoms of conscience, thought, religion and association.

Perhaps the most obvious freedom which is taken away under this construction of Sharia is the freedom of religion. This does not apply to any non-Muslim who wishes to become Muslim or to join any other faith. It does however apply to a Muslim who wishes to renege from his or her faith or convert to any other faith. A Muslim who makes such a claim would be instructed to repent. Failure to do so after a set number of days (the legal schools have various opinions) would mean that the Muslim remains an apostate and would therefore be killed. Some interpretations say that the apostate who remains silent should be left alone. Others say that if the apostate preaches his new faith to Muslims, he would be liable for capital punishments. The most 'liberal' of these opinions says that apostates who preach against Islam should be expelled from the land. This apostasy law has lingered in the Muslim mind to this very day even though it is not even mentioned in the Qur'an. It is not uncommon for us to read about former Muslims who had to leave the land of their birth because of persecution. Malaysia, once considered a shining beacon of Islamic liberalism, has a famous case where an apostate was not allowed to have her identity card changed to reflect her new faith. She then had to leave the country due to threats on her life. The apostasy law tightly regulates the Muslim population so no one leaves the faith. There is no conscious choice. Once you are born into the faith, it is your legal religion until you die. The apostasy law emerged as a tool used by the caliphs to strengthen their influence and ensure their populations remained loyal. This is why there is no distinction between apostasy and treason.

Religious minorities and women are also a persecuted section of the community under this perverse concoction. The fetishisation of women's dress and the necessity to be accompanied in public by a *wali*, guardian, is just one of many examples. Religions other than Islam are not allowed to preach to Muslims (regardless of the fact that Muslims are not allowed to leave their faith anyway). But Muslims can actively preach to members of other faiths. Not only that, Muslims are not allowed to read scriptures of other faiths in case they become 'polluted' with falsehood. In Malaysia, Malay-language Bibles are emblazoned with warnings to Muslims that they are prohibited from reading them. Not only that, the use of the word 'Allah' is forbidden in Bibles published in Malay in case Malaysian Muslims who read them (despite not being allowed to anyway) confuse the Bible for Islamic scripture.

The Islamofascist now has an Islamic State and the laws to govern it. All that is needed is a population. The Muslim community provides, willingly or unwillingly, the human subjects for Sharia: the ummah. Unpacking this term is no easy task. From an early age, Muslims are taught that they belong to the Muslim ummah, a religious community of sorts. However, upon deeper analysis, it becomes apparent that the word ummah transcends all notion of religion and may not even refer to religion at all. Consider a Muslim who is new to a particular locality or geography. How does he recognise other members of the ummah? He could identify them by making assumptions about their dress, social habits and even names. As a new arrival to the UK many years ago, I did not even have to seek out the local Muslim population. Someone read out my name for attendance during the University's orientation, which was enough for devoted Muslim students to find me, say salaams, and inquire if I needed any assistance. This is the beautiful aspect of the ummah. It is not dissimilar to a cultural affiliation that draws individuals together on the semblance they have something in common.

However, this very same concept of inclusivity can morph into exclusivity. What if I was a Hindu student? I would not be included in the

ummah and the Muslim students would not have inquired after me. From
the Islamofascist perspective I would be considered a kafir (infidel) and my
welfare would not be of any interest. It should be noted that my actual
piety never came into question. I was identified by my name and assumed
to be a member of the ummah.

The concept of ummah is also used to demarcate spaces which are then
deemed to be Muslim domain. These could be public spaces such as
government buildings, parks or even certain housing areas. During
December 2013, a handful of young extremists took it upon themselves to
create a zone of Sharia in East London. They harassed members of the
public for drinking or wearing inappropriate dress in what they had,
without any authority, designated to be 'Muslim areas'. The incidents were
swiftly condemned by the management committee of East London
Mosque. But the fascist understanding of the concept of Ummah was given
a public airing. Indeed, in countries like Saudi Arabia all public space is
Sharia space. The religious police go around with big sticks to ensure that
women are dressed properly, complete with black abaya, and everyone is
present and accounted for during the times of prayer. In a northern
Malaysian state, Muslim men who do not attend the Friday prayers three
times consecutively will be liable for a fine or jail-time or both. Muslims
who eat or drink in public during the fasting month of Ramadan can also
be fined. Enforcement of the ummah's morality is tied strongly to race as
Malays are constitutionally defined as Muslims. Ironically, Chinese and
Indian mixed race individuals tend to look like Malays and sometimes
become victims of this draconian law.

The concept of Ummah is also manipulated by clergy to usurp the voice
of the Muslim masses. This representational fascism manifests itself in
phrases employed by the clergy such as 'Islam believes that..', or 'Muslims
are offended by…', as if the entire community feels as they do. Any
incident concerning visual representations of the Prophet Muhammad can
predictably lead to such pronouncements, which are then mistakenly
assumed to be the majority view.

To preserve the ummah's integrity, steps must be taken to ensure that its
cultural identity is not diluted by illicit interactions. Here, the concept of
the ummah is subjected to meticulous social engineering. The most
damaging way to dilute the purity of the ummah, according to Islamofascist

ideology, is inter-religious marriage. The children of such marriages could be lost to Islam forever. Thus conversion of potential spouses is demanded to protect the ummah's progeny.

In order for Muslims to accept the total denial of their basic freedoms, a framework of doctrines are set in place to which all must adhere. This body of sacred knowledge is contained within the corpus of Islamic tradition and strikes awe in the typical Muslim mind. It is the only acceptable truth; and its monopoly and power to dissuade, even intimidate, believers from thinking for themselves and challenging prevailing opinion is awesome. This has evolved into what I would term 'knowledge fascism'. But this body of literature was not constructed overnight; it took a few hundred years after the death of Prophet Muhammad to emerge, stabilise and be officially recognised. Once the absolute truth was formalised, all other opinions were regarded as heresies, contrary to Sharia and punishable by death.

The religious scholars, ulama, derived their name from the singular term alim which is itself related to the word ilm or knowledge. Thus the ulama are people with knowledge — those who know. But what do they know? Apparently, they have sacred knowledge acquired through an elaborately devised system, which they claim enables them to attain the correct knowledge as intended by Allah. The fifteenth-century Egyptian scholar, Jalaluddin Suyuti enumerated some eighty different 'sciences' that an alim must be schooled in before he has the authority to interpret a single verse of the Qur'an. This includes obscure scraps of information such as the mood of Prophet Muhammad when a particular verse of the Qur'an was revealed to him. In the case of Hadith, the demands were even more daunting. Hadith scholars such as al-Bukhari had to travel far and wide to gather information about the Prophet. They then exacted a rigorous process of authentication on all that they accumulated and hundreds of years later this fragmented data came to be codified in hadith collections. It should be noted that these tomes, even if deemed to be authentic, have been criticised for their shortcomings even by members of the ulama class themselves.

The subjectivity of this system is inescapable. It is inconceivable that sacred knowledge can be construed as divine just because it is scrutinised for consistency. Yet it is considered taboo if not outright blasphemy for one to disagree with the ulama. The body of sacred knowledge can only be critiqued if one acknowledges the fundamental principles of the knowledge regime. In other words, disagreements can only be within given parameters. So the whole system follows a circular logic; and can only be sustained if you begin with what the ulama are trying to achieve in the end. The ulama class itself drive their legitimacy from the dictum that they are inheritors of the Prophet. Hadiths of the Prophet, they tell us, confirm that 'the Ulama are inheritors of the Prophet' and 'Ulama of the Islamic Ummah are like Prophets of Israel'. With such accreditation, the Ulama's position becomes impeccable. But the reverence given to them by the ummah is actually incidental and a by-product of the reverence afforded to Prophet Muhammad himself.

The Prophet is not a divine figure in Islam. The Prophet represents a rallying point and a human ideal to which Muslims aspire. However, there is a specific religious piety that is centred upon him. This includes marking his birthday with celebrations, prayers and even music. It also includes the retelling of the mystical night journey during which he ascended to the heavens to meet Allah and receive the command for the ritual prayers. This aspect of religious observance is considered particularly objectionable by certain schools of Islamic thought. But for the Islamofascist, there is another level whereby the Prophet Muhammad is seen to be the supreme personality in the history of mankind.

The Qur'an frequently states (for example: 2: 62, 5:69, 29:69, 5:48 and 2:148) that there are many paths to God. This should entail an attitude of acceptance of all religions. The Qur'an also states that the only right path to God is Islam. While a reconciliatory reading would mean that the term 'Islam' is inclusive of multiple paths, a fascist reading would abrogate those verses that suggest plurality. The Prophet is thus lauded as bringing the final, absolute and only version of God's faith. Other paths are declared as utterly unacceptable. The Prophet is also given a central role in the scenario of judgement day. In this scenario, he is seen to be bringing his ummah for judgement before the other ummahs of the previous Prophets. He then intercedes on behalf of his ummah which enables even hardened sinners to attain paradise. His capacity for intercession is unique and is denied to even the major Prophets according to hadith. The Prophet Muhammad thus becomes superior to all other Prophets and his vivid superiority extends to the superiority of the Ummah itself and its manifest destiny.

Much of the dogma of the Islamic tradition thus contains elements that contribute towards the construction of a system of oppression. Some of these factors are in themselves benign and only become malignant if deliberately manipulated to serve a particular agenda. Other characteristics are quite malignant such as the capital punishment meted out to apostates. When brought together, all these elements produce a system which creates and perpetuates oppression. It is this system that I am calling Islamofascism. Of course, many Muslims will not be happy with the term. Fascism is something that exists only in other societies. The pure ones are not tainted by such ideologies. But sticking your head in the sand does not stop you from being blown up. We have to recognise the evil within our own community; and call it by its true name. What ISIS, Boko Haram, the Taliban and their ilk seek, and what we have seen in Islamic history, is a system led by a dictator caliph with total power, forcibly suppressing opposition, criticism, plurality, outlawing basic freedoms, regimenting religion, culture and even dress, and emphasising an aggressive outlook – well, that's the definition of fascism.

Of course, Islamofascism is not the view of the vast majority of Muslims. Most Muslims simply wish to carry on with their lives. Any complicity with Islamofascism is likely to be passive, possibly even a passing phase and not akin to the unhelpful comments of David Cameron who insinuates that the British Muslim community quietly condones the likes of Islamofascists ISIS. But what can be asserted with a degree of confidence is that we are not challenging the engineers of Islamofascism, the conservative ulama, to the degree that would motivate them to reform. Unless we Muslims, of all types and sects, assert our agency, and force the ulama to change, the enemy within, Islamofascism, will bludgeon on.

PAUPERS AND PLUTOCRATS IN EARLY ISLAM

Benedikt Koehler

Each year the world's shakers and movers descend on Davos for shop-talks at the World Economic Forum about trends affecting the state of happiness of mankind in general and, coincidentally, of their own in particular. For the global elite, taking time out from their busy lives to muse about the future is time well spent, since they, after all, have a great deal more at stake than most of us, and anyway, their interests are in sync with those of society at large. Or so one would like to think. 'The rich are like us,' wrote Hemingway, 'they just have more money,' a quip which, glossing over the irony of the subtext, could serve as a WEF motto. But of late, the feel-good atmosphere enveloping Davos Man has come under strain as austerity policies seem to bite every section of society bar the one at the top of the income scale whose members in the midst of global belt-tightening seem to be doing rather well for themselves. In particular, the Davos Man's comfort zone has been punctured by stark statistics tabled by Oxfam. Accordingly, the world's eighty richest people hold as much wealth as the bottom 3.5 billion, moreover, on current trends by 2016 the top one per cent of the population will hold more than half of the world's wealth. Such data suggests the economy is a turbo-charged wealth machine for a happy few feeding crumbs to the rest of mankind, but if it is, what should and could be done about such extreme wealth inequality? In a charged debate, taking a step back to gain a historical perspective can help clarify the issues. Tracking back to the very beginning of Islam, to Medina in the seventh century, shows already the debates over wealth distribution, income policies and tax fairness were front and centre of policy discussions.

When Arabs first stepped out into history, what puzzled observers more than anything else was what to make of their attitude to wealth. Ragged camel drivers descended from across desert dunes on towns near

Mediterranean shores, in Gaza and elsewhere. Greeks searching for words to describe these newcomers pitching camp called them '*sarakenoi*', meaning 'people who dwell in tents.' The term stuck. Saracens became a blanket reference for all Arabs, with a whiff of condescension towards a people who seemed quite content to make do with the most basic accommodation. But these tent-dwellers, when it came to positioning themselves in markets, proved surprisingly nimble in cornering market segments where profit margins were highest, in luxury goods such as perfumes, pearls, and silk. Commercial savvy belied their tatty attire. When Arabs, after concluding business, turned back East and again were lost to sight, they left behind a reputation for uncommon bargaining skills and, by inference, of extraordinary riches accruing from it. That reputation travelled widely. When the Roman poet Horace, famous for extolling moderation in all things, looked for a suitable phrase to censor a friend whose mind was set on accumulating riches, he lit on 'your heart on Arab wealth is set'. Into world literature entered a new figure, the Arab as epitome of a plutocrat. Ibn Khaldun echoed the voices of Greek and Roman Antiquity since he, too, remarked Arabs embodied instantiations of opposites. 'The story goes,' wrote Ibn Khaldun of Arabs in early Islam, 'that when they were given a pillow they supposed it was a bundle of rags,' and then he contrasted this image of privation with a mention of the caliph al-Mamun's wedding gift to his bride Buran: a thousand rubies. Largesse on such scale betokened affection, surely, but whatever was Buran meant to do with a thousand rubies? If switching between rags and riches was a trait so marked in Arab culture that Horace and Ibn Khaldun called attention to it across a distance of 1400 years, it is unsurprising one of the defining policy issues when Arabia was transformed by Islam was the proper treatment of wealth to redress the existing extremes.

In Mecca, during the formative years of Islam, poverty and prosperity existed side by side. Mecca was a city where to be member of the ruling class one had to be a merchant. At the opposite end of the social scale, life was grim, as anyone who defaulted on a loan was banished to the desert, a punishment tantamount to a death penalty. Prophet Muhammad knew what it was like to be poor. He had grown up an orphan and in his youth shepherded camels, then worked his way out of poverty and married Khadija, herself a member of Mecca's merchant elite, and so belonged to

Mecca's establishment. Many of Muhammad's first converts to Islam were from Mecca's underclass, slaves, but also included merchants, in particular Abu Bakr, Umar, and Othman, one day to succeed one another as Islam's first three caliphs. As merchants, they were in the business of making money, and converting to Islam did not make them change their mind about the merit of the profit motive. Another of Muhammad's companions, Abdurrahman ibn Auf, had a reputation for 'finding a dinar under every stone he turned over' and soon after settling in Medina set out at the head of caravans numbering hundreds of camels. Another Companion, Talha, did not fight in the Battle of Badr because he was out of town away on business. Abu Bakr, the first caliph, although he drew a salary during his tenure in office left instructions for after he died to pay it back, something he was able to afford as he had an independent income from investments in mining. In sum, Muhammad recruited a significant following amongst Mecca's lower classes, but he also drew support from entrepreneurs who were as devout as they were acquisitive.

When Muhammad died the borders of the Islamic Empire expanded and so did opportunities for business. Medina became a boomtown. It was not hard to spot ready cash being spent with abandon, for example on properties, upgraded with marble and imported wood, even on fripperies, such as tableware worked from gold and silver. Such tastes were a far cry from the spending priorities of Islam when it began, when, in fact, the Qur'an propagated Islamic income policies in the shape of *zakat* with the effect of levelling income disparities that in pre-Islamic Mecca had gone unchecked. Income policies, one should add, were a top policy priority also for Muhammad's first two successors, the caliphs Abu Bakr and Umar, who expanded the reach of Islamic welfare policies. Abu Bakr put *zakat* on a new footing by converting it from a voluntary to a mandatory contribution. His successor, Umar, overhauled the Islamic benefits system from top to bottom: he set up a financial clearing-house to log tax receipts, the *diwan*; carried out a census; and introduced a comprehensive income support scheme. Entitlements covering every man, woman, and child were pegged on a scale against social rank or personal merit, but even the poorest sections of society were afforded a living income. In effect, what Umar had put in place, for the first time anywhere in the world, was a social security plan. Thus the first two caliphs made use of a growing budget surplus to fit social policies to changed circumstances. Umar's financial integrity was scrupulous and exacting; he did not shrink from forcing officials to disgorge illicit gains, and even Khalid al Walid, a popular war hero, after he was found guilty of misappropriating funds could not escape dismissal from the military. Indeed, so innovative and radical were welfare policies introduced by Islam that one of Muhammad's biographers, Hubert Grimme, considered Muhammad a practitioner of socialism, a contention he underpinned by citing many Qur'anic verses. Hubert Grimme's biography appeared in the 1890s, at a time the European welfare state was beginning to take shape, and however much contemporaneous events may have coloured his views, he correctly perceived income distribution as a social flashpoint of early Islam.

The tenure of Abu Bakr and Umar was a high water mark of the Arab economy, and when Othman, the third caliph, took office, he could take stock of what was the most propitious set of circumstances any Arab could remember. It would have been hard to discern symptoms advertising the onset of social stress. Consumer spending brightened Medina, no doubt, and, everyone, whatever layer of society they belonged to, enjoyed a standard of living that was appreciably rising. This was true nowhere more than at the top end of the income scale. Othman's residence used luxurious building materials – teak, cypress, marble – imported at great expense. It was not uncommon to own second and even third homes abroad, for example in Alexandria and Basra. Nor were properties abroad modest. Masudi, the tenth century historian, related that one of Medina's seventh century magnates had built a property in Basra so substantial that two hundred years later it was still in use as a hotel. Masudi offered another telling story, this one involving Muawiya, a cousin of Othman and governor of Syria, who was known for his repartee as well as his fondness for fine living. Muawiya afforded himself and his family properties that were big – indeed, very big. Once, one of Muawiya's sons-in-law asked him for a large sum to carry out improvements to his home in Basra, and when Muawiya asked for an explanation why quite such substantial sums were needed, his son-in-law explained the expense was only reasonable, elaborating the size of the building, its many rooms, its extensions. When at last he had finished, Muawiya, who had patiently heard him out, retorted, was the residence in question truly located in Basra, or rather vice versa? Clearly, a building boom was under way and property prices were increasing at a fast clip. Medina was no exception. Muhammad's widows took advantage of a bull market to move up the property ladder. Their home was situated in a prime location adjacent to the Medina mosque, and Aisha, Hafsa, and Umm Habiba all sold their apartments but then made their own arrangements: Aisha remained in her home as a sitting tenant; Hafsa bought a house from Abu Bakr; and Umm Habiba moved to Damascus (she was a sister of Muawiya who no doubt found luxury accommodation for her).

But Othman failed to detect a fuse had been lit that in due course would blow up and bring down the social structure that had been crafted by his predecessors. For even though everyone was better off than ever before, some were getting richer more quickly than everyone else, and at the top end of society what seemed a small coterie was seen indulging in material comforts that to most citizens were unobtainable, even unimaginable. This began to rankle with anyone in Medina who felt they, too, had endured hardships when they emigrated to Medina leaving behind in Mecca all they owned, and had laid the foundation through their dedication and sacrifice for what had become an empire – and now felt slighted by the super-rich flaunting their wealth. With every new imposing façade presented to the streetscape of Medina, the social fabric of a society bound together through shared effort during the lifetime of the Prophet began to unravel.

Othman ought to have sensed his extravagance alienated even his key supporters, the top tier of Medina's plutocrats, when on one occasion he settled a high-price property transaction with Talha on the spot, and Talha said it was offensive for anyone to be in possession of so much ready cash and distributed the sales proceeds in alms. This was a snub that should have made Othman consider changing tack, but Othman, instead of reining back his extravagance, openly disregarded any financial distinction between his personal income and monies that came to him in an official capacity. Othman shocked public opinion by taking valuable items from the state treasury and giving them away to personal favourites, worse, assigned them claims over tax receipts. The caliph had turned into a kleptocrat, and distaste over his spending habits escalated into undisguised insubordination. Othman's chief treasurer declared his accountability was to the people rather than the caliph, resigned in protest, and affronted his master when he returned the keys to the treasury by hanging them in public view from the *minbar* in the mosque instead of handing them back to Othman. But Othman was oblivious that he was painting himself into a corner.

Othman's most glaring misstep was his handling of criticism voiced by Abu Dharr, one of Muhammad's earliest converts who by now was much too old to worry about damaging his career prospects. Abu Dharr aired grievances to Muawiya whom he confronted over the money he had spent on his residence in Damascus. There were only two conceivable explanations, Abu Dharr accused Muawiya, how you could have built a residence of such extravagant size, you either spent government money or else you spent your own; in the first case, you are a thief, otherwise, a spendthrift. These words were harsh, and Muawiya for once was speechless.

Altercations over income policies were the thin end of the wedge of public discussions on Othman's stewardship of office more widely, disputes where Othman first lost public approval, and ultimately his office and his life. A swelling tide of discontent that would eventually sweep away Othman's rule gathered strength once Abu Dharr hardened his contention that Othman's material self-indulgence was wrong because it conflicted with the true mission of Islam. Othman, however, was unrepentant, on the contrary, he pointed out he had never neglected paying alms and so was fully compliant with the Islamic faith. But this rebuttal did not silence Abu Dharr, who raised the stakes by claiming Muhammad once had confided to him if he owned a pile of gold the size of a mountain he would give it all away. Now, Othman found himself on the horns of a dilemma, because he could not rebut Abu Dharr without seeming to defy Muhammad. Once Othman realised Abu Dharr was not for turning, he sent him into exile, and from that moment, Othman was a caliph in office but not in power.

Disputes over income policies had become an issue that refused to go away once Abu Dharr had invoked the authority of Muhammad, and thereby widened into the even more weighty issue of correct compliance with the Qur'an. Inevitably, the Prophet's own approach to private property became a matter of public interest, stirring up another divisive dispute, that of the settlement of Muhammad's estate. As was known, two parties had filed opposing claims to Muhammad's property: Muhammad's daughter Fatima and her husband Ali against Abu Bakr and his daughter Aisha. Abu Bakr's ruling had turned on evidence given by Aisha,

Muhammad's widow, whose testimony carried particular weight since she had been married to him longer than any other wife. Aisha testified that Muhammad had held no personal effects of any consequence at the time of his death, and therefore had been indifferent to accumulating possessions. As Aisha might have added, the plain appearance of Muhammad's home corroborated her testimony; Muhammad's home had no pretensions to elegance and Muhammad did not even have a private room, in fact, he resisted his wives' aspirations to home improvements. Once, Muhammad returned from an absence to Medina and discovered his wife Umm Salma had added an extension to her apartment, which precipitated a row with Muhammad who scolded his wife for incurring an unnecessary expense.

But, on the other hand, Aisha's testimony alone fell short of a full audit of Muhammad's income status. To begin with, Muhammad at the time of his death had been married to eleven wives, and maintaining a household at such scale must have incurred recurring expenses of some size. Moreover, it was obvious Muhammad had had access to significant amounts of income because in his capacity as military commander-in-chief he had been entitled to one fifth of booty, *khums*. Convention demanded he pass on three quarters of his lion's share, but the residual personal entitlement was hardly inconsiderable. In relative terms, in fact, Muhammad's portion from booty was astronomically high (this will show from a back-of-the-envelope calculation of the division of booty: as *khums* was 20 per cent, Muhammad's entitlement to a quarter of one fifth equals 5 per cent of the total. Splitting the remaining 80 per cent between, say, 1,000 warriors, then the ratio of Muhammad's share to that of an individual soldier was about 60:1). However, Aisha, strictly speaking, was correct: Muhammad never cared much about acquiring money for its own sake. So where had all that income gone? Muhammad indeed had not cared to accumulate property for himself, he did, however, provide for his family and his Companions – this transpires from accounts of Muhammad's household income following the conquest of Khaybar.

The division of spoils after conquering Khaybar, which occurred four years before he died, presented Muhammad with a logistical challenge, one that he used to introduce a financial innovation that enabled Islamic society to reconcile rewards for entrepreneurial success with the need to provide welfare. The settlement of Khaybar was a seminal moment in

Islam's financial history, one that resulted in the introduction of private provision of welfare through a *waqf*, and given the importance of this institution for Islamic society the circumstances leading to this innovation deserve remark.

The conquest of Khaybar, a cluster of farming estates north of Medina, presented Muhammad with a novel challenge. Previously, Muhammad's raids had yielded assets that were easy to sell off straight away. But on this occasion, booty consisted of farms where the value critically depended on retaining skilled labour to cultivate them. Conventions for dividing booty on this occasion were inoperable, and Muhammad had to find a way to keep farmers in place whilst also distributing rewards.

The Khaybar booty was huge, broken down into 1,800 lots. Muhammad awarded exceedingly generous land grants to his wives and to his daughter, Fatima, consisting of land holdings yielding annual harvests far in excess of what was needed for personal consumption. Thus Muhammad ensured financial security for all members of his family. But Muhammad's allocation of land grants had impacts that went far beyond making his family members rich. This transpired when Umar, on receipt of his award, was moved to ask what thoughts Muhammad had in mind how he should use it, and Muhammad directed him to apply his future income to charity. At that moment, this provision may have seemed an isolated, impromptu recommendation. All it meant, ostensibly, was that land grants to Umar came with strings attached: Umar was a nominal owner, but was obliged to reserve the income accruing from his property to provide welfare. On close inspection, however, this arrangement was complex – it contained ramifications that in the final analysis led to an altogether new approach to property ownership. Until then, anyone who owned land could deal with his possession as he pleased. Whereas before, title to a property was held by a single party, now, there were two: the first was Umar, the landowner, and the second, beneficiaries entitled to future income. It did not take long to realise that if conflicts of interest were to be avoided, this scheme could only work if an independent administrator stood between Umar and future beneficiaries, and further, the independence of the administrator needed to be enshrined in a binding legal agreement. Such was duly achieved, through a legal contract governing the rights and duties of the independent administrator, a *mutawalli*, who could ask for protection of the courts in the event someone tried to tamper with the assets of a *waqf* (pious foundation). Umar ceded control of assets to the first *mutawalli*, Hafsa, his daughter and a wife of Muhammad. (Hafsa was the second of Muhammad's wives who took on executive responsibility; Khadija, his first wife, had been a professional investor.) Thus disbursement of alms through *zakat* now had a complement, welfare provision through a *waqf*. But whilst *zakat* was collected and distributed by state authorities, a *waqf* was set up and managed by private individuals.

Later, Abu Bakr set another precedent for widening the range of eligible purposes of a *waqf* (plural: *awqaf*) by endowing one where he nominated as beneficiaries his family. The *waqf* sector then expanded quickly, wealthy donors endowing mosques, schools, libraries, orphanages, hospitals, and many other civic institutions. *Awqaf* proliferated throughout the realm of Islam, and the creative energy of this thriving philanthropic sector remained in full flow throughout the Middle Ages. In Alexandria, rents from shops funded *awqaf*; in Aleppo, urban expansion clustered around new mosques funded by rents from shops in the vicinity; and in Jerusalem, entire villages provided rents dedicated to funding hospitals.

To return to Othman's policy failures. Both he and Abu Dharr had failed to grasp the dynamism inherent in Muhammad's approach to income policies. Abu Dharr's insistence that Muhammad, through a demonstratively modest standard of living, had set an example to every Muslim overlooked the fact that those who had been closest to Muhammad already during his lifetime had become quite wealthy. Othman's counter, on the other hand, whereby paying *zakat* was enough to discharge one's dues to those sections of society who found themselves in less fortunate circumstances, also missed the point. When Muhammad established the *waqf* he had paved the way for an innovation, one that allowed for the acquisition of wealth whilst enabling a mechanism for providing welfare, and that step was epoch-making and formative for the way welfare would be provided within the realm of Islam and beyond. The creative flair that Muhammad, Abu Bakr, and Umar displayed in their dispositions was lost on Abu Dharr but, because he did not hold office, in the wider scheme of things was inconsequential to the fate of the Islamic polity. Whereas for Othman, the caliph, inability to match the competencies of his predecessors in fiscal matters ultimately proved fatal. Muhammad, Abu

Bakr, and Umar had found means to reconcile support for wealth creation by entrepreneurs with fostering civic institutions for provision of welfare, and Othman demonstrably fell short of the ingenuity of all three leaders of Islam who had preceded him.

The shadow cast on Islam during Othman's caliphate was long and ominous. A successor to Othman came forward within days of his assassination, Ali, a contender for the caliphate thrice passed over whose hour at last seemed to have arrived. But before long, Ali's rivals and adversaries strew rumours impugning his integrity, whispering Ali all along had reckoned the caliphate would fall to him if Othman was killed. A many-sided conflict erupted, and Ali met the same fate as his predecessor, knifed by an assassin, and civil strife flared up again and again and did not run its course until after another pretender to power, Abdullah az Zobayr, barricaded at the last in the confines of the *kaaba*, was put to death. A civil war that had its roots in contentions over fair distribution of wealth had taken over thirty years to run its course.

To return to the present. If an Oxfam panel discussion in Davos were to include Othman and Abu Dharr, it would be easy to write the script and picture the scene: Abu Dharr — sincere, earnest, compassionate — defying tycoons; Othman — suave, confident, sophisticated — brushing him off. As it happens, Oxfam supplemented statistics on wealth disparity with suggestions what to do to close income gaps, and it would also be easy for listeners to match Abu Dharr's policy stance to Oxfam's agenda today, and Abu Dharr would not need much prep time to master his brief. Oxfam's recommendations include closing tax loopholes, and opening up public services free of cost to the needy. Discussions over wealth distribution in Islamic societies today may wish to consider they have venerable antecedents, since Oxfam's policy analysis and prescriptions match those disputed in seventh-century Medina to a tee.

IN NO UNCERTAIN TERMS

Gordon Blaine Steffey

In January 2008 the Office for Civil Rights and Civil Liberties in the US Department of Homeland Security (DHS) published a memorandum of mark: 'Terminology to Define the Terrorists: Recommendations from American Muslims.' As its title suggests, the memorandum was built atop counsel from 'influential Muslim Americans,' and proposes to map the 'difficult terrain of terminology' so as to avoid dancing to the tune of recruiters making hay on the 'clash of civilisations' narrative. Its opening gambit was that 'words matter,' but the matter of which words to prefer above others proved to be trickier terrain than anticipated. Initial talks about what to call 'terrorists who invoke Islamic theology' bore smoke but not flame. In the end, a group identified as 'US-based scholars and commentators on Islam' drafted an easy reference guide for 'describing the terrorist threat.' These unidentified consultants urged officials to favour terminology carrying a negative charge, for example, cultist or sectarian. By contrast, officials ought to avoid terms that glamorise or legitimise extremist activity and that may be too nuanced to be 'strategic' for a general audience, for example, jihadist, Salafist, or Islamist. On the trail of off-putting terminology, the memorandum's authors soberly weighed the merits of 'takfiri death cult.' After all, the 'Three Points' of *The Amman Message* had recently ruled *takfir* or declaring apostasy impermissible between the vast majority of Muslims worldwide. In the end, 'takfiri death cult' ran afoul of the memorandum's sage instruction to eschew Arabic and religious terminology. The wider Muslim population ought to be described in terms counterpointing cult and sect, for example, 'mainstream,' 'ordinary,' or 'traditional.' 'Moderate' should be binned on grounds that 'many Muslims' rejected it as code for the West's 'good Muslim,' the marginally religious Uncle Tom. In 2007, Turkish Prime Minister Erdogan reviled the logic of moderation as 'ugly' and 'offensive,' titillating his base with the dictum, 'there is no moderate or immoderate Islam. Islam is Islam and that's it.' Erdogan's observation lit up right wing media in the US, who fancied it to be confirmation of their insight into the secret depravity of Islam (see, for example, Robert Spencer's 2008 *Stealth Jihad*, which hurrahed Ibn Warraq's distinction between moderate Muslims and immoderate Islam). In the nine page DHS memorandum, the term 'extremist' appeared six times, but never as recommended lexis, a tacit recognition of the obstacles to its 'strategic' appliance.

Published twelve months ahead of the inauguration of Barack Obama, the 2008 DHS memorandum reflected a course adjustment to the severe route struck by the 2006 National Security Strategy (NSS) of the George W. Bush administration. The 2006 NSS held infamously that 'the struggle against militant Islamic radicalism is the great ideological conflict of the early years of the twenty-first century.' That claim sat cheek by jowl with friendlier locutions like 'Islamic world,' 'responsible Islamic leaders,' and lumbering attempts to distinguish the 'proud religion of Islam' (a construction so painstakingly formulaic that it verges on Homeric) from its 'perversion.' Granting that 'proud' sometimes signifies a salutary quality, it has sometimes enjoyed a darker acquaintance (e.g., 'Death be not proud' or 'Boast not, proud English'). Suffice it to say that the NSS spares neither jot nor tittle on other 'proud' religions. Its engagements with Islam evoke something out there, a portentous and foreign matrix mysteriously generative of 'peaceful' Muslims (our allies in the great conflict) and 'the terrorists.' The forty-nine page policy document spars only briefly with 'religious extremism,' 'terrorist extremists,' and 'terror-supporting extremism' before retreating to box comfortably and tirelessly with 'the terrorists.' 'Terror' and its cognates register one hundred and twenty-five appearances, a close second to 'free' and its cognates at one hundred and thirty, tallies that could prompt charges of over-lexicalisation.

To be fair, the 2006 NSS constituted a thawing of the frigid rhetoric that marked Bush's first term. His administration took onboard a few suggestions from residents of the 'Muslim world' and US diplomats steeped therein that routine reference to 'Islamic extremists' was sinking the ship. The thaw (however negligible or considerable) was hidden behind several ongoing and prodigious policy howlers that precipitated the Republican surrender of the White House to Barack Obama. 'Change we can believe in' was in the offing, oratorically and rhetorically if not otherwise. The framers of the 2008 DHS memorandum conceded the rare necessity of deploying the term 'Islamic' in order to discriminate between groups 'claiming' Islam and 'extremist groups' that do not. They nevertheless counselled circumspection in the exceptional use of 'Islamic' and urged that such use be attended by 'strategic' emphasis on the exploitation of Islam in the service of mundane and mercenary political ends. Dilating on embryonic impulses ineptly expressed in the 2006 NSS, the DHS memorandum envisioned the abolition of the 'negative climate' endured by many Muslim Americans or at a minimum the abolition of an administrative vernacular aggravating that climate. Under the heading 'Emphasize the Success of Integration,' its framers stated what they termed a 'simple and straightforward truth,' to wit, that 'Muslims have been, and will continue to be part of the fabric of our country. Senior officials must make clear that there is no "clash of civilisations;" there is no "us versus them." We must emphasise that Muslims are not "outsiders" looking in, but are an integral part of America and the West.' However tonic the perspective, this assurance was still more prescriptive than descriptive, a bromide drafted in part to acknowledge that Muslim Americans suffered abuse and alienation in the broad wake of 11 September 2001. It effectively allowed that 'integration' was more unreflected and incipient than intentional and in evidence. Realising integration will require a broadly consultative process generative of educational and community initiatives at the national and local levels of American government.

The Obama administration's 2010 update to the National Security Strategy embodied the good sense of the 2008 shibboleth 'words matter.' It sketched a comely image of America after Bush, and it built atop the 'new beginning' promised by President Obama in his 2009 speech at Cairo University. Specifically, the 2010 NSS retired rhetorical efforts to map the ideology of the 'killers' and 'terrorists' vis-à-vis Islam. Rather it identified definite antagonists, all to the intense pique of hard-right unveilers and neocon straight-talkers. In one of only two references to Islam, a reference hard pressed by dire syntax, the 2010 NSS clarified that 'this is not a global war against a tactic – terrorism, or a religion – Islam.' The antagonist of the moment proved to be the 'specific network, al-Qaeda' and its affiliates, whose terroristic tactics 'neither Islam nor any other religions condone.'

President Obama was soon blistered for 'underplaying' or 'downplaying' what the risibly styled 'non-partisan' Washington Institute for Near East Policy (a 1985 spin-off of AIPAC) identified as the essential ideological ingredient to 'domestic and foreign radicalisation,' namely, 'radical Islamic extremism.' Despite being roundly discredited by John Horgan, Arun Kundnani, and Scott Atran among others, a surprisingly tenacious and facile radicalisation thesis remains a favourite instrument of indolent American media and neocons. Other pundits and talking heads of sundry hues grieved the Obama administration's capitulation to political correctness and to 'Muslim intimidation.' Detractors impeached the President for pusillanimity and delusion, and the routes of media clogged with lamentations over this latest infidelity to the American masculine. Obituaries of the American cowboy noticed but dismissed as gutless equivocation the robust deployment of a language that long sat on the rear burner. The locution 'violent extremist' or –ism transitioned from wallpaper to heavy furniture, occurring twenty-three times in the 2010 NSS. The slow march across the 'difficult terrain of terminology' seemed to be nearing its terminus, but the new vista unsettled specialists in security studies. They worried that failure to 'define' and 'circumscribe' extremism would scuttle security-related policy objectives, but efforts to define and circumscribe tended to replicate the problems that occasioned the lexical change, to wit, the alienation of Muslim Americans, the Muslim World, and potential international partners. At the World Economic Forum in February 2015 Secretary of State John Kerry warned against 'vilifying potential partners,' a warning ignored by French President Hollande and British Foreign Secretary Hammond who beat their chests at the threat of 'Islamic' and 'Islamist' extremism. Abroad and at home, all sides to the debate insisted that 'words matter,' and each side chastened others for failing to fathom the critical role of words in the exercise of liberty, the pursuit of social integration, and the attainment of domestic and global security objectives.

In the twenty-nine page recension of the National Security Strategy published by the Obama administration in February 2015, the renovation of the world and words seemed complete. A singular reference to Islam appears, a stouter assertion of a claim made in Cairo's 'A New Beginning' and untroubled by the syntax of the 2010 NSS. Ploughing over established views well irrigated by Orientalist scholarship, the 2015 NSS proclaimed: 'we reject the lie that America and its allies are at war with Islam.' The message was convincing in its clarity and concision. 'Violent extremism' remained the locution du jour and featured in February's White House Summit on Countering Violent Extremism (CVE). CVE named a new policy paradigm that emphasised the integral role played by local communities and constituencies in preventive counterterrorism, for example, through outreach to 'at-risk youth' and the development and promulgation of counter-narratives to extremist scripts. Some were troubled that the paradigm presupposed a contested radicalisation thesis. CVE events populated the months trailing the White House summit, and a series of regional CVE summits concluded in late summer ahead of the 'Leader's Summit on Countering ISIL and Violent Extremism' scheduled for late September. The dawn of the CVE industry signals the terminus of the quest to locate strategic terminology for 'terrorists who invoke Islamic theology.' To the surprise of some and the vexation of others that terminology is nonspecific. 'Violent extremism' embraces both the depredations of the foreign ISIS and the 'lone wolf' action of 'homegrown' shooter Dylann Storm Roof.

Critics of this lexical change to the NSS argue that 'violent extremism' has been gelded of ideology markers critical to security strategy. Muslim American groups counter that what looks like a gelding is in fact business as usual. They contend that the cannonade of summits, papers, and initiatives rounds up the 'usual suspects' despite the chummier language. The national legal advocacy group Muslim Advocates thunders away at federal and state CVE initiatives for concentrating resources on immigrant Muslim and Muslim American communities in wild disproportion to the rate at which those Muslims engage in extremist violence. They charge that CVE pilot programs treat violent extremism as an 'almost exclusively Muslim problem' in extravagant neglect of data sets indicating that Muslims have no hand in the staggering majority of domestic incidents of violent extremism. Indeed, CVE programs proliferate a 'false perception' that 'Muslims pose a special threat to America,' a perception that critical attention to the matter of words was intended partly to abate. In May 2015 a coalition of Minnesotan Muslim groups posted a letter formally requesting sponsoring government agencies to 'discontinue' the 'stigmatising, divisive, and ineffective' CVE pilot program. The coalition argued that the program's 'false premises' about 'problematic' religious commitments exposed resident Muslim and Somali communities to stigma and abuse and muddled the boundary between community outreach and counterterrorism. They argued too that surveillance, immigration slowdowns, airport and border detentions, and selective criminal prosecution at once intimidated the Muslim community and held the entire community responsible for the lunatic fringe who 'usurp our faith and ethnic identities.' Coalition concerns were shared by the American Civil Liberties Union, Council on American-Islamic Relations, and Muslims leaders in Boston and Los Angeles who opposed CVE pilot programs in their cities on similar grounds. Writing in *The Atlantic*, Peter Beinart observed that 'for the most part, both sides agree that when Obama says "violent extremists" he actually means "violent Muslim extremists,"' an observation confirmed for many Muslim Americans in the implementation phase of the CVE policy paradigm.

Specialising in civil rights legislation and advocacy, the Southern Poverty Law Center (SPLC) publishes an annual monitoring report of US extremist groups. In its 2015 edition of 'The Year in Hate and Extremism,' the SPLC reports a significant contraction of active hate and extremist groups for the second consecutive year, a contraction all the more striking given the historic waxing of the lunatic fringe in 2012. In exposition of an organised radical right on the wane, the SPLC points to a convalescent economy, effective policing, and the flight of American radicals into the 'anonymity, safety and far-reaching communicative power of the Internet.' More troubling is its suggestion that this contraction reflects the normalisation of 'hard-right ideas' or the runoff of extremist ideology into the mainstream. In that case a declining tally of extremist groups would be a 'strong' indicator of a brisk trade in US extremism. Why suffer the premium cost of membership in an extremist group if its ideology infiltrates the political mainstream? No hard-right idea has more successfully infiltrated the US political mainstream than the notion that Islam is a threat to US security. In 'The Year in Hate and Extremism,' the SPLC recalls the misadventure of Steve Emerson, executive director of the Investigative Project on Terrorism and self-styled 'expert' on terrorism and security. Prime Minister David Cameron styled Emerson a 'complete idiot' in the wake of remarks Emerson made to Fox News, the most watched cable news channel in America for more than 150 consecutive months and counting. Emerson described for viewers the existence of 'no-go zones' (and 'no-go' cities like Birmingham, England) where 'Sharia courts' operate in defiance of duly-constituted French, British, Swedish, and German governments and whither non-Muslims 'simply don't go.' As a consequence of fear-mongering by right-wing media outlets and 'experts' like David Yerushalmi, Steve Emerson, Pamela Geller, and others, eight US states have passed and twenty-four more pondered legislation to prevent the consideration of 'foreign laws' in judicial deliberations, where 'foreign laws' transparently conceals Muslim law and jurisprudence lest the legislation be overturned as unconstitutional on appeal.

In the immediate aftermath of the *Charlie Hebdo* killings, Steve Emerson surfaced to lament left bunkum on a peaceable Islam. Citing the morphological affinity of Islam and salaam, Emerson bristled, 'No, I'm sorry, Islam means a lot of things, and to these people it's Islamic extremism, and there's a lot of support for it in the Islamic community.' From his cloudy belvedere, Emerson has long reproached Muslims for failing to produce 'detailed rebuttal' of radicalisation scripts. Such failure he reckons as evidence of strong 'support' among Muslims for 'Islamic extremism' of the *Charlie Hebdo* variety. His opinions brim with a rhetoric of frankness that must be de rigueur for pundits espousing this view: insistently bluff, artlessly informed, and ruefully apocalyptic. With eyes trained on the causal pathway from radical ideology to violent extremism, Emerson stumbles on: 'it has to be said – and unless that's said and acted upon – we're going to see attacks like this occur over and over and over again.' In short, the Obama administration's refusal to say 'it' exacts a premium in blood. Emerson will surely claim as evidence of his percipience the violence in Paris on 13 November. Some will yawn. On the heels of his Birmingham howler, surely the batty Emerson entertains a mere and meagre fringe.

The *Charlie Hebdo* killings prompted Andrew C. McCarthy to 'flip through' a fourteenth century CE manual of Shafie fiqh. Findings from this amateur audit of al-Misri's *Reliance of the Traveller* were printed in the 'conservative' conduit *The National Review* (wherein McCarthy's ravings abound). The former federal prosecutor fulminates that its 'anti-liberty, supremacist, repulsively discriminatory, and sadly mainstream interpretation of Islam must be acknowledged and confronted.' His comity sorely taxed by the burden of insight, McCarthy explains that 'Al-Qaeda and the Islamic State did not make up Sharia law. Islam did. We can keep our heads tucked snug in the sand, or we can recognise the sources of the problem.' Behind a wave of incendiary proof-texting from al-Misri, McCarthy pleads with readers to resist the summons to term '"violent extremist" doctrine' what is in fact plain 'Islamic doctrine.' In short, ISIS is Islam and not 'some purportedly "extremist" fabrication of Islam.' Those acquainted with *The National Review* and McCarthy will yawn, 'this too is vanity and chasing after the wind.'

In March 2015 *The Atlantic* magazine carried a feature promising to reveal 'What ISIS Really Wants.' *The Atlantic* aligns more to centre than *The National Review*, and author Graeme Wood seems to prefer truth to swagger (unlike several of his interviewees). And this is why 'What ISIS Really Wants' is finally so toxic. Wood urges readers to see ISIS as 'a religious group with carefully considered beliefs.' The religion is not in question. Wood insists that 'the reality is that the Islamic State is Islamic. *Very* Islamic.' Granting that ISIS attracts psychopaths and thrill seekers, he soberly observes that 'the religion preached by its most ardent followers derives from coherent and even learned interpretations of Islam.' By 'Very Islamic' Wood means just that ISIS is earnest about religion and that its Islam is neither preposterous nor pathological. This neither-nor he seems to accept on the testimony of ISIS and Near Eastern Studies Professor Bernard Haykel. Haykel persuades Wood that 'these guys [ISIS] have just as much legitimacy [vis-à-vis Islam] as anyone else.' This is a fevered claim that substitutes the rule of dealer's choice for the constraint of normative traditions, and betrays Haykel's indifference to centuries of Muslim scholarship on notions and judgments of 'legitimacy.' Haykel blusters on that Muslims who disavow ISIS as 'un-Islamic' suffer from a 'cotton-candy view of their own religion' or surrender their good sense to 'an interfaith-Christian-nonsense tradition.' Do Christians who disavow The People's Temple of the Disciples of Christ suffer a similar sweet tooth?

Ultimately Wood cautions 'Western officials' to 'refrain from weighing in on matters of Islamic theological debate,' specifically, the sorting of

Muslims from non-Muslims. His own emphatic assessment of ISIS as '*Very* Islamic' is presumably covered by his employment outside government. In his exposition of ISIS, Wood makes heavy weather of steering between 'facile' fingerpointing at Islam and 'counterproductive' rejection of ISIS as 'un-Islamic.' It is difficult to detect this middle way in the face of his claim that ISIS is '*Very* Islamic,' or his claim that Muslims cannot unconditionally oppose slavery or crucifixion 'without contradicting the Koran and the example of the Prophet.' The latter view he learns again from Haykel, who opines that the 'only principled ground' from which to oppose ISIS is to invalidate 'certain core texts and traditional teachings of Islam.' McCarthy concurs that the 'literalist construction of sharia that Islamic supremacists seek to enforce is "literal" precisely because it comes from Islamic scripture.' The conclusion seems to be that criticism of ISIS requires a standpoint outside of 'core' Muslim texts and traditions (or inside but compromised by contradictions with the core – this is to leave untouched suppositions about the term 'literal' and literalism). In passing Wood notes that 'most' Muslims 'appreciate' Obama's refusal to treat ISIS under the heading of Islam, but how will Wood explain this? If ISIS is as 'Islamic' as he insists, are most Muslims pleased because Obama gallantly papers over an embarrassing truth about the 'core' of Islam? Or because Obama's refusal affirms their own 'cotton-candy' view of Islam? At the same time Wood warns that for a minority of Muslims 'susceptible to jihad' Obama's refusal to treat ISIS under the heading of Islam confirms that 'the United States lies about religion to serve its purposes.' What conclusion shall we draw from this? Should the Obama administration watch Muslim Americans twist in the public square so as to avoid aggravating the fringe 'susceptible to jihad'? With anti-Muslim sentiment and violence on the rise, does good government consist in enabling a religiously minded but religiously illiterate society to muddle ISIS and Islam, accurately or otherwise?

Pointed criticisms from Shadi Hamid and J.M. Berger of the Brookings Institution prompted Wood to concede that ISIS operates in ways 'antithetical to traditional interpretations of Islam.' One is tempted to insist: *very* antithetical. Berger argues that the extant mysteries of ISIS are better framed through the lens of identity-based extremism than Islam. Writing online in *The Guardian*, Shiraz Maher agreed, 'The roots of radicalisation? It's identity, stupid.' Berger contends that 'exclusive identity' matters far more than religion to ISIS, which engages in 'virtually unlimited theological gymnastics' to protect its identity formation. He has in mind the infamous ISIS pamphlet 'Question and Answers on Female Slaves and their Freedom.' The pamphlet turns a tin ear to the emancipatory ethos that infuses the Qur'an and cushions its treatment of chattel slavery so as to legitimise its masculinist fantasy of licit conqueror sex with pre-pubescent non-Muslim slaves. Wood describes his ISIS interlocutors as amiable, earnest, and scholarly, but anthropologist Scott Atran describes ISIS partisans as largely uneducated, religiously illiterate youth aching for a sense of identity and significance in a flattened world. They find in ISIS a 'countercultural' movement that welcomes them into a 'band of brothers' and sisters who together will struggle and sacrifice in the exercise and pursuit of a life of meaning and consequence. In Atran's view, 'violent extremism represents not the resurgence of traditional cultures, but their collapse, as young people unmoored from millennial traditions flail about in search of a social identity that gives personal significance and glory.' Atran's broad but trenchant counsel on how to convert the 'youth bulge' into a 'youth bloom' sadly underscores the deficits of CVE programs in the US, which focus primarily on security rather than soft-power initiatives like community development and youth engagement.

In February 2015 former New York City mayor Rudy Giuliani put the following question to a room that listed heavily to starboard: 'What the hell? What's wrong with this man [Obama] that he can't stand up and say there's a part of Islam that's sick?' Giuliani surely applauded former Congresswoman Michele Bachmann's jibe to the 2014 Values Voter Summit: 'Yes, Mr. President, it is about Islam.' Hardboiled indictments of Islam are more commonplace than may be indicated here. The Center for American Progress has carefully documented the key players and deep pockets of the 'Islamophobia Network' in its 2015 report 'Fear, Inc. 2.0.' Between 2001 and 2012 ten anti-Muslim organisations and think tanks received contributions totalling 57 million US dollars from the top eight donors. Steve Emerson's Investigative Project on Terrorism received almost 1.5 million US dollars. Is the 'Islamophobia Network' titillating a lunatic fringe or achieving its aims? On the morning after the arrest of fourteen-year-old Ahmed Mohamed for engineering a timepiece to impress his teacher, I was persuaded of the profound threat posed by

'Islamophobia Network.' Writing now in the hours after presidential candidate Ben Carson declared Islam to be 'inconsistent' with the US constitution (thus disqualifying a Muslim candidate), I am persuaded that the left should prioritise the dismantling of the network. A 2014 Arab American Institute poll reported a decline in favourable attitudes towards American Muslims (from 40% in 2012 to 27% in 2014), and a rise in unfavourable attitudes (from 41% to 45% in the same period). Fourteen years after 11 September 2001 prompted so many to look into Islam (however misleading that prompt), too many Americans have come no further in their understanding of Islam than they were in the immediate wake of that catastrophe. The broad response of the American right and its cardboard candidates to the extremist violence of 13 November fortifies that ignorance.

As heartening as it is to see constructive change in policy language (from jihad to violent extremism), it is dispiriting to find such change mitigated at the level of CVE policy implementation. Is this disjunction between language and program initiatives more strategic than bureaucratic? It is troubling to think so. As 'Islam' and its cognates ebb from US policy language, federal and state CVE initiatives remain trained on Muslim American and immigrant Muslim communities. The success of the 'Islamophobia Network' in mainstreaming hard-right ideas about Islam aggravates this stigma. The next US administration ought to realise more closely the integrated society envisioned by the new language of the Obama administration. Obama's refusal to criticise Islam and reproach Muslims must be seen as the requisite foundation for a more sustainable dwelling. Giuliani huffs and puffs: why will 'this man' simply not say that a 'part' of Islam is 'sick'? For the record, he should not say it because data sets pertaining to the threat of violent extremism cannot support a policy focus on Muslims. He should not say it because to adopt such a focus in the face of contravening data is to mismanage finite resources. He should not say it because it too intimately merges, as Berger observes, 'a mainstream demographic with identity-based extremists who claim to be its exclusive guardians.' He should not say it because such merging exposes 2.5 million Muslim Americans to unmerited and surplus suspicion and molestation. He should not say it because such merging incapacitates international cooperation on hard- and soft-power initiatives to prevent extremist violence. He should not say it because such rhetoric works in concert with the binary framing routinely promulgated by identity-based extremists like ISIS. He should not say it because ideological radicalisation does not predispose to extremist violence. He should not say it because neither the whole nor a part of Islam is 'sick.' Americans must finally jettison the toxic tale of the causal pathway from their religion (Islam) to our woe (9/11, etc.). Striking references to Islam from the National Security Strategy was a step forward, the next step is to match the walk to the talk. This is not a proposal to take religion off the table, to neglect the roles played by religious discourse and iconography in extremist and violent extremist groups, but such assessment must be the province of both religiously literate professionals and specialists from across academic disciplines.

STATUES OF IDENTITY

Elma Berisha

Early last year, in a spontaneous and unplanned meander, I visited some of the landmark Buddhist and Hindu temples in Malaysia, Thailand and Cambodia. I was quite unprepared for all that I encountered. The visions before my eyes were undoubtedly an extreme form of religious sculptural symbolism and mythological bas-relief. Paradoxically, these forms were as abstractly symbolic as concretely cast in stone: miniatures of multi-armed divinities with elephant heads, monkey faces and female curves in Batu Caves; golden dragon wings and snake statues stretching dozens of metres long, circling Thai temples; the majestic Apsara heavenly maids, as well as headless Buddha statues in Seam Reap, town after town, beheaded by, we were told, the interim conquerors of other faiths in the past.

Headscarfed, I was permitted to climb the central highest temple in Angkor Wat, unlike a few other tourists who were not permitted to climb this sacred tower, either due to their occasional headwear or less than modest attire. Rumours abound that in local culture headwear was disrespectful to the temple. 'Muslim?' I was asked and 'Muslim' I affirmed. That sufficed. Intriguingly my permit was based on the assumption that a Muslim headscarf is not necessarily symbolic like the other headwear sported around me. Although, given the endless queuing in the tropical heat for the sacrosanct gates to open, the latter one might have been deemed, at best, necessarily functional. While I unsymbolically ascended to the apex of Khmer civilisation, notwithstanding my limited background knowledge of the subject matter, I could still wonder to the tour guide: 'What is a Vishnu statue doing here, in the prime nest of the Angkor Wat temple?' Our tour guide revealed some bias as he lamented the many decapitated Buddha statues and excavated bas-reliefs dominating the landscape, for it ultimately turned out that, in fact, the vast historical site stretching beyond 400 square kilometres was originally built as a Hindu temple. Therefore, it was Buddhists who had been the conquerors throughout the sixteenth to nineteenth centuries. I pondered the irony of our guide explaining the presence of the eight-armed Vishnu statue at the apex temple, albeit, with a forcefully replaced, still intact, Buddha head! A few months later, amidst other daily work, I came across an online news headline that a Vishnu statue in Angkor Wat was reported to have been damaged by a tourist (other sources were rather citing a 'damaged Buddha statue'). I was never able to establish whether the motive of this incident was symbolic extremism or otherwise.

The experience resonated within me. I grew up in an ex-communist country where religious symbols were but conspicuous by their absence. Accustomed to a barren, atheist topography of public space, spiced up by one or two national symbols at most, the contemporary Southeast Asian Pantheon invoked an inquisitive self-awareness. How do we win or lose anything by the sheer facile transposition of our symbolic identity upon otherness? How does one religion or ideology win or lose a 'battle' by remoulding or distorting the shape or the symbolic identity of statues and images of another? In that instance, as a detached outsider I could ponder over this, as if it were a very remote, unfathomable phenomenon. At that point in time, I did not know that soon I would be confronted with IS's heart-breaking destruction of ancient artefacts and sacred shrines in the Middle East. Then I realised that this was not as 'remote' and exotic a curiosity as I initially thought. I vaguely recalled the 1990s when Serbian emergency police entered some of the neighbourhood schools in my hometown to extirpate the statues of our national heroes. This was despite the fact that most of these were the statues of common heroes: heroes of our shared past of multinational communist glory. It must have been a great priority for the Serbian authorities, based on how much care they took, in their all-encompassing platform to banish and downplay anything of ethnic Albanian significance. It was an extreme form of evidence demolition or invisibilisation of national identity. As if the statues were the only 'proof' of the Albanian blood spilled to earn itself a spot in the peaceful commonwealth of ex-Yugoslavia.

One of our deepest needs is for a sense of identity and belonging. Cultural heritage is crucial 'proof' of who we are and perhaps of 'why' we are here too. Cultural icons that awe and inspire communities around the world are an indispensable mnemonic to people's ideals and achievements fulfilled. The paramount relevance projected on cultural heritage is not new, however it is becoming increasingly asserted in the face of newly emergent uncertainty and threat of indiscriminate destruction. Recent turmoil in the Middle East and North Africa consequent to the 'unhistorical' advent of the rebellious groups of so called 'Islamic' militants, has ushered us into an era of unprecedented archaeological terror. Thanks to the so-called 'Islamic' militants and prolonged wars in the region, the 'symbol attack' has reached extreme proportions. Ancient archaeological sites of universal value and sacred shrines rooted in nuanced multi-religious narratives are being jettisoned from human civilisational consciousness.

It may be assumed that this 'cultural genocide' in the Middle East might have been initiated with the mass looting of the Iraq National Museum in 2003, after the invasion of Iraq. However, this phenomenon was preceded by other appalling incidents ranging from Europe to Afghanistan. I find myself recalling the destruction of three million books and dozens of artefacts in the National Library of Sarajevo, burned to the ground in 1992 by Serbian militants claiming to defend Christendom by correcting, via forced erasure, half a millennium of local history. Another widely disputed case is that of the demolition of the Ayodhya Mosque in North India, provoking a springboard of inter-religious bloodshed across many decades. Much international uproar was caused when the Bamiyan Buddhas were blown up by Taliban terrorists, aiming to purify the universe by imposing a sanitised version of their exclusivist truth. What is common to all these incidents is that in each case the target of violence was not a population or a strategic point in a military sense. Rather they were attacks on what is perceived as symbolic targets or evident traces of history. Yet multiple meanings are attached to the attacks just as multiple interpretations of the symbolic target itself can be found. In a distorted account, cultural icons risk the perception of becoming symbols of dominance. Thus, inadvertently, the historical monuments and artefacts are caught in specific groups' spatio-temporal struggles for identity as well as power and dominance. Perhaps, more of the latter than the former, as building dominance and power is predicated on initial forging of an identity, as no citadel stands in a vacuum. In this present quest of erecting predominant structures of power, culprit hands reach out to an overarching past to correct it in retrospect, to ensure that the monochromatic identity needed is there – standing alone and undiluted. There must be no hubris of the unwanted elements left over. The so-called 'Islamic State' wishes to wipe 1,400 years of rich and diverse Islamic civilisation from the mental map of Muslims. The Serbs sought to remove the evidence of five centuries in Bosnia when Muslims, Christians, and Jews lived in harmony just as the many remnants of ancient multicultural Andalusia are now part of collective amnesia.

Islamists of the Ansar Dine rebel group destroyed at least eight Timbuktu mausoleums and several tombs, centuries-old shrines monumental to the local Sufi version of Islam in what is known as the 'City of 333 Saints'. Other archaeological heritage remnants of the great Sahelian empire states that flourished and then died out centuries ago, are under persistent threat. Pundits recalled other times in the past when Timbuktu was sacked but they highlighted the fact that, in this part of the world, destruction of monuments, especially mosques and tombs, is unprecedented. Much concern was voiced about the fate of tens of thousands of ancient manuscripts, some from the thirteenth century, proof that the African continent had a written history alongside her much lauded-oral one, at least as old as the European Renaissance. Similar horrendous attacks on cultural heritage were reported to have been committed in Syria, Egypt and Libya in the past years by extremist groups and as collateral damage of ongoing wars. Most recently, shock-waves were sent across the globe as a result of the vividly brutal destruction of the ancient remains of the 2,000 year old city of Hatra in northern Iraq. Hatra is famous for its hybrid ancient architecture which blends Greco-Roman and Eastern styles. The ruins of Nineveh, in Mosul, were attacked too, one of the greatest cities in antiquity and former seat of the Assyrian Empire. Mosul is one of the oldest cities in Iraq and it is said to have been home to Persians, Arabs, Turks, and Christians of all denominations across the centuries. The rich multi-layered religious and cultural profile of the past, made me question titles like 'Iraq Crisis: Ancient Hatreds Turning Into Modern Realities'. Is it, in fact, quite the opposite: Modern hatreds and fictional totalitarian extremisms turning against historical realities of multicultural ethos and coexistence.

Whether there is a cure to such barbarism remains an unanswered question. However, a definitive hope would be a realisation of the universal educative value of all that has passed. Diverse cultural heritage is a natural antidote to the myth of homogeneity and exclusivity seeking to untimely re-emerge its devious tentacles in today's world. In every inch of the global landscape, cultural heritage illustrates the natural tendency of the hybridisation of cultures, consensual tangents of religious narratives and the ultimate stamping of equally valid contributions to the world history by a spectrum of identities and cultures. It defies the modern myth of homogeneity whereby only an isolated puritanical entity, be it religious or otherwise, had supposedly operated and enshrined the roots of a worthy legacy. By sanitising the cultural heritage into a singular legacy, the extremists of all kinds are trying to impose, in hindsight, this myth of homogeneity to the detriment of the reality of intercultural hybridisation. The Tomb of the biblical prophet Jonah, or Nabi Yunus in Muslim parlance, recently wired with explosives and detonated by ISIS terrorists, is a tragic illustration of this common thread of shared narratives and values under threat of oblivion. Though it had a mosque built over it, it stood on top of a mound that was believed to be an Assyrian temple. After the Assyrians it became a Zoroastrian temple and then it became a church. Ironically, during Saddam Hussain's regime it underwent extensive renovation and preservation.

Alternatively, in Islamic discourse, group identity and the exploration of diversity is considered to be a positive incentive. We are taught that plurality encourages creativity and healthy competition, which can, in turn, advance engagement and participation in community and government and is a human method of social adaptation. Thus, racial, religious and cultural differences between populaces may be 'signs of God' as stated in the Qur'an, and exactly by virtue of this diversity, they emphatically point towards shared human origin and visionary ideals. 'Have they, then, never journeyed about the earth, letting their hearts gain wisdom, and causing their ears to hear? Yet, verily, it is not their eyes that have become blind – but blind have become the hearts that are in their breasts!' (Qur'an, 22:46)

The wide-ranging social and political implications of representing and narrating the past continue to posit a challenge for archaeology. Studies have shown that archaeology was employed to foster national identities and to fend off the counter-claims of other groups and nations. Linkage between national identity and the heritage preservation is widely known as the concept of cultural heritage in the West. It is this affinity that is historically connected to the Enlightenment. Cultural heritage not only involves the past but, through contemporary ideological prisms and socio-political realities, it also involves the reconstruction of the past and the projecting of the future. A cursory glance at the UNESCO world heritage list will suffice for an indication of selective valuation. Not that nation-statehood has proved an ideal preservation model, given the political dimensionality of cultural heritage, and what constitutes worth saving. For instance, present Israeli law, which protects only sites dated to pre-1700 AD, serves to selectively privilege only the ancient biblical past over the more recent past. Meanwhile, Saudi Arabia has been accused of a 'cultural massacre' by the Turks in trying to erase any monumental memory of the Ottoman Empire in the holy lands. The Turkish cultural minister likened the vandalism perpetrated by the Saudi government to the Taliban's destruction of the Bamiyan Buddhas. Yet none of these Saudi acts had attracted the proportionate attention of UNESCO. Stretching to extremes, in Europe the selective valuation and proactive care and preservation of cultural heritage is also evident in 'negative heritage' instantiated in deliberate policies to erase Nazi-related artefacts. A recent Hitler statue in the Warsaw ghetto museum had proved controversial at best and deeply offensive at worst.

In Siem Reap, in Cambodia, the abject poverty surrounding the ancient towns and temples I visited was painfully striking. The communist regime of the Khmer Rouge had exterminated almost two million Cambodian citizens, a quarter of the entire country's population, over the duration of a few years, in its efforts to socially engineer a utopian, classless, pure agrarian society. The Khmer Rouge moved precious gems and antiquities across the Thai border to finance their war efforts prior to their seizure of power. Cambodia's ancient sculptures and ceramics are considered amongst Southeast Asia's finest and can be compared to the value of Egyptian or Roman or Chinese antiquities in the international art market. However, it seems that antiquities looting has a long tradition in Cambodia. It began with André Malraux, French novelist, theorist and Minister of Cultural Affairs, who removed nearly a tonne of stones from Angkor Wat in 1924. Moreover, it is reported that in 1993 as many as 300 well-armed bandits used rockets to blast their way into the Angkor conservancy: they removed eleven statues worth up to a million dollars.

So it turned out that the image of excavated Buddhas in Siem Reap engraved in my memory was not due to Hindu extremists or dogmatic feuds over symbolic images. It seems to have been more likely a result of brazen, profit-driven looting and vandalism, and highly organised communist war-mongers that were self-sponsoring parasitically on the flesh of a glorious past.

CHARLIE HEBDO AND EXTREMISM IN THE ARTS

Samir Younés

Intellectual meanness procures satisfaction to the minds of those who enjoy inflicting emotional pain with the intention of causing feelings of inadequacy in a victim. Intellectual meanness requires a double talent: that of aiming correctly, and that of fittingly expressing meanness in a visual or verbal medium. The greater the wit with which meanness has been expressed, the greater it grows in acceptance, even in prestige, and thus becomes established as the ritualisation of moral injury – an activity at which the French critical mind excelled. 'What a man could have been [Honoré de] Balzac if he only knew how to write', quipped Gustave Flaubert. Speaking of dramatist Victor Hugo the novelist Jules Barbey d'Aurevilly bellowed: 'You can relinquish the French language, and it will not complain because you have sufficiently tired it out. Write your next book in German'. Referring to the members of the French Academy, writer Georges Bernanos wisecracked: 'The day when I will have but my buttocks to think, I will sit them down at the Académie'. Such mean jocularity made the fortune of satirists from Apuleius, Horace and Juvenal, to Al-Jahiz and Tha'alibi, to Giovanni Bocaccio and François Rabelais, to Jonathan Swift and Daniel Defoe, to Voltaire and Benjamin Franklin, to George Orwell, Aldous Huxley and Joseph Heller, and a proliferation of recent television programmes.

Meanness can be developed into an art and can become accepted as an art by artists who gratify their adulating public with their personal opinions. Meanness becomes a form of entertainment that operates on the principle of the emotional elimination of the other. An increase in artistic meanness is also accompanied with an increase in the demand for such meanness. The more humour is allied with insolence, irreverence, irony, cynicism, sarcasm, mockery, sadism, and above all, iconoclasm, the more of it is needed. Intellectual meanness reaches particular effectiveness once the visual and verbal arts combine as they do in paintings and their titles, in caricatures and their captions, and especially in the ever-present empire of television. Mean and cruel thought, ever a companion of criticality, is probably as old as humanity itself. This disquieting phenomenon links the mural painting entitled *The Universal Judgment* by Giovanni da Modena in Bologna (1412-1415), Andrés Serrano's cibachrome print known as *Piss Christ* (1987), and the cartoons collectively published by Charb, Cabu, Tignous, Honoré, and Wolinski, at *Charlie Hebdo* (in particular since 2006). In the terrible events in Paris on 7 January 2015 the issues of artistic freedom, the freedom to offend, and extremism were confronted in a most agonising way. Understanding these events requires an intense historical knowledge of socio-political ills, but the present essay concerns itself only with the artistic expressions of mean thought.

The Universal Judgment by Giovanni da Modena

San Petronio, Bologna's magnificent and still incomplete cathedral, contains the Cappella dei Re Magi (the chapel of the Three Kings), also known as the Cappella Bolognini. This fourth chapel from the entrance – to the left of the nave – conserves almost intact the original murals of Giovanni da Modena who painted a three-part cycle: *The Consecration of San Petronio* in the middle wall over the altar; *The Universal Judgment* on the left wall; and *The Story of the Three*

Kings on the right wall. Giovanni da Modena painted the cycle between 1412 and 1415 at a time when the papacy and Christendom were assembling, in vain, their military forces to launch another crusade with the intention of preventing the Ottoman expansion in the Balkans and in order to save Constantinople. *The Universal Judgment*, arguably the most renowned and at the same time, infamous of the murals, is composed of three registers, with Paradise on the top and Hell at the bottom. The hellish part of the mural depicts a well-known passage from Canto XXXVIII of the *Divine Comedy* in which Dante calls the Prophet Muhammad a disseminator of scandals, blames him for the schisms between religions, and relegates him to the bedlam of heretics. Dante condemns Muhammad to an eternally sorrowful path along which his wounds will temporarily heal but only to be reopened with sadistic blows dealt by a sword-wielding devil. Additionally, Muhammad's head was to be severed from his body, and Giovanni da Modena depicts this lugubrious act being completed by yet another very industrious devil. In 1998 seventy-three homeless immigrants occupied a part of the cathedral of San Petronio for twenty-four hours in protest against the mural during the Muslim Feast of Ramadan until the police disbanded them. Following this event, the president of the Muslim Union of Italy asked for the demeaning and violent depiction of the Prophet Muhammad to be erased from the mural. This demand was rejected by most of the Muslim community in Italy as well as the Italian authorities.

In 1987, New York artist Andrés Serrano won the competition for the Awards in the Visual Arts held by the Southeastern Center for Contemporary Art – a competition that was partially sponsored by the National Endowment for the Arts. Known as the *Piss Christ*, the work was a photograph of a plastic crucifix submerged in a glass that contained the artist's own urine. Many, including myself, found the photograph to be profoundly offensive and vilifying – which was no doubt Serrano's manifest intention. Many, including myself, decided that the best way to deal with this kind of expression was to ignore it. But ignoring this image poses difficulties in an age where the dissemination, or rather proliferation of images on a vast scale is fervently linked to the belief that artistic freedom has no bounds and should never have any bounds. One's daily consumption of countless images is only partially conscious, partially voluntary; and much of it requires an unavoidable participation into which one is unwillingly drawn. The images associated with commercial advertising are an example. The daily blitz of images is of such intensity that one rarely has the respite needed to sift through them, and one is forced to make immediate judgments regarding which image to dismiss on account of it being aesthetically or morally displeasing, or to mentally retain it on account of it being aesthetically or morally gratifying. Ignoring artistic expressions that one finds aesthetically or morally condemnable is no easy matter; it requires sustained and disciplined restraint. Much opposition was voiced in the United States to the *Piss Christ*, and the reader may recall that one US senator vehemently denounced the vulgarity of Serrano's work before tearing up a photographic reproduction on the Senate floor. In 2007, another photograph of the *Piss Christ* was vandalised in an art gallery in Sweden by a group that claimed to be on the far right politically; and on 17 April 2011, the same photograph was destroyed using a hammer and pickaxe in the Musée d'art contemporain in Avignon. The exhibition was part of the Collection Lambert entitled *Je crois aux miracles*: I believe in miracles. More than one thousand opponents demonstrated in Avignon, and thousands more Catholics signed a petition to remove the photograph from the museum. The local bishop, Jean-Pierre Cattenoz, declared: 'I cannot approve the destruction of this work... but we have demanded that this work be simply withdrawn. If someone spits or 'pisses' on me, I would know that I am being disdained. Similarly, to exhibit as a work of art that which for us Christians is a sign of disdain toward the Cross is grievous'.

As a successor of the banned satirical journal *Hara-Kiri*, *Charlie Hebdo* took aim at many social and political dimensions of French society with satirical cartoons, irreverent jokes, and jarring news polemics. (*Hara-Kiri*, also known as *L'Hebdo Hara-Kiri*, was founded in 1960 by François Cavanna and Georges Bernier and soon employed France's most vituperative satirists. It was banned twice in 1961 and 1966 for its offensive caricatures and language. President Charles de Gaulle's death in November 1970 in his native village of Colombey-les-deux-églises occurred a few days after a fire in a discothèque took the lives of nearly one hundred and fifty people. The editors of *Hara-Kiri*, deciding to satirically comment on the French media's frenzied coverage of the fire, published a cover headlined 'Tragic Ball at Colombey, one dead'. The journal was banned again in 1970 and changed its name to *Charlie Hebdo* in order to circumvent the ban). With relentless obsession, especially since 2006, the cartoonists at *Charlie Hebdo* (the self-described '*journal irrésponsable*') employed themselves in depicting Islam and the Prophet Muhammad in degrading cartoons. One cover page was headlined 'The Koran is sh..t' with a cartoon depicting bullets piercing both the Qur'an and a man holding it with a caption pointing to the Qur'an saying that 'It does not block bullets'. Another cover page titled 'The film that enflames the Muslim world' illustrates the Prophet naked and laying on a bed with a cameraman behind him. With buttocks prominently displayed to the camera behind him, he says to the viewer 'And my thighs. Do you like my thighs?'. The cartoon suggests that the Prophet is the protagonist in a pornographic film while the cameraman, in apparent disgust, covers one eye. A third cover illustrates pregnant and angry African Muslim women demanding that their welfare rights not be touched. The cartoon occurs under a cover headline that identifies these women as those that had been kidnapped by Boko Haram in order to make them sex slaves, but the title and the cartoon suggest that the women's anger was not at being enslaved but rather at the reduction in their welfare benefits, in reference to African women living in France.

In 2006, *Charlie Hebdo* reprinted the infamous twelve cartoons of the Danish journal *Jyllands Posten* and added several new ones, resulting in a dramatic increase in its copies in circulation. Following many demonstrations against the journal throughout France, President Jacques Chirac and several ministers and public figures condemned *Charlie Hebdo*'s provocations and called for a wilful avoidance of offending the religious convictions of others. Presidential hopefuls Nicholas Sarkozy, François Bayrou, as well as François Hollande, expressed their support for freedom of expression as one of the foundations of the values of the republic. Three Muslim organisations sued the journal for defamation, and in particular for two of the cartoons that conflated Muslims in general with extremist Muslims, but the journal was acquitted because the court concluded that the journal intended to offend the fundamentalists and not Muslims in general. The leadership of the CFCM (Conseil français de culte musulman) declared that it was hoping for a 'symbolic condemnation' in order to discourage those who are engaged in the clash of civilisations from further provocations. 'Muslim federations are constrained to appeal to the judiciary given the absence of dialogue. Judicial action is our last resort', said Mohammed Bechari, president of the FNMF (Fédération nationale des musulmans de France).

The murals in Bologna occurred at a time of terrible ethnic and religious antagonisms, and any observer of current affairs cannot but feel the dreadful return of these hostilities which one had hoped had been superseded by an increased tolerance between cultures. But beyond open hostility toward Christianity and Islam, the cibachromes of Serrano and the cartoons of *Charlie Hebdo* operate on the basis of an artistic phenomenon that has long been accepted as part of modernist art, namely shock value. The main value of shock value is the emotional charge that it delivers both to the artist and the approving observer. This emotional charge is like a bad infinity, being continuously fuelled by the renewed momentum of the emotional charge itself. Consequently, a gradual increase in shock value is needed by a consciousness ever in demand of expanded emotional charges, and ever dissatisfied with the level of shock value itself. Too little of it is disappointing because the anticipated satisfaction was only partially reached. The phenomenon eventually leads to extremes, as both artists and their approving followers grow in their acceptance of artistic expressions that were previously considered extreme. Shock value then becomes an imitative quality as more artists and more viewers wish to express shock value for themselves. In this case, visual perception insistently participates in the formation and development of a desire for more shocking images and words. Shock value succeeds because it is a form of desire, an addictive desire to pass beyond irritation, to provocation, to incitement, to enflaming, to insulting, to humiliating another – all in the name of freedom of artistic expression. Artistic freedom, here, has come to be equated with a freedom to offend. Swiss intellectual Tariq Ramadan qualified the work of *Charlie Hebdo* and Charb (Stéphane Charbonnier, the chief editor of the journal) as *un humour lâche*, a cowardly humour, because these artists hide behind the law while hurling insults against others who are then condemned for being insulted by the offense. Naturally, none of this justifies the arson at the offices of *Charlie Hebdo* in 2011, or the murder of their cartoonists by the extremist Kouachi brothers in 2015.

When no extreme positions are disturbing the world of art many intellectuals make no trenchant opinions about limitations to artistic content or the limitations to socio-political expression in the arts. In fact these same intellectuals wish to maintain an ever-expanding range for artistic freedom, particularly in a society that claims democratic pluralism as one of its most valued virtues. They associate democratic pluralism with political freedom and with artistic freedom. Although both freedoms are not the same, it is usually held that political freedom encompasses artistic freedom, in the sense that political freedom is a necessary condition for artistic freedom to flourish. Even when artists abandon propriety and temperance and begin to pursue rupture and transgression, intellectuals still affirm political and artistic freedom because it is better to have artistic transgressions than to imply that artists should self-censor, or worse still, to imply that institutions should impose a form of artistic censorship. Citizens should not find themselves fearing censorship. And yet...

and yet, that very same French society that prides itself on its tolerance of conflicting opinions proffers severe punishments on those who insult the nation, the head of state, national symbols like the flag, or whistling during the recitation of the Marseillaise.

But when some artists adopt the position that rupture and transgression should constitute the very theory that guides their daily practice, it is quite possible that the artistic and political content that qualifies this work becomes extreme. Here, intellectuals are faced with a difficulty and their judgments begin to divide. Some, faithful to the old call for shock value, actually welcome extreme expressions. Others, will remind the public that art has had a decidedly confrontational role since the French Revolution's call *aux armes, aux arts* was used to justify politico-artistic belligerency, leading to the storming of the Bastille, followed by the storming of the academic Bastille. Some will decide to tolerate some transgressions while turning a blind eye to others. Others still, might be intimidated by artistic extremism and prefer to look the other way.

Fewer intellectuals will judge the transgressive quality of the art itself in relation to its mean effects on society and on the artistic image itself.

But even if intellectuals may not take trenchant positions, extremist artistic productions compel artists themselves to take a position on the limits of expression in the arts. Ordinarily most artistic productions are considerably more temperate in their socio-political content than the work of the satirists at *Charlie Hebdo*. So we are not comparing amusing satirical work versus non-amused observers, although most readers who disliked the work, including French Muslim readers, simply decided to ignore it. We are instead comparing extreme provocations that are artistically expressed (*Charlie Hebdo*) and extremely violent reactions to them (the murderous Kouachi brothers). This is not the old struggle between iconoclasts and iconophiles. Nor is it a conflict about the artistic freedom of expression versus those so intolerant of artistic expression that they are prepared to murder the artists themselves. Rather, it is on the more basic level, or rather base level, of emotional rawness where artistic extremism collided precisely with the violent extremism it has been actively taunting for years. The streets of Paris became the tragic theatre for this fatal embrace of extremisms. The caricaturists were extreme in their relentless affront and humiliation of certain religious beliefs by knowingly provoking those who adhered to the most extreme interpretations of their faith. The Kouachi brothers were extreme in their intention to vindicate the affront by committing the crime of killing the artists, as if murder somehow re-establishes the balance with respect to demeaning images and words. Although intellectuals in democratic societies will rarely admit it, the image and the word can still provoke violence; and let us not forget the verbal violence uttered by art critics.

Artistic freedom can also be turned into an abuse of the artistic image, and although the work of the caricaturists of *Charlie Hebdo* shares a tenuous relationship with the rich tradition of the *bandes dessinées* in Belgium and France, they are very far from the refined artistry of an Hergé (Tintin), a Jacques Martin (Alix), an Edgar-Pierre Jacobs (Blake et Mortimer), and even Goscinny et Uderzo (Astérix). In their stimulating stories these artists suggested social reforms and sometimes engaged in irony and satire with sharp humour. But with few exceptions, they rarely descended into bad taste or insulted the other, where otherness is understood as being inferior. Their work still upheld propriety (the Latin *decor*, the French *convenance*) in the sense that they voluntarily practiced temperance using their art as a departure point with which to look at society, and then looking at their own art taking society as a beginning point. In so doing, they used their art in order to build a common culture. Art can be used to build the City, the moral edifice in which we share our political life with the aim of living together justly. The fact that many artists have abandoned this aim is all the more reason to reaffirm it. The artistic practice of mean thought will certainly continue to give satisfaction to its authors and their public who can suspend propriety for the purposes of bathing in the relativist flux of entertainment empires. But if art is to express another of its roles, in particular its welcome reformatory and educational tasks, then it is more likely to achieve these tasks by appealing to the intellects and moral judgments of the citizenry, and their tolerance of the other.

Reprinted, with permission, from *America Arts Quarterly* Summer, Vol. 34, N°3, 2015.

CORRUPTION

Jerry Ravetz

Corruption is everywhere. It is one of the most extreme manifestations and a major endemic social disease of our time. It afflicts individuals and collectives, governments and businesses, and causes enormous loss and injustice. It destabilises many governments, and is an important cause of their collapse into gangsterism and tyranny. Indeed, it can be argued that the corruption of some key element of our civilisation could cause its downfall. We had a premonition of this in the great financial collapse of 2008–9. Then corruption at many levels enabled fantasy and greed, fuelled by computers and rationalised by junk mathematics, to bring down the world's banking system.

Can nothing be done about corruption? Frequently it is so blatant, that reformers can believe in the simple remedy: clean out the bad men, replace them by good men, and all will be well. And sometimes that works, at least for a while. The rankings of Transparency International, the anti-corruption agency, do show real improvements. But the evidence shows that corruption is systemic, and that good people as well as bad are engaged in corrupt practices. However, there are variations in the degrees of corruption, its prime locations in society, and the style of its operations. So it is not a simple infection, and better understandings might yield better management.

How are we to approach the understanding of corruption? We can start with the obvious example: public officials and politicians enriching themselves, either by simple theft or by selling favours. However it happens, it is a betrayal of trust, in this case of the civil service and of the electorate. But suppose that they are in a situation where they could not even have got to their position or kept it, without engaging in corrupt practices, and anyway where no-one trusted them to begin with? This example is the first lesson in the paradoxical character of corruption, so different from what is taught in schools and proclaimed by public figures, about society and its institutions.

Let's try again, now looking at the system. We might think of corruption as the social system whereby power and privilege are exercised, by means that are technically culpable. Because of this the actions will tend to be clandestine in some respects, belonging to a world of knowledge where 'everyone knows' within some small or large community, but nobody says — yet. And in that sense corruption is quite natural. For power and privilege are all about being exercised for someone's benefit, and if the formal structures prohibit them, then so much the worse for the formal structures.

As power and privilege are differently organised in different cultures, there will be an anthropology of corruption, as it were. If we are to believe what we see on television, even in uptight moralistic Scandinavia personal sexual corruption is prevalent among at least some of the powerful, people who would be outraged at the offer of a thick brown envelope. By contrast, the Mafia operate a code which equally prohibits informing to the police and seducing a colleague's wife, while permitting just about anything else. Mere passivity can constitute corruption. I once refrained from making a fuss about a colleague whose teaching was so bad that he actually harmed students. I knew that 'everyone knew' already, and I would only get myself into trouble if I made a formal complaint, so I was silent — and thereby was complicit in covering-up harm to students. This example is important as a reminder that the cover-up can be corrupt even when the original act, in this case genuine incompetence, is not.

The dividing line can become very shadowy indeed in cultures other than those of recent modern Europe, where public servants are expected to live on their state salaries. Elsewhere, in the traditional system where 'gifts' for services are the norm, the term lacks definition. The great philosopher and jurist Francis Bacon was trapped by this ambiguity, when his servant accepted a gift from a litigant just before judgement was given, thereby furnishing his enemies with a pretext by which to destroy him. Also, when the formal system becomes so out of touch with reality that informal means are necessary for its operation, corruption is quite functional. This seems to have been the case in the later Soviet Union.

Even in countries where corruption is relatively isolated, there is an enormous grey area. After all, institutions cannot run in the absence of a 'favours economy'. To try to put a price on every act of cooperation or help would bring collective work grinding to a halt. But can every favour or understanding be rigorously exposed to the searchlight of public scrutiny? The famous TV series *Yes, Minister* showed delightfully how civil servants and their supposed political masters worked in a network of confidential favours, which could become a mesh when someone (usually Sir Humphrey) pulled the strings.

There is also a sociology of corruption. For this we have two approaches. One is the institutional one, seeing every job as comprising a 'role' and an 'incumbent'. The role is defined by its place in a hierarchy, defined by its functions and specifying goals and procedures. The incumbent should do their best to satisfy these, but will actually have purposes of their own. We might say that when the private purposes of the incumbent dominate over the goals of the role, then we have corruption! To keep incumbents 'straight' requires an ideology to which they subscribe even at a cost to themselves. The later British imperial civil servants, trained to imagine themselves as Platonic guardians of Empire, were accordingly incorruptible to an exceptional degree, even while their system exploited the natives vigorously.

More interesting, perhaps, is the hierarchical analysis of corruption, which becomes apparent through the phenomenon of cover-up. For, while corruption occurs at all levels, cover-up is the task of the higher levels responsible for direction and control. From this the lesson is that those at the top are never innocent. Indeed, it can be argued, the lower-level corruption is the price of higher-level corruption. Once the police chiefs are on the take for big rewards, they must tolerate the low-level stuff. There may be exceptions; thus in the recent cases of widespread toleration and lengthy cover-up of horrendous crimes against children (mostly girls) committed in England by men with no status (taxi drivers of Asian-origin), it does seem unlikely that leading local politicians, police and social-work officials were collaborating as well as complicit. On the other hand, in the Roman Catholic Church the structures of re-victimising the victims of sexual abuse, in requiring them to participate in their cover-up on pain of theological fates worse than death, were operated at the top by at least some who shared those particular delights.

What is emerging from these examples is the intimate connection between corruption and cover-up. It's not just that one could not happen without the other. It's more that the systems are deeply intertwined. One reason why this has not been so clear up to now, is that it is far easier for the public to be told about the corruption than about the cover-up. After all, crimes of all sorts happen all the time. But when those charged specifically with protecting us against the corrupt turn out to be on the game themselves, the prospect becomes frightening. Whom indeed can we trust? This is the situation in Britain today. Indeed, in some ways the cover-up is morally worse. Taking sexual corruption as an example, it does seem that many of the perpetrators are genuinely sick, with this particularly horrible addiction. But those who cover up are not; they are generally upright citizens doing a professional job who in this instance are just following orders.

Further complicating the analysis of corruption is the way that the cover-up modifies reality. We might use an analogy with treason, which never succeeds, for if it does it is a service to a new legitimate government. Similarly, corruption never officially happens now. Accusations of corruption are either suppressed or officially denied. In every case of major corruption there have always been some who saw it and tried to expose it. They are now called 'whistle-blowers' rather than troublemakers, at least in some places. Only when the dam of cover-up breaks, is past corruption recognised by the appropriate authorities. What is going on now, with its supporting hierarchy of cover-up, is still outside the category of 'all the news that's fit to print' as the *New York Times* proudly announces.

This sudden bringing of past non-existent events into an historical reality has drastic effects on the past cover-up. Ignorance, even culpable ignorance, turns out to be less damaging than culpable knowledge. So a leading question in modern public life becomes, 'Who knew what, when?' This takes its place alongside the traditional maxim, 'Don't believe it until it's been officially denied!'

I believe that we need a model for understanding the way that corruption can be so intertwined with the body politic, sometimes contained and tolerable, sometimes rampant and lethal. I can offer an analogy in the contemporary understanding of disease. A long time ago this was understood as resulting from some sort of invisible 'influence', partly physical and partly magical or supernatural. Then came Science and the 'germ theory': those nasty super-small bugs that invaded us and ate or poisoned our body tissues until we either expelled them or died. Now we have a more nuanced understanding. Some microbial creatures can coexist with us quite happily, sometimes even performing essential physiological services, like those trillions of bacteria in our guts. They can be associated with us in all degrees of intimacy, either coming in occasionally from the environment, or being carried over at birth, or even sharing our genetic material. Then something happens to disrupt the harmony of their coexistence, and they begin to run wild. We lose our ease, and become dis-eased. Then, worst of all, they invade our whole body, as when Candida burrows through our intestinal wall and even infects nerves and brain cells. Then we are really sick, or moribund.

What makes the analogy work is this: our physical body organs and processes are to a greater extent developed together and controlled together, with well defined control centres (brain, heart, gut) and systems of communication. This reminds us of the formal, public aspect of the social order. Then in an elaborate symbiosis, there are rather more freely-living organisms who join the dance but are not totally absorbed in it. The distinction is very far from absolute, of course. In this analogy, we are reminded of the myriad of informal interactions, in many ways constrained by the formal, public system, but still distinct. With this analogy we can think of corruption as a sickness of the body politic, a dis-harmony between the formal and informal, where the informal runs wild, freed of the constraints of the formal. Occurring in its various manifestations and degrees, corruption can be seen as an infection, a tumour, or a cancer.

Can the analogy extend to the cover-up, which as we have seen is just another facet of the corruption? In physical terms, this would be a process of the infection actually subverting the system of control. In medical terms we imagine the immune system recognising pathogens; and with a successfully established disease the immune system has been tricked or disabled, or perhaps even turned in on itself, as in an auto-immune reaction or disease. And almost by definition, the disease could not flourish in the absence of a disabled or corrupted immune system.

Again, just as disease is not a simple on-off condition, so as we have seen corruption can infect insidiously by stealth. We can map this in the reactions to increasing degrees of covert selfishness. It starts with special favours, perhaps quite small. Then there is 'fiddling', cheating on such a small scale that nobody is hurt and it isn't worth the authorities cracking down. Eventually when word gets around, there arises an attitude, '*così fan tutti*' – 'that's what they all do'. Then anyone who plays by the formal rules is something of a fool. To accommodate to this situation there develops an ethic that I have called 'the pyrites rule' (for 'fools' gold'). This is that 'Each should strive to get ahead by betraying the trust of all the others'. This might seem extreme, or rather abstract; but we observe that this became the ethics of international investment banking some years ago. In spite of its destructiveness (as when mutual trust collapsed in 2008/9), all the evidence is that it still rules today. When the pyrites rule is generally adopted, those naïve outsiders who are involved in corrupt payments become dismayed and outraged, for then the bribed officials become corruptly corrupt and break their promises.

Out of all this analysis, is there anything constructive that can be said about curing corruption? Again we can draw lessons from the medical analogy. In the golden age of germ theory, health was a simple affair: identify the germs and kill them. In our case, this would be to expose corruption, remove the evil agents and replace them with good ones. Now we appreciate that the problem of health is more complex and subtle. In many ways we are going back to the classical principle: '*mens sana in corpore sano*' – a healthy mind in a healthy body. Bodily health is a systemic property, and so is societal health.

Given the special character of corruption, with its dependence on cover-up, there is an effective path to its management (I will not say prevention and elimination). This is to invoke the American bumper-sticker wisdom: 'Sunshine is the best disinfectant'. Whistle-blowing, leaking, and investigative journalism, best focused on the respectable men at the top rather than the squalid characters at the bottom, become our societal immune system. Thomas Jefferson said, 'the tree of liberty must be refreshed from time to time with the blood of patriots and tyrants'. We need not invoke such sanguinary measures, but since corruption is among the worst enemies of liberty, his words ring true today. The most hopeful aspect of our very mixed contemporary world is the spread of ungovernable communications. With all their evils, they are the social sunshine that we need for penetrating cover-up and exposing corruption.

This objective analysis of corruption should not obscure its character as a crime against society, people and civilisation itself. Outrage against it is the strongest basis for its management. But in the absence of understanding, the best intentioned campaigns for reform will yield only frustration, disappointment and cynicism. That is why we need more thought and more discussion, necessarily including those who become its victims by being among its perpetrators.

SIKH EXTREMISM

Sunny Hundal

In 2005 Rajinder Singh made history by being the first non-white Briton to feature in an election broadcast by the British National Party. Ironically, he wasn't even allowed to join the BNP, but he didn't care. 'I say adapt and survive and give the brave and loyal Rajinder Singh the honour of becoming the first ethnic minority member of the BNP,' their communications officer wrote at the time. The party ignored that advice. Singh had developed a deep hatred for Muslims from India's partition of 1947 when he blamed them alone for the violence and carnage that took place. 'Britain had a role to play,' he admitted to the *Guardian* in 2009, 'but the violence [during Partition] sprang from the Qur'an. The Muslim answer to reasoned argument is knife, dagger and bomb.'

Such open displays of xenophobia aren't frequent among British Sikhs, but scratch the surface and they can be found all too easily. As the BNP started faltering from 2008, the rise of the English Defence League (EDL) was similarly characterised by outreach towards Sikhs and Hindus. In 2010 an EDL rally featured a Sikh speaker called Guramit Singh, who told a reporter: 'We're not here to be anti-Muslim, anybody in the group who is anti-Muslim will be kicked out. We're here to fight against Muslim extremism.' But a trawl through his Facebook page found comments like: 'the muzzies wanna keep away from me im just looking for an excuse im fucked off at the mo fuck the pakis. i just think we shud burn the cunts now!' – and others in a similar vein. He claimed he had been provoked into them by death threats he had been receiving. Guramit Singh was eventually arrested by the police for religiously aggravated harm and later jailed for a robbery. But he was the first to publicly try and help the EDL broaden their appeal. In response some Sikh and Hindu groups released a statement in 2011 condemning any association with the EDL, but many Sikhs never really shunned the EDL as they were urged to.

Indeed, they were to be seen rubbing shoulders with the EDL in 2012 when tensions had flared up in Luton at the rumour that a Muslim man had abused a Sikh girl. *The Mail on Sunday* revealed that a secret meeting took place between some Sikhs and EDL leaders two days after the protest to discuss 'acts of vigilantism'. Fortunately, cooler heads prevailed after Sikh and Muslim leaders worked together to reduce tension. But the flirtation continued. The EDL even created its own 'Sikh Division' and it has over 12,000 Likes on Facebook. As recently as April 2015, the former leader of the EDL (who has several names including 'Tommy Robinson'), was warmly welcomed on to the Sikh Channel for an interview. Astonishingly, he wasn't asked about numerous examples of the EDL's racism, but instead allowed to pitch for Sikhs to join his campaign against Muslims without challenge.

While most British Sikhs are unlikely to be seduced by such overtures, these episodes illustrate the dangerous actions of a loud minority. But the antics of this extremist community seldom get noticed in the British media. There is an implicit assumption that the Sikhs are a model minority that aren't plagued by social ills or religious extremists like Muslims. Nor is there a regular slew of controversies to make it an ongoing worry.

Within the community however it is a different matter. A number of recent controversies illustrate that a cultural divide is opening up between more liberal-minded and conservative Sikhs. Many fear that a growing movement of puritanical Sikhs could create a schism, leaving the global Sikh community badly fractured and divided. Moreover, as Sikhs are predominantly Punjabi and come from highly patriarchal families, there is a deep blindness to social problems that will likely have big repercussions in the future. But it is difficult to discuss these issues because the shadow of Prime Minister Indira Gandhi's assault on the Golden Temple in Amritsar in 1984 looms large over everything. The attack, called Operation Blue Star, was bloody and heinous enough, but worse were the repercussions: Indira Gandhi was assassinated by her Sikh bodyguards and in retaliation thousands of Sikhs across India were murdered in orchestrated pogroms or wrongly jailed. Many still rot in prison. These events made louder the calls for an independent Sikh homeland, more so in the British and American diaspora communities than in India. As successive Indian governments deny justice to victims of 1984, the big debates among Sikhs continue to revolve around the events of 1984 and the aftermath, at the expense of all else. The discussions and campaigns around 1984 are important, but so are many other problems that threaten to destabilise the entire global Sikh community.

The rise of Sikh extremism is one of the main problems. I define Sikh extremism in two ways: open xenophobia that can fuel hate-crimes; and attempts by some to impose their views on others under the guise of religious puritanism. Most Sikhs are liberal-minded and secular, but they live in denial about extremism within their own community. Of course, I'm not referring to the violent extremism of the Taliban or al-Qaeda type, but low-level coercion that still impacts lives and makes problems worse.

Let's begin with xenophobia. Animosity between Sikhs and Muslims (and in some case, Hindus) was rare in the UK until the 1980s as most focused on battling racism. Under the banner of 'black unity', Asians identified themselves more along racial than religious lines and fought racists together. The burning of the Hambourgh Tavern pub in 1981, when men from Southall fought with skinheads and police and which was widely seen as a symbolic defeat for the far-right, was one such example. Around the 1980s and 90s, especially after the controversy around Salman Rushdie's *The Satanic Verses* in 1988, an increasing number of British Muslims became politicised and identified along religious lines. That helped push Sikhs and Hindus along a similar path. Tensions didn't come to the forefront until the rise of Hizb ut-Tahrir and its flamboyant leader, Omar Bakri, who actively sought to inflame frictions to push his agenda. Most famously, controversy erupted in Luton in the mid-90s when a leaflet was found offering a reward to Muslim men to convert Sikh and Hindu women to Islam. No one admitted ownership (though Bakri was widely suspected) but it played into fears that Muslim men were preying on Sikh and Hindu girls. Later, while leading the splinter group al-Muhajiroun, Bakri was banned from staging an event in London where Sikh and Hindu girls would apparently publicly denounce their old religions and convert to Islam. Omar Bakri's raison d'etre was to incite a clash between communities so he could get more recruits. Other Muslim groups shunned him, but it gave the impression to Sikhs and Hindus that they silently condoned him. After Bakri left the country, his tactics were adopted by protégé Anjem Choudhary, who became the leader of the extremist al-Muhajiroun.

A decade later, some Sikh and Muslim groups sought to play on this urban legend to advance their own agenda. The Hindu Forum of Britain told newspapers that Muslims had 'aggressively' converted 'hundreds' of British Hindu girls to Islam. Newspapers initially repeated his allegations without proof, until an *Evening Standard* investigation exposed its leader Ramesh Kallidai as the 'fundamentalist father' whose claims didn't stand up. Similarly, allegations by the Sikh Awareness Society (SAS) that Muslims had forcibly converted Sikh girls were investigated by the BBC Asian Network and found to be without evidence.

When I was at university in the late 1990s, a group of Sikhs broke into the room of a Muslim man one night and stabbed him in the leg because he was dating a Sikh girl. What was also remarkable about the incident was how many people shrugged it off as a danger that cames with the territory of a Sikh-Muslim relationship. Gangs such as Chalvey Boys (mostly Muslim, based in Slough) and Shere Panjab (mostly Sikhs, based around Southall) clashed frequently during that era, sometimes over inter-religious relationships.

Not much has changed since. Of course, inter-religious relationships have been frowned upon by many of both religious groups. But some Sikh groups insist on claiming that girls were being duped by Muslim men who merely wanted to convert them for money. Of course, their focus has always been on women – as if men were too intelligent to fall victims to such ploys or it didn't matter if a Sikh man was dating a Muslim woman. In 2013 a documentary seemed to confirm their worst suspicions. A BBC1 investigation found cases of Sikh girls being groomed by Muslim men. The Sikh Awareness Society claimed it had been right all along. But this is disingenuous. In this case, young impressionable children were being groomed for sexual exploitation, not conversion to Islam. The men who perpetrated these crimes were not religious but sexual predators, targeting white and Muslim girls too. Their aims weren't religious but to prey on girls regardless of their backgrounds.

Worse, the abused girls in the BBC1 report were stigmatised by their families and other Sikhs. One victim was warned by her mother not to tell anyone; another was banished to the United States to recover. Mohan Singh from Sikh Awareness Society carelessly said: 'we know that a girl who is tarnished with this kind of thing would never get married anyway'.

Why not? Were they defiled property now? The shame and stigma perpetuated by Sikhs also applies to discussion about sexual abuse within Asian families. When Sikh women have raised or campaigned on these issues they have been shouted down or ignored, as if the subject wasn't worth discussing.

This strain of xenophobia invents conspiracies about Muslims and casts a shadow of doubt on all Muslim men. Not only is it utterly patronising (are Sikh women so stupid they are so easily duped into conversion?), but it perpetuates the view that Muslims should be viewed with suspicion because they have bad intentions towards Sikh women. Meanwhile, of course, bad intentions of Sikh men are ignored.

Religious intolerance is not far behind xenophobia. The controversy over Gurpreet Bhatti's play *Behzti* ('shame') in December 2005 was a significant marker of growing intolerance among British Sikhs. It featured a segment where a disabled woman is raped in a Sikh Gurdwara – not acted out but as part of the story. Some Sikhs walked out of the play in protest, saying it should have been set in a community centre not a Gurdwara. It wasn't a slur on Sikhism and the writer refused to relent. Radical groups organised protests in front of the theatre until windows were broken and the police could not guarantee security. The play had to be shut down. The furore shocked many in the mainstream media who had earlier assumed Sikhs wouldn't do anything like the events around *The Satanic Verses*. But the parallels were there. Some wanted to sue the writer, herself a Sikh, for incitement of hatred against Sikhs; others started spreading baseless rumours about the play and the writer; there was the inevitable cry that people shouldn't be allowed to insult Sikhism (the play didn't). Of course, she got death threats too, but since the notion of Sikh extremism doesn't fit the media narrative there was little focus on that. Some claimed the play was inappropriate because women had never been raped in a Gurdwara. In one notable interview, when a Sikh woman called up BBC Radio 5Live debate to say she personally knew of one such incident, the Sikh 'leader' on air dismissed her.

I asked writer Sathnam Sanghera, who wrote the acclaimed family memoir *The Boy with the Top Knot*, whether he self-censors on issues regarding Sikhs. His book attracted criticism from people who claimed it was insulting the community, even though it was about his personal experiences. 'I definitely self-censor. I avoid discussing all religious issues and refuse all invites to speak at community events, although sometimes I would actually like to do so. Because as a community, we haven't yet learned to talk about ourselves, and it's just not worth the aggro that always results,' he says. And adds: 'the Jewish people have had centuries of being able to analyse and even laugh at themselves. Muslims were forced to learn to discuss themselves as a result of *The Satanic Verses*. But the Sikh community has no real tradition, past or present, of self-examination... the level of debate is either appalling or non-existent. We're at the stage where to even use the word 'Sikh' as an adjective, a label, in the course of just describing one's life (as a secular Sikh), is to attract the allegation that you are somehow criticising the religion or community'.

Like many younger Muslims, there is a growing tendency among second and third generation Sikhs to adopt a puritanical version of their religion as their principal identity. Any challenge or criticism of their religion (as they see it) is therefore taken as a personal insult and they become willing to take action against it. The recent campaigns against inter-religious marriages is a good example. In 2012, a group of around forty Sikhs stormed an inter-religious marriage between a Sikh woman and her Christian fiancé, posting a video of the incident online as a warning to others. A BBC Asian Network documentary in 2013 found that some Sikhs had become afraid to speak out because of a continuing campaign of harassment and intimidation; people had their windows smashed and faced other forms of intimidation simply because they wanted a religious ceremony at a Gurdwara.

Underneath the radar of the national media, such events have escalated. A group calling itself Karaj has repeatedly disrupted inter-religious weddings at Gurdwaras, claiming they go against Sikh tenets. 'On the weekend an outerfaith [sic] wedding where a Punjabi bimbo was marrying a non-Sikh (white Christian) was forcefully stopped by the Khalsa. Respect to these lads for standing up for whats right and standing up to a corrupt gurdwara committee', they boasted last year after one event. Such incidents prompted one group of self-appointed 'community leaders' from the Sikh Council to release a set of 'guidelines' in 2014 to further stamp out inter-religious marriages from Gurdwaras.

Fundamentalists say a strict interpretation of the *Rehat Maryada* (a set of codes set out by scholars in 1950), which prohibits marriage between

Sikhs and non-Sikhs at a religious ceremony, must be enforced. They would rather have Sikhs who marry non-Sikhs be driven out than be welcomed so perhaps their children may still grow up Sikhs. In effect, they would rather have more liberal and secular Sikhs ex-communicated than have the religion 'corrupted' as they see it. Their thinking is that it's better to have a community that closely follows a narrow interpretation of the religion than deal with a myriad of actions and opinions outside that.

Due to the centralised nature of Sikh officialdom – religious edicts are only meant to come from the central authority ('*Akal Takht*') at the Golden Temple in Amritsar – there is a growing cultural divide between conservatives and liberals. Religious leaders in India are not just opposed to inter-religious marriages but have also issued edicts against gay marriages and, until recently, banned menstruating women from helping inside the inner sanctum of the Golden Temple.

The controversy over the film *Nanak Shah Fakir* in April 2015 perfectly illustrates this growing intolerance. The Indian-made film, a biography of the first Sikh Guru, Nanak Dev Ji, was abruptly taken off cinemas worldwide after Sikhs protested in the UK and in India. Mohan Singh, of the Sikh Awareness Society, told the BBC: 'The sister of Guru Nanak is played by a human being, and we are also led to believe that a human actor played the role of Guru Nanak Dev ji, and that is blasphemy and is one part of why Sikhs around the world are objecting.'

Let's leave aside the fact that Guru Nanak was a real human being who lived between 1469 and 1539, so it would be impossible to portray him as anything other than human. In fact a human actor didn't play him in the film: the director stated repeatedly that he was briefly illustrated with CGI as a person hidden mostly by a shining light. Sikhs have had illustrations of the ten Sikh Gurus in human form for hundreds of years, so to say it is blasphemous to depict him as human is absurd. Sikh leaders in India, who had earlier commissioned life-like paintings of the Sikh Gurus and signed off on the film, now claimed to crowds that such depictions in films were blasphemous. Meanwhile many British Sikhs were openly disappointed and angry that they were denied from seeing it.

A conversation around Sikh extremism and its impact is urgent partly because the community is in the midst of a crisis. Sikh women do face considerable problems, but the uncomfortable truth is that they do so at the hands of Sikh, not Muslim men. The state of Punjab, where most Sikhs are based, is in a mess. Across India it has among the lowest ratios of women to men, due to a mixture of factors that include unusually high ratios of gender-selective abortion, infanticide, neglect of girls, rapes, and dowry related deaths. In 2009 an Action Aid report found there are areas in Punjab with just 300 women to 1000 men; the usual rate is around 1050 women to 1000 men. Parts of Punjab are referred to as '*kuri mar*' ('girl killer') areas where it's not unheard of families to dispose of unwanted baby girls by burying them alive in a pot in the ground. Punjab is also awash with alcoholism and drug abuse. Some call it a 'drug epidemic'. Punjabi women are even trying to organise themselves against this but face a herculean task.

In the UK, British Asian women are twice as likely to commit suicide as white women. There have been numerous cases of so-called 'honour' killings of Sikh girls. When Jagdeesh Singh's sister was murdered by her in-laws for daring to seek a divorce, he told the *Independent* that he was shunned by Sikhs for wanting to talk about the issue. 'The so-called community leaders, the influential religious groups and the local language newspapers remain deafeningly silent when these killings happen. But that silence makes them just as guilty as the people who kill in the name of honour'. Sathnam Sanghera says that when he wrote that Sikh Punjabis had one of the highest rates of alcoholism in the world, a problem that had claimed several members of his family, he was accused of insulting the Sikh religion.

I asked Herpreet Kaur Grewal, a British writer and journalist, whether women were excluded from debates among Sikhs. 'I feel Sikhism is interpreted from a male perspective – as so much of everything in our modern world is. I accept this but seek to change it by asking what it is that women think and put across? It is sometimes so easy to accept the often heard and loudest interpretation! It takes guts and muscle to really dig out new perspectives. Any debates are mostly addressed by male voices from the community'. She adds: 'Having said all this I feel Sikh men are very open to the idea of equality between the sexes and listen when issues are brought up. Some are stuck in that old patriarchal, Punjabi way of thinking but they need to be reminded Punjabi does not necessarily mean Sikh.'

Since it inception, the Sikh community has been a minority community. As Sikhs started becoming a distinct and large community in the 1500s, they came under attack from the Mughals and Hindu rulers. Some Mughals admired them, such as emperors Humayun and Akbar, but a number of the Sikh Gurus were distrusted and attacked by the Mughal emperor Aurangzeb. Even as Sikh numbers prospered and grew, they faced a constant threat from the British. During the partition of India, many Sikhs were resentful because there was little regard paid to Sikh autonomy, as promised by Mahatma Gandhi, despite their over-proportionate sacrifices to gain independence. Even the sole Sikh empire created by Maharaja Ranjit Singh (1799 to 1849) was not a majority Sikh state. Currently 80 per cent of Sikhs live in the Indian state of Punjab, where they form just about two thirds of the population. In India, they are about 2 per cent of the population, but contribute over-proportionally to the army and police force. But, to the chagrin of some, Sikhs are frequently portrayed in films as objects of ridicule or as simpletons.

Constantly protecting their identity and being a minority in every country has inevitably made Sikhs a very defensive community. There has always been a long-standing intolerance of religious diversity within the community for fear it would splinter and disintegrate. But it was the events of 1984 that cemented the defensive mentality and persuaded many Sikhs that they needed an independent homeland ('*Khalistan*') to flourish. Subsequent campaigns focusing on justice for victims of the 1984 pogroms have been important, but the debate about *Khalistan* has frequently crowded out everything else.

But here's the irony. Sikhs are heading for a schism precisely because of xenophobia and intolerance – the two mechanisms they have adopted to keep the community intact. They have just not adjusted to being a globally dispersed minority community on a diverse and pluralistic planet. In other words, they haven't yet addressed how to keep Sikhs within the fold even if members start to adapt to different lifestyles and cultures.

Meanwhile, more secular and liberal Sikhs in the US and UK are not going to take orders from ultra conservative elements. They want to know why their co-religionists favour censorship over minor issues, or find it difficult to intellectually discuss controversial issues, or want to discriminate against gays, or reject non-Sikhs, or demand a theological state that could never survive the modern world. Inevitably, some will just move away from Sikhism and further shrink the community. Others will likely try and start their own movements, raising the prospect of a schism. There are plenty of parallels – the split in the Anglican and Catholic churches over women Bishops is just one example.

The Sikh community, in Britain as well as India, needs self-reflection. The Sikhs need to focus on internal problems which are not about religion or religious education, but a deeply entrenched culture of sexism, alcoholism and anti-intellectualism. The most ironic thing about Sikh extremists is how much their tactics, rhetoric and world-view mirrors that of the group they most claim to hate – Muslim extremists.

If Sikhs want to prosper and survive, they need an open and vigorous debate about how the most pressing challenges they face come from within, not outside. The defensive mentality that has suffocated important, intellectual debate has to come to an end, or else it could end up suffocating the Sikh community itself.

THE NEW ATHEISTS

Andrew Brown

The idea of a fundamentalist atheist seems a contradiction in terms. Fundamentalists, at least since the emergence of the term in the early twentieth century, are people committed to a particular interpretation of a text: at least that's what they claim to be. Atheism has no sacred text, although there are atheist cults. Some people would enlarge the definition of fundamentalist to include dogmatism, and tribalism but I think the defining quality of a fundamentalist is a certain style of the imagination. It is not so much the imposition of a particular set of ideas on the world as it is a sense of the self-evident that is out of key with that of the surrounding world. I want to say 'self-evident' rather than 'sacred' because disorder and disagreement are threatening to the fundamentalist in ways quite different to those in which blasphemy shocks a believer.

It seems at first that the defining quality of a fundamentalist's imagination is that they can't themselves see it: they are convinced that they deal only with facts and their logically ineluctable consequences. Metaphors are simply decorations – the flower beds around the power station, in Mary Midgley's phrase – but the fundamentalist believes that his central beliefs are not in the least bit metaphorical. This is true as far as it goes, but it doesn't actually separate out the fundamentalist from the rest of us very well. For we all base our thinking on imaginative constructs and metaphors which have through long use become invisible to us. The only way for most of us ever to notice this is to be immersed in a foreign culture and language where all of a sudden nothing can be taken for granted. And it is not surprising that fundamentalism has its greatest appeal to the uprooted.

For the fundamentalist starts their journey when they find that the things they take for granted are all of a sudden pointed out as of questionable sanity and rationality by the society around – which is of course pursuing its own equally irrational and arbitrary habits as if those were perfectly normal. Some people can handle this and some can't. It's not that the fundamentalist needs security more than is psychologically healthy: it's that they find themselves in a situation where this security can't be achieved in socially acceptable ways – and once you start to feel like that, the consequences are entirely self-reinforcing. The further you get from the assumptions of mainstream culture, the more grotesque they appear, and with that grotesquery comes an assumption that they are evil too.

In this sense, the New Atheist movement shares some important characteristics with religious fundamentalism. For a start, it was a social rather than an intellectual development. The two intellectual novelties associated with it have now been quietly forgotten as being too embarrassing to mention. So let's bring them up:

The first was the doctrine that moderate religious believers are actually more wicked and dangerous than the ones who burn witches or blow up children. This was prominent in Sam Harris' early works, though it seems to have been dropped quite smartly once it was realised what the implications would be for such things as relations with Muslims. After all, if Harris is right, Ziauddin Sardar is a more dangerous figure than the Caliph of ISIS, and how then do we justify locking up Abu Hamza when we let that man Sardar roam free?

The second, of course, was the nonsense of 'memes', which speaks to a deeper or at least more imaginative longing: that the world works according to a few lovely simple and comprehensive explanations – in this case, something supposedly Darwinian. In the late Nineties some very intelligent people spent time trying to understand culture as a selective process; variations on this work are still being done by Dan Sperber and others: it is after all interesting and worthwhile to ask if there are sub-rational reasons why some ideas and stories survive while others do not. But no serious researcher now thinks in terms of fundamental cultural units called 'memes' and indeed Sperber himself has completely demolished the concept.

Now, one of the most unattractive characteristics of the New Atheism is actually a protection from the fundamentalist mindset. This is its sheer exuberant nastiness. I find it disgusting, but one has to admit that shared hatred is a wonderful solvent of anxiety and can make all manner of misfits feel at home, as any vicar in a football crowd can tell you. Take the

Australian entertainer Tim Minchin. There is a Youtube clip of one of his
performances in front of an enthusiastic crowd:

'Fuck the motherfucker.' he sings: 'He's a fucking motherfucker!' and
then repeats variations of this for three long minutes while the crowd
giggles and the rain comes down. The fucking motherfucker who should
be fucked was the Pope, whom Minchin holds guilty of rape – you see:
'Rapist/papist' – they rhyme so it must be true. Indeed the whole Roman
Catholic Church is apparently guilty:

'So fuck the motherfucker and fuck you motherfucker. If you're still a
motherfucking papist (fucking motherfucker).'

The joke – and there has to be some reason why YouTube comments call
Minchin 'hilarious' – is that this was all sung at something called 'A rally
for reason' which was meant to celebrate the superiority of reason over
the adolescent fantasies of religion.

I watch the clips and remember George Orwell's claim that in the end,
you cannot be a Christian and be quite grown up. It appears from Minchin
that you cannot be an atheist and even in the least bit grown up. The
problem is not just that he's nasty, but that he's entirely infantile. The
mixture of jeering and execration from a position of impregnable self-
righteousness is simply a slow-motion tantrum. If toddlers used words
better, they would sound just like Minchin, and be every bit as reasonable.

One point to notice is that they are claiming a kind of special privilege
for criticism of religion which does not apply in other social contexts.
Atheism in this sense and in the Western world is better than football
because it's less likely to get your head kicked in. If you were to sing 'The
Pope Song' at a football match the world would turn on you as a repulsive
thug, and in Scotland you might very well be jailed. Even if you turn it on
other religions – 'Fuck you, motherfucker, if you're still a motherfucking
raghead' – it still somehow doesn't sound quite like a hymn to reason.
Minchin's excuse is that he's outraged about child abuse. He introduces it
by saying 'This is a song about choosing where to place your anger'. Well,
no: it's a song about the pleasures of self-righteous posturing. In the cold
light of reason, the most shocking thing about the various Catholic child
abuse scandals is that they were not exceptional. The few statistics that
there are – and the evidence of such things as insurance premium rates in
the USA – show that the problem of child abuse is widespread, found in all

religions and in entirely secular institutions. Nor can you consistently maintain, as many people seem to do without a thought, that secular humanism is a huge moral improvement on religion, but that scandals in secular children's homes don't discredit the moral claims of secularism, while scandals in Roman Catholic homes discredit the whole religion.

No: the point of this song, and the pleasure that it gives, is the promotion of hatred and of a smug contempt for the less fortunate. And that is a value in itself for the Extreme New Atheists. Here is Richard Dawkins, finishing his speech at the same rally:

> When you meet somebody who claims to be religious, ask them what they really believe. ... Mock them! Ridicule them! [applause, whoops] In public! [laughter!] Don't fall for the convention that we're all too polite to talk about religion. Religion is not off the table. Religion makes specific claims about the universe which need to be challenged and, if necessary, need to be ridiculed with contempt.

Now, if you make a mash-up of the more respectable bits of Dawkins' speech with Minchin's song – and this is not unfair, since Dawkins promoted Minchin in the issue of the *New Statesman* that he guest-edited – we get a flavour of the peculiar quality of the New Atheism:

> Science makes us see what we could not see before/Fuck the motherfucker, fuck the motherfucking fucker/Religion does its best to snuff out even what we can see /Fuck the mother fucker, fuck the motherfucking fucker/So we're here to stand up for reason/Fuck the motherfucker fuck the motherfucking fucker/to stand up for logic/fuck you motherfucker for a motherfucking papist/to stand up for the beauty of reality/Fuck you, motherfucker' da capo.

Put together like this, it actually makes more sense than either of the constituent parts on their own. Minchin's whole persona, with eyeshadow and long hair, is that of an adolescent misfit. It fits wonderfully with a comment by one of the regulars at American biologist PZ Myers' site Pharyngula:

> Personally I don't see what's uncivil about saying things like 'that's so unbeliev-ably goddamned stupid' when something really is so. Nor is there anything wrong with saying 'only an ignoramus can believe crap like that'. If we put up with nonsense and idiots we'll surely have to suffer more nonsense and idiots,

and personally I think there is way too much nonsense and far too many idiots to begin with.

So what are sophisticated intellectuals like Dawkins doing in front of this crowd? One of the things that Dawkins, and the late Christopher Hitchens contribute to this mix was the same contempt but with an Oxonian gloss. There are some things you can only teach people young, and the easy, unshakeable assumption of superiority that Oxford teaches the British ruling class is impossible to fake. Contempt and ridicule come naturally to these people, and nowadays, of course, they are more urgent because there is no real superiority behind the rhetorical manner.

The old British ruling class, into which both Dawkins and Hitchens were socialised, no longer rules or even administers anything much. But the trauma of that loss is mostly over. In America, things are different. Power is still being transferred there away from the classes most drawn to the new atheism. You can put this politely, as Charles Taylor does:

> It's very much like the reaction of Victorian bishops to Darwin. There was a certain view among Protestants, in the late nineteenth and early twentieth centuries, to the effect that civilisation and democracy were progressing and that they came from Christianity. And then this torpedo [Darwin] came from the side and they were very upset by it.

> Similarly, many of the liberal intelligentsia in the late twentieth century thought that we were moving towards a higher civilisation, that religion was disappearing. Then suddenly, it seemed to return. So a kind of panic and anger arose. It's the outlook of an emerging establishment that finds itself destabilised.

Or you can simply say, as I prefer, that in the USA the New Atheism is fundamentalism for the college educated.

Either way, what we have here is a social and emotional movement that officially understands itself as a purely intellectual one.

I see the American movement as a response to the destruction of the old, valued and valuable role for a particular sort of labour: in this case, the labour of the intelligentsia. There once was a dignity to all kinds of work which the progress of capitalism and – if you like – modernity has undermined. Ordinary people could believe that their lives and their work mattered, especially in America – and one way to look at the last forty or fifty years is one long lesson in just how mistaken they were. Now this process is moving up the social scale. College-educated intellectuals, scientists as well as humanists of all sorts, are finding that the world no longer needs nor respects them.

And, in the USA, atheism is a class marker. To despise the religious is, as new atheists will endlessly tell you, to despise the poor, the uneducated, and the stupid. The more 'the religious', and their Republican puppet-masters, gain power, the more urgent becomes a class warfare against them.

But because it is pitched as a cultural war, it doesn't feel as if you're siding with the rich against the poor: in fact, to the left-wing New Atheists, it seems that they are siding with the poor against their exploiters by tearing down illusions that hold them in bondage. If that feels like a largely religious idea, it's no coincidence.

This has some interesting consequences when you look at the way in which these people, many of whom would think of themselves with complete sincerity as left-wing, react to contact with the real proletariat. Here, for example, are the instructions that PZ Myers gave his followers when they went off to disrupt a creation museum:

a) 'We shall descend upon them as a horde and sweep through their "museum", documenting the foolishness and mocking the silly.

b) 'the Christians running this show, and the Christian attendees, are the delusional victims here. Feel some pity for them. Do not, however, forget that this is an institution dedicated to promoting lies and ignorance. Do not pull a Michael Ruse and start admiring what they've accomplished'; and

c) 'you are not a gang of hooligans planning to vandalise the place, you are sceptical anthropologists there to observe the peculiar and pathological folkways of a backwards, intellectually impoverished people.'

This is a remarkably mixed message, but with one constant theme: never for one moment forget that you are superior to these miserable, common, twerps. Real anthropologists, whether sceptical or not, don't tell themselves, or their grant committees, that they are going to observe 'the peculiar and pathological folkways of a backwards, intellectually impoverished people.'

Perhaps it is worth mentioning here that Myers claimed once that 'My personal image of religion isn't fundamentalist at all, but the quietly gullible, unquestioning, moderate faith of my mother's family.'

But then many of us regard some of our relatives as backwards and intellectually impoverished. It's practically part of the definition of a family.

The mention of Michael Ruse brings out another characteristic of the New Atheists. Although they despise Christian believers, and they are frightened of Muslims, the people they really purely hate are other atheists. One has to be careful here, for they hate as well as fear Muslims. They don't fear moderate or non-fundamentalist atheists ('Atheists But' in Dan Dennett's phrase, or 'Neville Chamberlain atheists' as Dawkins calls them) but they surely do hate them. There is an interesting parallel here with Christian fundamentalists like Ken Ham, who runs a 'Creation Museum' and claims that liberal Christians are much more dangerous to the truth than open atheists.

Ruse has been a particular target of this kind of hatred from fellow atheists (as have I, in a small way: I offer these thoughts in my capacity as 'the *Guardian's* resident moron' in the phrase of Jerry Coyne). But Ruse ... a quick Google of the Myers site brings us posts headed 'Michael Ruse: incoherent and annoying'; 'I am so good at making Michael Ruse cry '; and 'Waaaah, Michael Ruse, waaah waaaah waaaaaah ...'.

Myers is admittedly a man with an almost Trotksyite capacity for invective and splittism. An Irish blogpost announcing with all the solemnity of the Popular People's Liberation Front of Judea that 'Atheists Ireland' would no longer associate with him and listed some of his rhetorical charms:

> He has said that 'the scum rose to the top of the atheist movement', that it is 'burdened by cretinous reactionaries', that 'sexist and misogynistic scumbags' are 'not a fringe phenomenon', and that if you don't agree with Atheism Plus, you are an 'Asshole Atheist'. He agreed that science fetishism reproduces the 'white supremacist logic of the New Atheist Movement.' He said 'I officially divorce myself from the sceptic movement,' which 'has attracted way too many thuggish jerks, especially in the leadership'.

He said Richard Dawkins 'seems to have developed a callous indifference to the
sexual abuse of children' and 'has been eaten by brain parasites', Michael
Nugent is 'the Irish wanker' and a 'demented fuckwit', Ann Marie Waters is a
'nutter', Russell Blackford is a 'lying fuckhead', Bill Maher's date at an event
was 'candy to decorate [her sugar daddy's] arm in public', Ben Radford is a
'revolting narcissistic scumbag' and his lawyer is 'J Noble Dogshit', Rosetta
scientist Matt Taylor and Bill Maher are 'assholes', and Abbie Smith and her
'coterie of slimy acolytes' are 'virtual non-entities'. He called Irish blogger Zen
Buffy a 'narcissistic wanker,' after she said she has experienced mental illness.

One need not have heard of any of these people to understand the way
in which movement Atheists love one another.

But I don't think this is fundamentalism, exactly. For one thing both
Myers and his enemies are far too exuberant, and far too open about their
hatreds, to catch the particular spirit of fundamentalism, which appears
from the inside as entirely rational. Fundamentalism in this sense is a
phenomenon of the twentieth century. It is part of the modernity that it
rebels against, and it shares the belief in the prestige of science, and of
reason. For truly fundamentalist atheist reasoning you have to go back to
something like Sam Harris' first book, *The End of Faith*, and consider his
justifications of torture.

He now claims to have been misunderstood in that book, and quotation
is an activity by its nature selective. People say what they don't really
mean, and they even write what they don't really mean. In the end, there
is a judgement call involved; there must be.

Here are the relevant passages, from *The End of Faith*, with page numbers
drawn from the British paperback.

I believe that I have successfully argued for the use of torture in any circumstance in which we would be willing to cause collateral damage.(p198)

Given what many of us believe about the exigencies of our war on terrorism,
the practice of torture, in certain circumstances, would seem to be not only
permissible, but necessary. (p199)

Two questions then arise: is this enthusiasm? And does he think that the
circumstances are such that torture is justified today? As to whether it's
enthusiasm, he admits that we may feel a certain squeamishness at the

results of his reasoning; he says he does so himself. But – and this is rather more important – he thinks this squeamishness, this ethical revulsion, is misplaced and mistaken.

I believe that here we come across an ethical illusion of sorts, analogous to the perceptual illusions that are of such abiding interest to scientists who study the visual pathways in the brain. The full moon appearing on the horizon is no bigger than the full moon when it appears overhead, but it looks bigger, for reasons that are still obscure to neuroscientists. A ruler held up to the sky reveals something that we are otherwise incapable of seeing, even when we understand that our eyes are deceiving us ... (p198)

(p199) ... the reasons for [our inability to understand that torture is necessary] are, I trust, every bit as neurological as those that give rise to the moon illusion ... Clearly, these intuitions are fallible ... It may be time to take out our rulers and hold them up to the sky.

So Harris believes that there are scientific ('neurological') grounds for supposing that his moral reasoning is correct and that we ought to be torturing people. Parenthetically, this reasoning from dodgy science to mistaken morality is exactly the fault of which he accuses Francis Collins, though in a rather more egregious form.

The second defence that has been made of him is the claim that he's not really talking about real torture at all. The circumstances under which he talks about it being justified: the ticking bomb, the villain who knows where the kidnapped child has been hidden, will never arise. So it is all theoretical, and it's quite wrong to claim that he wants it done in the real world. There are two reasons to reject this view. The first is that these kinds of arguments are never made in a vacuum. They gain currency only when there is real torturing to be done. The second is that Harris himself rejects it, first implicitly and then explicitly.

Torture, remember, is to be justified – sorry, necessary – wherever we would accept collateral damage from bombs and other modern weaponry. That covers any war that the US might possibly be involved in. And he believes these wars are necessary and we should not recoil from them:

Fearing that the above reflection on torture may offer a potent argument for pacifism, I would like to briefly state why I believe we must accept the fact that violence (or its threat) is often an ethical necessity. (p199)

Has he any particular war in mind? As it happens, yes: the war that the US was just then starting, with British help, in Iraq:

We are at war with Islam. It may not serve our immediate foreign policy objectives for our political leaders to openly acknowledge this fact, but it is unambiguously so. It is not merely that we are at war with an otherwise peaceful religion that has been 'hijacked' by extremists. We are at war with precisely the vision of life that is prescribed to all Muslims in the Koran. (p 109) ... No amount of casuistry can disguise the fact that the outer of 'lesser' jihad – war against infidels and apostates – is a central feature of the faith. Armed conflict 'in the defence of Islam' is a religious obligation for every Muslim man. (p111)

Islam, more than any religion humans have ever devised, has the makings of a thoroughgoing cult of death (p123)

And, in case you hadn't quite got the point,

Is Islam compatible with a civil society? Is it possible to believe what you must believe to be a good Muslim, to have military and economic power, and not to pose an unconscionable threat to the civil societies of others? I believe that the answer to this question is no. (p152)

In other words, we are at war, we must be at war; and in this war we must accept collateral damage, because that's the way wars are; and if we accept collateral damage, we must also accept, and practice torture (see above).

But he doesn't stop with the general case. On page 197-8 of the *End of Faith*, Harris specifically demands the torture of one named person.

Enter Khalid Sheikh Mohammed: our most valuable capture in our war on terror ... his membership in al-Qaeda more or less rules out his 'innocence' in any important sense, and his rank in the organisation suggests that his knowledge of planned atrocities must be extensive. The bomb is ticking. Given the damage we were willing to cause to the bodies and minds of innocent children in Afghanistan and Iraq, our disavowal of torture in the case of Khalid Sheikh Mohammed seems perverse. If there is even one chance in a million that he will tell us something under torture that will lead to the further dismantling of al-Qaeda, it seems that we should use every means at our disposal to get him talking. (p198)

So, yes. I do rather think that Sam Harris can reasonably be described as a defender and advocate of torture, at least when it is practised on Muslims. Plenty of people share his views: a majority of American evangelicals favour torture; the Bush/Cheney/Rumsfeld gang followed Harris's prescription exactly in the case of Khalid Sheikh Mohammed, who was at one stage waterboarded 185 times in two months. But what is shocking is that people who denounce American Evangelical Christianity as a threat comparable to the Taliban, aren't shocked at all when Sam Harris reproduces the same reasoning. They care much more about his attitude to imaginary gods than about his attitude to real torture victims. This is nothing I can understand as humanism. But it is, I think, entirely characteristic of the mindset, shared with the religious fundamentalist, that says the maintenance of a particular imaginative picture of the world, and the consistency of reasoning within that imaginative frame, is much more important than anything in the messy world outside: the screams and smells aren't nearly as real as ideas.

This is connected to the widespread view that there is an absolute divide between 'facts', which are real, and accessible to third parties, and 'values', judgements, morals, all that squishy stuff, which are ultimately matters of personal preference and meaningless.

That is also the view that connects scientism to the wider culture and gives it plausibility. It was crystallised for me by a comment quite early in the history of Cif belief, when a Christian was trying to explain herself and someone interrupted – discussions online consist almost entirely of interruptions – with the phrase 'But this is an appeal to personal experience. Personal experience can't explain anything'. The words personal experience were italicised to underline the contempt and incredulity that anyone in this day and age should believe their personal experience proved, or could prove, anything.

To discount personal experience absolutely is a fairly radical form of nihilism. Modern science is of course based on the discovery that the readings of instruments can be more reliable and more sensitive than the impressions of our senses. It also demands reproducibility. But reproducible results aren't just impersonal. They're also interpersonal. To pretend that nothing is real except the position of the instruments on the dial and that all our feelings are just frothy swells of emotion beating against these rocks of truth is not to eliminate value judgements but to make the judgment that they are valueless. Yet it turns out we can't easily live without them. Nor is it obvious that we should.

It's actually very hard to live as a nihilist and all but the most determined will end up concluding that other people's lives and loves are notably more meaningless than their own. Which explains, I think, why we are right to fear people who suffer from fundamentalist imaginations, whatever the paradise they imagine may be.

THE MAN WHO HID IN AN AEROPLANE TOILET

Rahul Jayaram

Humsari Hussain turns away from the small, barren patch of land that she and her husband once owned near the two-room house they still live in. The patch is roughly the size of a tennis court, though once it had seemed to be enough. Surrounding it are well-demarcated rectangles of land owned by neighbours, where cabbages, sugar cane, and wheat are in varying stages of fruition. The patch is barren because the new owner has not worked it yet. Children from nearby homes use it as a playground. They have abandoned the hopscotch squares they etched on the hard brown earth and will soon switch to cricket.

This land once kept Humsari's family fed and was, for a poor family such as hers, the umbrella for a rainy day. Her husband, Habib Hussain, grew up working it. As did his father and his father's father. Then he sold it. For a dream.

'It was our mistake,' says his wife. 'We made a big mistake, which we are paying for.' Her voice chokes up and her eyes fill with tears. Then she gets agitated and begins to shriek, looking at me, though the person she seems to be speaking to is herself. 'We were cheated,' she says. 'We didn't do anything wrong. We didn't do anything wrong.' Her two small children tug at her knees, consoling her.

Habib sold their land to pay for his passage to Saudi Arabia. The strategy had seemed foolproof. Habib would leave his home and his family and his village and travel a great distance in the belief that – like so many Indian men before him – he would earn enough money to return a man worthy of admiration.

Instead he changed his family's fortunes in ways he could not foresee. Then he escaped, in a most unusual way, and in the early winter of 2010, Habib Hussain was briefly a footnote in the national conversation. His face, bearded and drawn, flashed on the television and in the newspapers, not as a symbol of a successful man of the world, but of something else.

*****

It is not difficult to imagine the appeal of seeking one's good fortune in a place far from Kundarki, the village of some 26,000 souls where Habib Hussain lives.

Kundarki is about one hundred miles northeast of New Delhi, in the state of Uttar Pradesh, India's most populous province. Its market street is so narrow it does not allow for two-way traffic. The ground is half-hardened sludge. Sewage spills over onto the path, where it mingles with wet earth and is carried on by cycles, motorbikes, and rickshaws. Lines of grocery stores, stationery shops, and clothing sellers face each other along the route. Lamb and mutton carcasses hang from shop fronts, where flies buzz in circles around the suspended meat, like satellites. As buyers line up in front of the butcher shops, street dogs, their legs as grimy as the lane, bark at their rivals for a bone.

What little work there is to be found in Kundarki is in the fields, where Habib Hussain toiled. But for twenty years, Indian agriculture had been in a freefall, wreaking such human devastation in the interiors of north and central India that, according to a report by the National Crime Records Bureau, between 1995 and 2010, a quarter of a million Indian farmers committed suicide. Many poor Indian farmers and sharecroppers left for the cities. Millions of others, drawn by stories of the money to be made for those willing to journey to the Gulf, headed overseas, as many Indian men have since the oil boom of the 1970s.

Habib Hussain was better off than most people in Kundarki in that he owned land. The land yielded little; its worth was in its value to a buyer, and even that was not a lot. But selling it would allow him to afford his airfare, the cost of a visa, and the fee charged by an agent who would make his passage possible. Luckily, or so it appeared, the agent was a relative – Imran, his sister's husband.

Imran himself had made the journey. He had left behind a small farm and travelled to Saudi Arabia where, for three years, he worked for an Arab sheikh. When he returned, in 2008, Imran was able to set up a shop with a photocopier, a fax machine, stationery items, and a telephone booth with long-distance calling capability. Habib saw how Imran had become a man of respect in his village. Imran bought a new Maruti car for himself and a Hero Honda motorbike for his younger brother. Imran began scouting for people who wanted jobs in Saudi Arabia as labourers, coolies, shop workers, electricians, plumbers, and carpenters. He became the local manpower consultant for the Middle East. Habib heard that Imran had sent four people from his village to Riyadh, Medina, and Jeddah, two of them to work for the same sheikh for whom he had worked.

Habib, meanwhile, was making only enough money to feed his family, the equivalent of perhaps $100 a month – a fifth of what he said Imran told him he could make in Saudi Arabia. Habib had studied till the fifth grade at a municipal school in Kundarki. He could read with some difficulty and could sign his name in Hindi. 'I wanted change,' Habib would later say. 'I wanted to do something else with my life. Give my family better things.'

In May 2009, Imran began visiting his relatives in nearby villages. His sister spoke with Habib's sister, who, in turn, spoke with Habib's wife, Humsari, about him going to Saudi Arabia. But the trip would come at a cost and no one was willing to lend Habib the money.

But then there was the land.

The family was divided about selling it. Habib's older brother, Jalaluddin Hussain, who lived next door and who tilled the adjoining parcel of land, opposed the idea. But Habib was determined. He told Jalaluddin that because Imran was a relative, nothing could go wrong. Habib prevailed. He sold the goats, a buffalo, and the land. He used some of his money to host a feast for his family and friends in Kundarki.

Then, a week later, he left to seek his fortune.

He would return six months later, in circumstances far different than he, his wife or anyone in Kundarki could have imagined, escorted from detention to courtroom, again and again, as a judge in Jaipur tried to determine whether Habib was a threat to the nation's security or, as he claimed, a victim of what amounted to indentured servitude, servitude so humiliating that he sought his freedom by stowing away in the toilet of an Air India flight out of Medina.

*****

The big water tank at Kundarki stands over a wide swath of land that is the bulk vegetable market. At one corner, just before the main entry to the market, Kalway Ali sits in a chair by his furniture shop.

Kalway is in his early forties and sports a beard and prayer cap. We exchange pleasantries and he sends a boy in the shop to fetch special 'ginger-cardamom' milk tea. The villagers, wrapped in shawls against the December winter morning, gape and smile at me. Kalway and I begin talking. Others often interrupt.

'Habib will be here tomorrow,' he says. 'He has gone to work and could not get a day off today.'

I have come to Kundarki to meet Habib, to hear his telling of the events that led to his escape. First, I have a question for Kalway, who wants me to know that all of Kundarki was thrilled at Habib's return.

It's a matter of great honour to go to Saudi Arabia, I say. What do you make of how people are treated there?

Kalway gets animated. 'Oh Lord! Not good. Not good at all. People go there thinking we will make money and send it home. Leave their wives and children behind. Get our boys and girls a little more educated. Go for Haj. However, nothing of the sort happens in Saudiya,' he mutters. Saudiya is the local slang for Saudi Arabia.

The next morning I return to Kalway Ali's furniture shop. There are more villagers there than yesterday. It's nippier than the day before, too, and the village folk are tightly covered in shawls and caps. Tea is ordered again. Soon comes a ripple of cheers from the people gathered. A young man zips into the storefront on his bicycle. A boy calls me. As I proceed toward him, the man gets off the bicycle and greets me with a tight handshake. It is Habib Hussain.

He is slim and his thick black hair is oiled and neatly combed. Habib still has the stubble that I saw in the photograph that ran in *The Hindu*. But he looks fresh and energised. He seems far removed from his past. The eyes that looked so lifeless in the photo now look well rested.

We begin to talk and ten or so villagers seem eager to chime in. Habib and I move into a space where logs of wood are stacked.

The first thing Habib talks about is greed. 'I got greedy,' he says 'I was blind. And I paid the price for it. I should have been more smart while getting into all this.'

I ask what Imran, the agent, told him. Habib is convinced that Imran – whom he believed he could trust because they were relatives – deceived him. Still, 'Please do be careful when you write about him,' Habib says. 'It's a question of my sister's life.'

Imran, he says, 'promised I would find a job in a company or an office.' Yes, he concedes, the Saudi visa that Imran arranged for him clearly stated he would do the job of a cleaner. (All Saudi Arabian work visas specify the category of worker.) 'Yes, it was a cleaner's visa and I had made it clear to Imran that I wanted to work in an office. He said with the same visa I could do other jobs. The cleaner's visa was for just the purpose of first getting to Saudi Arabia.'

Imran got Habib's passport issued in June 2009. The total expense – including Imran's charges, the visa and immigration fees, and the air ticket – amounted to 110,000 rupees, or $2,227. Habib had been earning 5,000 rupees from produce he sold off the land. The money he spent to leave for Saudi Arabia was almost two years of what had been his income.

*****

When the journey began, Habib spent a week in Mumbai, at an accommodation that Imran arranged, a dingy room in a lodge in a predominantly Muslim neighbourhood, a small room he shared with two other people. Over the next few days, Habib underwent blood and urine tests at a hospital that issued reports recognised by Saudi Arabian authorities. Habib had expected Imran to hold his hand from the moment he left Kundarki till the time he reached Saudi Arabia, but he was on his own. 'He could at least call me and speak to me and stay in touch,' Habib says. 'He hardly kept in touch.'

Habib tells me about the day of the visa interview at the Saudi Embassy in Mumbai. 'I wanted last-minute instructions from Imran and we spoke after many days,' he says. 'He told me what will be asked and what to answer. But he had also promised to buy me good clothes and I didn't have any good ones.'

As he waited in line for his visa interview, Habib says, an officer looked at him, pointed to the slippers that he was wearing, and moved him into another line. Habib believes that the first line he was in was for those applying for a slightly 'superior' visa, one for a plumber or electrician or factory worker. But in Habib's telling, the officer looked at his appearance, muttered something in Arabic, and moved him to the section handing out work visas for 'cleaners.' Habib got the visa eventually, but was furious with Imran. 'I called him that evening, but he kept saying it would not be an issue,' Habib says. 'Deep down, though, I knew it was a problem.'

Habib doesn't remember the exact day he flew from Mumbai to Jeddah, but the month was July, in 2009. His first flight ever, and an international one at that, was on Air Arabia. Habib was excited about Saudi Arabia. But, he says, when he landed at King Abdulaziz International Airport, there was no one to pick him up or to give him directions. 'I waited for two-and-a-half hours at the airport, looking here and there,' he says. 'I did not expect this.' Habib had a few hundred Saudi riyals. He tried calling Imran but the call wouldn't go through. He did not want to call his family, though the thought often crossed his mind.

After two hours of waiting in the lobby of the airport with his luggage, a man turned up. He was an Arab wearing a traditional *dishdasha*. He looked at Habib, called his name, and checked his passport and visa. He asked Habib to come with him. For almost half an hour, Habib tells me, he followed this man, pushing his baggage trolley, until they reached a series of rooms in the airport. This man instructed Habib to stay inside till he returned. He told Habib he would be back in half an hour. When he left, Habib heard the door snap. The room had been locked from the outside.

*****

The room was large and occupied by five other men from different parts of India. It seemed to be a waiting room for transit passengers. There were rolled mattresses, rugs, and sheets in a corner. Most of the other men were sitting on a mat. Habib guessed that these men slept on the floor. 'They did not look happy to me,' Habib says. 'They spoke little, but they were friendly. They had been confined to the room for ten days.'

All of them had arrived in Saudi Arabia on 'cleaner' visas. Twice a day, the Arab man would open the door and a Bengali airport worker would bring them their food. This consisted of lentils, big rotis, and curries. Whenever Habib asked him about work or about Imran, the Arab man would get the

Bengali speaker to interpret. 'You will be fine, wait for some days,' the Bengali said. Habib says he remained in that room for twelve days. The room had a toilet, a refrigerator, and air conditioning. For the first four days the Arab man came in with the Bengali twice a day. Later, the Bengali dropped in alone for a third time in the early evening. It was then that the men in the room would plead with him to get them out, or at least to find out what was happening to them.

Habib doesn't know the Bengali's name, but all those in the room called him 'bhai,' brother. He assured them that they would begin working soon, that the Arab man would place them either with companies or with an individual employer. All those confined were devout Muslims. They had not prayed in days. Habib and others requested 'bhai' to take them to a mosque.

Habib describes, with some bile, the first time he prayed in Saudi Arabia. On a Friday several days after his arrival, bhai came to pick them up. There were two other Arabs with him. 'We walked some distance and then switched from elevator to elevator before we reached a big parking area,' he says. They crowded into the back of a van and drove for thirty minutes. It was Habib's first glimpse of the world outside the airport.

But at the mosque, Habib says, he and the other Indians were barred from entering. Instead they were told they could pray outside the mosque, in a traffic island, a hundred feet away. Bhai asked that the men be allowed inside but was refused. 'None of us said much, but we were all very angry,' Habib says. 'We stood there and then we prayed.'

On the drive back to the airport they stopped at a cheap roadside restaurant. Habib says it was the first good meal he had eaten since the flight from Mumbai. In the days that followed, the food bhai brought got better, too. Instead of two meals a day, they now got three. The men pooled some of their money and gave it to bhai.

After two weeks of this, Habib was finally put to work. First, he had to surrender his passport. Then Habib took his luggage and moved to another corner of the airport. Bhai told him that three of his roommates were going to Riyadh for work, at a company, while the fourth fellow went to work for a sheikh on the outskirts of Jeddah.

'And what about me?' Habib asked him.

'Wait,' said bhai.

Habib's first job was cleaning the men's toilets and urinals at the airport. 'It was the work of a very low person,' he says. 'I felt betrayed and embarrassed.' He worked with two other men, one a Bangladeshi and the other a Pakistani. Work began at six in the morning. Habib worked seven days a week, with a half-day off on either Tuesday or Wednesday. He did not get paid. 'When I would ask the Arab about my salary, he said he would give me money in two or three weeks,' Habib tells me. (Here one of the other workers helped translate what the Arab man was saying to Habib.) 'He would also say since I was new, I was being observed on how I was working,' he tells me, searching for the word, probation.

Through an arrangement with a restaurant not far from the arrival terminal, Habib and his colleagues ate at a price lower than that on the menu. And the owner let them have lunches and dinners on credit –'Two big rotis and a dal and sometimes chicken or mutton curry,' Habib says. Two times a day. He says he never got paid.

After two months, Habib started to get restless. He called home and spoke to his wife and children and broke down. His wife told him that she had not seen Imran. When she asked Habib's sister about Imran, she was told he was away from home and would return in two weeks. Habib told Humsari that he felt swindled by Imran. Humsari wept on the phone. The children, she told him, missed their father.

A few days after the call to his family, Habib was cleaning when another worker came to him with the Arab boss. 'Would you want to work in Medina?' asked the boss. 'Pay is better and the work is moving luggage.' Habib thought a little and then agreed to the Medina offer. The next day, he took his bags and flew to Medina. The flight was short. His Arab boss handed him his passport, which he would surrender after landing in Medina.

But things were scarcely different in Medina. He worked in another airport, one that looked identical to the one in Jeddah. It seemed to Habib that he had just moved to another section of the same airport, only he had flown by air to get there. For the next three-and-a-half months, Habib moved luggage. 'It was a little better,' he says. 'I did not have to deal with toilets anymore.' The rhythm of his life, however, remained almost unchanged: the room he shared with others would be locked from the outside. There would always be an Arab guarding the door. Habib's shift was always for twelve hours, but sometimes in the day and sometimes through late evening to early morning.

Habib was fed. But, he says, he had yet to be paid. Habib asked the other workers whether he should inquire about his wages. Two of them told him they had started getting paid after five months. Habib thought of asking, but hesitated. His confidence, he says, was shaken. He was afraid of upsetting his boss, who, he adds, retained a large man as his enforcer. When Habib spoke of the enforcer, I sensed something amiss.

'What happened?' I ask.

'He hit me,' Habib says, his mostly neutral tone now inflected by rage.

'Why?' I ask.

'I was late one day,' he said. The guards knew the schedule of their shifts – they kept a timetable. A guard would keep the door open for select workers to exit one by one, ten minutes before their shift began. On that day the others, he explained, took time to finish bathing in the room and he was the last to leave.

So when Habib readied himself to leave the room, he was fifteen minutes late. As he was leaving, the guard came with the Arab boss's deputy. Behind them was a horde of other co-workers. Before Habib could utter a word, the deputy struck him. He aimed for Habib's cheek but, Habib tells me, 'He hit me on the neck. Then he screamed at me in Arabic.' Almost immediately the Arab man turned back. It was a command for everyone to return to work.

*****

I wanted to speak with Imran, so that he could tell me his version of Habib's story, to understand how it was that Habib felt first confused and then betrayed. What had Imran promised? Did he tell Habib that his janitor's visa was merely a convenience for gaining entry to Saudi Arabia, and that it would keep him from a better and less demeaning job? Was Habib wrong to feel betrayed, especially by his brother-in-law?

But Imran refused to meet with me and did not reply to my messages and calls. He did try to clarify things a bit to reporters from *The Indian Express*, on December 28, 2009, where he washed his hands of the matter. He said that, along with Habib, three more persons had gone to Jeddah on job visas. Imran is quoted as saying, 'I contacted the other three persons this morning and they said Habib returned because he was missing his family. I took money from Habib only to arrange the ticket and the visa. I have come to know that Habib sent money to his family twice.' He said he had told Habib he would be working as a labourer at Jeddah airport and make 800 riyals a month. 'I am not in the business of sending people abroad. One of my friends in Mumbai who works in an agency asked me if anyone wanted to go abroad for work. So I contacted Habib and the others,' Imran said.

I had other questions for Imran that I couldn't ask. So instead, to better understand how this labour system works, I sought out those who understood something about the system that people like Imran are part of, and how a barely-literate farmer like Habib might feel that he had been led astray.

I travelled to the nearest city, Moradabad. There, along its anarchic main road, was a line of travel agencies. The poorly painted buildings wore a mossy, rain-drenched look. But their billboards claimed they could get you a passport, visa, and tickets for a low price. And inside they looked better. It was almost refreshing entering one of these offices, ragged on the outside but slick within.

Akbar Travels of India Private Limited is among the better-known international ticketing agencies in the city. Rifaqat Ali Khan, an affable Urdu-speaking man in his early forties, has been the manager of the Moradabad branch for four years. Though his company is not involved in manpower consulting, the business of ticketing and air travel has given him a close view into the workings of Middle East migration. The office is warm and shields us from the evening fog outside.

'I cannot tell you the number of instances of people coming into my office and asking for a job in Dubai or Saudi Arabia,' Khan says, shaking his head. 'Every day, at least one comes in. Two years ago, we even kept a big notice outside our door, explaining we are ticketing agents and not manpower consultants. Still, many people didn't understand.'

For Khan this misunderstanding is a symptom of a deeper confusion. 'The really poor class of this town, and its surrounding areas, does not grasp the fundamental difference between people who arrange work in a foreign country and those who arrange your travel,' he explains. 'Clearly, if they cannot follow this, they are easy prey for so-called agents.' The government's regulations have not been able to clarify the distinction between a manpower consultant and a travel agency, Khan explains. 'It's a gap that is exploited by all sorts of people. When a man says I am an "agent" he can be a manpower consultant or a travel agent or both. This allows anyone to become an "agent".' Thus, an individual can exploit the crack in the governmental regulations.

Khan, like many people in Moradabad, has immediate family in the Middle East. They have been residing there for the last twenty-five years. He has travelled there every other year and has conducted the Hajj prayers.

What meaning does the Middle East hold for him? I ask.

'My uncle, who runs a business in Dubai now, had to sweat it out in the early 1980s when he went there,' he says. 'Working conditions were, and still are, horrible – especially if you begin at the lower rungs of employment.'

Why are Indians so crazy about the Middle East?, I ask.

There is the Hajj, and the money, 'bogus' as Khan says it often is. But there is something more, too: 'Going to the Middle East was a status issue. It bought you respect in this town,' he says. 'If you were a father who had a young son working there, it meant the son would get better prospective alliances in marriage. In the culture of Uttar Pradesh and Moradabad, you could show off a little if you had a son working there.'

He explains that Moradabad's four-hundred-year-long reputation as a centre for brass works declined dramatically in the 1980s and 1990s, as cheaper Chinese goods flooded the market. 'We're still a big brass-producing city, but not in the way we were long ago. The working class that was employed in those units saw their incomes rise very marginally,' he says. 'So a lot of them caught the Dubai or Saudi flight.'

But the magic of the Middle East has, in Khan's view, waned.

'All the poor folk here would think if you got to Saudi Arabia there would be trees of gold,' he says. 'Instead you are working in a desert at 45 degrees Celsius, sometimes being abused or beaten, and the money is a few crumbs more than what you get here.' And with India's domestic economy growing, especially in the cities of Mumbai, Delhi, or even in the state capital of Lucknow, Moradabad's lower middle class began seeking work in distant parts of India, instead. 'People used to send a lot of money home from the Middle East. Now it comes from inside India.'

So it is, he says, that agents like Imran do not scout for clients in Moradabad proper. Instead, they operate in the interior, in the nearby villages. 'That's where the gullible catch is,' he says, speaking of the villages surrounding Moradabad with the same sort of hauteur that big-city Indians of Delhi or Mumbai reserve for places like Moradabad. 'People would go to Saudi Arabia, work for a sheikh for four or five years, and return. By that time, they had developed a good relationship with their employers. The sheikh would ask them to send more labourers. So when this person returns, he calls himself informally an "agent".'

Many of these travellers come back to their home village and would not want to go back to the Middle East. Yet they wouldn't consider doing the same work they did before they went away; that would imply loss of status and of face. Besides, the riyals or dirhams earned abroad would now come in handy. 'So, this kind of man would set up a small shop with a photocopier, phone booth, passport-size photo facility, or a stationery business that would earn him a decent monthly income,' Khan says. For banks, such a returnee has a creditable profile, worthy of a loan if he wants to start a business.

Which sounded very much like Imran's story.

But what of the men like Habib – the dupes, the innocents, the ones whom Habib himself called 'airport coolies.'

'Since you are from Delhi, you should go to the centre of such agents,' he says.

Where? I ask.

'Have you heard of Khizrabad?'

*****

Its formal name is Khizrabad Bhagol but it is better known as just Khizrabad, a blue-collar borough in southeast Delhi. For workers from Delhi and its outskirts wanting to work in the Middle East, Khizrabad is the Mecca they come to before taking off for the real Mecca.

On the facades of the offices there, dozens of billboards draw your attention. Most of them promise to take you to Middle East nations like

Saudi Arabia, the United Arab Emirates, Kuwait, and Qatar. A few also offer services to Tanzania, Ethiopia, and Kenya. Unlike Akbar Travels, many of these firms combine the functions of getting a job for a labourer, procuring his visa, and also arranging his international travel – a one-stop shop for those eager to work in the Middle East.

Khizrabad is the hub for emigration agents and small agencies. Though many are affiliated with firms, some are not. The non-associated agents mostly bring in clients from outside New Delhi. The ones within an agency attract dozens of aspirants from the city proper. When you speak to any agent, he will always claim that he is working for a firm, even if he is not.

Pervez Ahmed is one such man. He is in his mid-thirties and has been in the business since his late teens. 'I work for all these offices,' he says, pointing to the roughly two-dozen firms in the area. He has worked for most of these firms and has since gone freelance. 'With a job there is security and growth is steady,' he explains. But 'in freelance there can be more money, if you calculate on the basis per client, but business can be shaky. That's why most agents are all with companies now.' He gets a phone call and excuses himself, saying it will take him a long time to return. I look out from his office onto the street. I see two men wrapped in shawls, smoking beedis – thin South Asian cigarettes with tobacco wrapped in leaves. I head out to talk to them.

Mintu Singh and Bijayant Singh are both pipe fitters in their early thirties. They are waiting for Ahmed to call them, once he readies certain documents. They have travelled far, having come to Khizrabad from Siwan district, six hundred miles away in the province of Bihar. They want jobs in Dubai. Both are clear they don't want to go to Saudi Arabia or Kuwait, considered by many Indian lower class labourers as rigidly Islamic and demanding environments.

Why did they come all the way here? I ask.

'We didn't trust the agents in our hometown,' says Mintu. 'Also, Bijayant and I have a friend who is now working in the U.A.E. Pervez got him the job. We trust him.'

Bijayant concurs. Both he and Mintu have been in Delhi for a month. They've been staying at the homes of friends from Siwan who are working in Delhi. 'The training here is very good,' Bijayant says. 'And they conduct interviews here also.'

Bijayant tells me of one nearby office that arranges for interviews for housekeeping, cleaning, carpentry, and electrical jobs in the United Arab Emirates. A door opens and both are called inside.

*****

To perform well at an interview for a decent job in the Middle East, a man must be prepared. And that, in turn, has spurred yet another industry – job training for work in the Gulf. G.M.C. Trade Centre for Mechanical and Technical Training is just such a place. It has the appearance of a warehouse that has been converted into a training space. There are niches with pipes, plumbing materials, welding machinery, furniture kits, painting and fabrication equipment, brass and steel polishing items and liquids, and a tiny classroom with a blackboard. In the middle of the hall is a bench where two applicants are paying fees to join the course. Facing them are a young man and a middle-aged one. They run the centre. The older man is K.M. Khan.

Khan is bearded, smiling, and has a sturdy millworker's handshake. He takes me for a little guided tour of G.M.C. Khan was a facilities manager in a building in Abu Dhabi for many years before returning to India for good. 'What I see is that those with skills like plumbing, carpentry already have the raw talent,' he says. 'We make the finished product before they take off.'

To illustrate, he takes me to the plumbing niche of the hall. He lifts two pipes fitted to washbasin taps, one in the left hand the other in the right. 'This one' – he raises the tap on the left – 'has a conventional system.' He disassembles the tap to show the pattern of the washer, the pivot, the valve and the nut that holds the tap together. He then shows me the other one, which 'you will see in a five-star hotel bathroom.' This one is more complex. 'The simple one is what the plumbers coming here will have worked on for years in India. The other one, they wouldn't have seen much of. Those are only in big houses or hotels.'

Khan's explanation of the fine points of, and differences between, the water tap and the pipe, applies to almost everything else inside the G.M.C. training centre. These include mechanical and technical apparatuses, and pipe fitting, carpentry, and building materials, to name a few. All the types of fixtures common in India and prevalent abroad are kept to educate students about the differences between each particular piece of equipment and the techniques required to work them.

In short, G.M.C. brings the working world of the Middle East to Delhi. 'Our purpose is to get those who want to go to Dubai to know what it is like to work there, even before they go,' Khan says. Among the other interesting things he does is to hold classes in the small classroom in another corner. On the blackboard is a diagram drawn in chalk. It shows the drainage structure of a building in Dubai. One day a week, Khan becomes a teacher in the classroom, explaining how civic and sanitation systems function in the Middle East. For applicants who want to work as company van and tempo drivers, he deputises another person at G.M.C. to teach them right-hand driving. (India, like many countries of the Commonwealth, drives on the left.)

Speaking to Khan, it becomes evident the kind of pre-departure exposure is something that someone like Habib missed out on. All this priming before travel makes one look at agents a little differently. Clearly, not all of them can be painted with one brush.

*****

By December, 2009, Habib Hussain had been at the Medina airport for a little more than three months. He worked almost entirely with a company that deals with passengers on Hajj flights. Many of those flights came from India on the Indian national carrier, Air India.

Though Habib primarily moved luggage and helped in the upkeep of the arrivals area, he also cleaned Air India flights. Having so much wanted to flee the task of cleaning urinals, Habib now found himself cleaning the toilets on Air India planes. He did it, he says, because he lacked the will to complain. He says he was still unpaid.

On December 25, 2009, he entered one such Air India aircraft. This one was flying to the northern Indian city of Jaipur. The flight was scheduled to depart in two hours. Habib cleaned the aisles and went into one of the toilets with his equipment. Once he got in, he says, he began rinsing the rim of the washbasin. He finished it and dealt next with the toilet seat. He had closed the door. As he was scrubbing, he shut the door tight.

'I didn't know how it all happened. I don't know how I got locked from the outside,' he says. He tried yanking the doorknob but the door wouldn't open. He banged and shouted for some time, but heard nothing. He kept at it for ten minutes and then gave up.

Then he sensed the aircraft move – on the ground, for about half an hour. In the course of that time, he made up his mind: he would stay silent.

He thought this was his best chance to escape from Saudi Arabia. He knew doing what he was doing – 'no ticket, no passport' – was like a leap into the ocean. Quietly, Habib prayed and wept.

He heard faint noises outside the door. He wiped the sweat off his brow. He felt cold. He was sure the plane was going to take off.

He sat back on the toilet seat and waited. Then, he felt the plane begin to roll fast.

He held the doorknob tight with his right hand. With his left hand he held the washbasin faucet. This position helped him keep balance. In time, the wobbling of the aircraft subsided and Habib released his grip on the knob and the water tap.

A few minutes later there was a thud at the door. Somebody tried to yank it open. Habib then heard a fiddling sound and the door spun open. It was an Air India stewardess, and she let out a scream. Habib joined his hands into a *namaste* and pleaded to be spared.

More flight attendants rushed forward as passengers looked on. 'I told them about my condition, and what had happened,' Habib says. Soon there were other people, even some passengers who got involved. The stewardesses gave Habib a vacant seat. Habib told them the story of his time in Saudi Arabia. The attendants called the pilot. By now many curious passengers had gathered. Most, if not all, were Muslims. Habib's tale of privation was an often-heard one. It was the manner of his exit that was new.

Habib reckons the staff felt convinced he was telling the truth. He was given biryani to eat, and a blanket. The flight had a scheduled stop in Jeddah, he was told. When one of the pilots came back to the scene, Habib says he screamed at the attendants for the breach in security that had allowed Habib to somehow stow away. 'The pilot told her, "I knew there was something wrong with one of the toilets, and I had told you to check it,"' Habib recalls. (Air India planes have radar sensors in the cockpit. The sensors indicate any intrusive presence during the time before a plane takes off. Air India officials later conceded to the press that Habib's presence on the flight was not only a huge embarrassment but a major security lapse. Air India declined to return calls for this story.)

Then the pilot turned to Habib. He questioned him for twenty minutes. The pilot asked him if he wanted to get off at Jeddah. Habib refused. 'I pleaded with him to take me to India,' Habib says. The pilot warned him about the repercussions of landing in Jaipur without a passport or ticket. He would be handed over to the police. 'I was fine with going to a jail in my country, rather than rot in Saudia,' Habib says he told him. He was allowed to remain on the plane.

When the aircraft finally landed in Jaipur, one attendant remained with Habib. As the rest of the passengers left, some offering him their good wishes, Habib was instructed to stay where he was. Finally, he was escorted off the plane. The pilot and attendant walked him into the immigration section, where he was interrogated again. Soon police officers arrived. An immigration official helped Habib fill out a document regarding his arrival in India, which Habib signed. And then he was led away.

At the police station, Habib was booked under a provision of the Passport Act of India that treats entry into the country without a valid passport and visa as a crime punishable by five years in prison. He was placed under arrest. But by now, the Jaipur press corps had been tipped off to the story and reporters and cameramen descended on the police station.

That night the nation watched Habib Hussain – flanked by two uniformed officers; bearded, drawn, and dressed in a striped brown sweater – being led into detention. The reports not only told of his curious and remarkable escape, but of the miseries that had led him to flee.

Habib himself was not shy about speaking, even if he did colour his escape as somewhat more calculated than merely accidentally locking himself into an airline toilet. 'I had no money,' he told a throng of reporters. 'My employer used to beat me up and treated me badly. That is when I started planning my return to India. I hid in a plane and came here.'

Reporters travelled to Kundarki to find his wife. She sat on the ground outside their sparse house, a blue scarf covering her head, as her young children stood nearby. 'He had been very unhappy since he left India,' she said. 'He used to tell me on the phone that his employers delay making salary payments and that they sometimes made him work thirteen hours nonstop.'

The questioning of Habib went on for ten days.

'I pray to the government to release me so I can go back to my wife and two children,' Habib told reporters. 'I think of them all the time. All I can do is sit in a corner and cry.'

At last he was brought before a judge, who concurred with the police that Habib, who by now had become known as the 'Air India stowaway,' was telling the truth, and that while he had surely exposed a breach in airline security, he posed no further risk to the nation's safety.

'He is a poor man who was tortured,' the judge told the reporters waiting outside his courtroom. 'and he has come back in desperation.'

His elder brother Jalaluddin came with others to Jaipur and took Habib back to Kundarki.

*****

Habib pauses as he recounts his story. There are more people surrounding us in Kalway Ali's shop where we sit and talk. 'When I got back home, I felt like I got back my self-respect,' Habib says.

The villagers around us in Kalway's shop now take over the conversation. 'The whole village came out to greet him. Our brother Habib had returned,' says Salim, a worker in Kalway Ali's shop.

'Do you still hold a grudge against Imran?' I ask.

'Of course, I don't talk to him,' Habib says, but adds, 'It's in the past now,'

I asked Habib about what life back in India would be like for him. After all this, I said, 'What does the future hold?'

'Life is good,' Habib says. 'I am home with my family. I work in the brass unit. I can take care of them with whatever I earn. What else should a man want?'

ARTS AND LETTERS

LONG WAY HOME *Ivan Carromero Manzano*

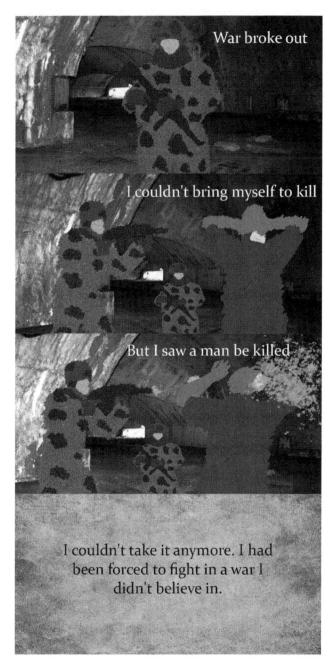

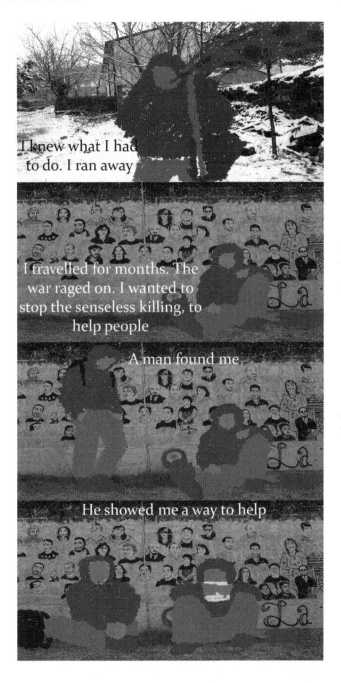

I knew what I had to do. I ran away

I travelled for months. The war raged on. I wanted to stop the senseless killing, to help people

A man found me

He showed me a way to help

He belonged to a clandestine group informing people that they were dying in a war that had no just cause. They called for an end to the hate.

He showed me I wasn't alone

We made leaflets and posters in secret basements

And handed them out

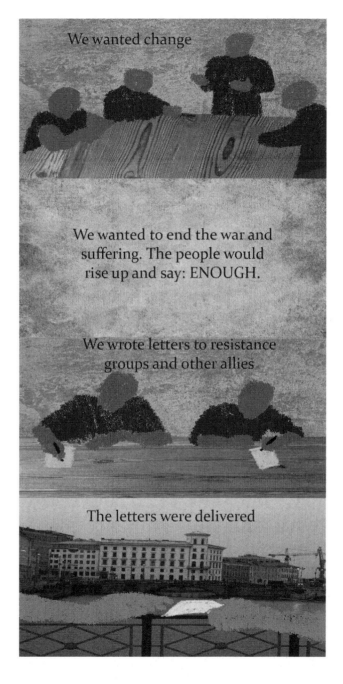

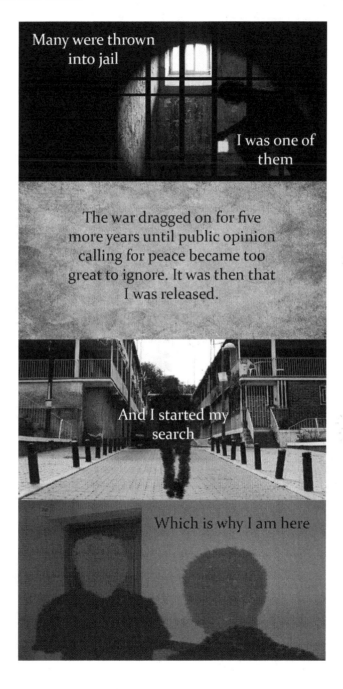

Many were thrown into jail

I was one of them

The war dragged on for five more years until public opinion calling for peace became too great to ignore. It was then that I was released.

And I started my search

Which is why I am here

PILLAR BOX

Navid Hamzavi

I've lost my wife and in case I die before turning seventy-five and do not find her, I have left a will in English on a scrap of paper that is of no use. As the sequence of the text is mysteriously out of my own control and constantly muddled up, it is strictly recommended to follow the numbers in order from latest to greatest. So, let's say, if the writing starts with No. 4, just ignore it, look for No. 1 then start reading from there. You'd then read it with ease. And if you find my wife, or have any clue how to reach her, or even any idea how to get to her, it would be easier to inform me. Here is my address:

Pillar Box EN 101
Spring Close
High Barnet,
Greater London
EN5 2UR

4. My wife had a dream

Our visas expired and we moved back to Iran. It started to rain the very night we arrived. People were falling down on the road along with bits and pieces that smelt of burnt meat. She ducked over and over in the downpour so that nobody would crash down on her. One of her shoes got tangled up between a charred torso and an arm. Manoeuvring between the deluge of corpses, she saw herself in a store window, black and sooty like someone who had climbed down from a chimney, then she jumped out from a deep sleep in the middle of the night and said: we are better off applying for asylum than moving back.

When she woke up that morning, one of her socks had gone missing (she was in the habit of sleeping with her socks on) and there were a few black traces on the sheet. I can vouch for that. The missing socks were never found. To not frighten her, I said: 'the traces are of the eyeliner that you dumped on the bed.'

1. In Iran, I had a girlfriend who committed suicide, unexpectedly. She threw herself from the eighth floor window of a building in Pasdaran Street, Tehran. Tangled up again and again in the cables of a three-phase power pole, she was just ashes drizzling down softly like rain, before she could hit the asphalt with a thud. It is I who is to blame. She had warned me, several times, that she would commit suicide if she couldn't escape Iran. I couldn't do a thing for her; only buy her some cheap, shoddy self-help books. When the rainy season passed, I married: the wife I am looking for from door to door, at this moment.

9. I was determined to find a job, a very English one. So finding a career became the most important thing in my life. After months and days looking for a job and getting rejection letters, I was eventually invited for an interview with Royal Mail. It has 'Royal' in its brand and the Queen's Crown is its logo. Preparing very hard for my interview, I delved deep into postal history as far back as Henry VIII. I have been rewarded for the effort I've put in; three weeks after the interview I received a job offer: three months' fixed term contract, 25 hours a week. And then officially, I became a Royal Mail part-time temporary employee.

I must have been a good employee. They extended my contract before it came to an end. After six months service you can order your uniform and be a real postman.

Two hats, one for winter and one for summer, a red pen holder classic polo shirt, a blue long-sleeved formal shirt, fingerless gloves, a belt, combat style patch-pocket trousers, a pair of combat style pocket and D-ring key-holder shorts, and shoes.

The shoes arrived first. They clung to my feet so tightly that I realised they were a good half size too small. I was hesitant to return them, and waited for about two more weeks to get a fresh pair, up until the day that they pinched my toes so much I had to take them off and post all the Chaucer Street letters barefoot, till I reached No. 161. A thin layer of skin, flaky, like pasta dough about the size of a restaurant portion, peeled away off my sole and convinced me to return the shoes. There were none my size though. I am now wearing one size too big. Though I adjusted them with thicker socks and insoles, they are still loose, like two people walking in them at the same time. Then the trousers arrived. I became grey up to my waist, the shirts turned me blue up to the neck, and with my hat on I became such a typical postman that even the dogs barked at me louder.

12. My dreams fluctuate widely; I am having a nightmare: Someone strips me bare by force so the only clothing I have on is a tattered white pair of men's briefs. He makes me run down the length of Chaucer Street, to No. 161; he walks behind me collecting the flakes of skin peeling off my feet. Piling his plate with flakes, he squeezes my feet until a few drops of blood trickle down on the plate. Said plate turns into a pasta dish with red tomato sauce on a restaurant table. And me, with only my briefs on, hands cupped on the window glass, staring at pasta disappearing into his mouth. No sooner is the pasta finished than my legs disappear from the knees down and I am toppling over.

6. The very same day, I made a serious decision. I became determined to integrate into UK society. With the little money left over and our government aids we rented a studio flat which turned into a bedroom when we unfolded the sofa bed. Watching English soaps was my very first step toward integration. I was always wondering if I would have been learning much faster had I had an English girlfriend instead of my wife, and perhaps sex with an English native speaker could make integration happen much faster whether I wanted it or not.

14. Now, with the aura of rickety crooked headstones mixed up with the stale odour of the decrepit residents of the care home, I've accomplished my goal of being integrated into UK society. My only concern is to find my wife, get the contact's attachment complete, sign it and send it back.

I should be grateful for achieving my goal and being among those few who fulfilled their dreams. Being an inseparable part of the UK, my one and only wish is to find my way into an Archive of the British Postal Museum and be selected as a Type B Pillar Box in its letter box collection, which in fact reflects a part of postal legacy and a glorious chapter in the history of Great Britain.

3. A visa running out is the most awful nightmare, like an ice-cream dripping and melting away when you are not eating it or disappearing all at once while you are gulping it down. The only way to slow this down might be just licking. We were looking everywhere to find a way to stay while our ice cream was about to dribble away, that's why we came to think about claiming asylum. In fact, claiming asylum was quite straightforward. What you need is to erase your history, at least for the Home Office, and carve out a fresh identity from a solicitor's recommendation. Which my wife was not happy to do. In panic, she looked into every single possibility, any offer, any solicitor's recommendation to find a way out of it. She even had some crazy idea of flying back to Iran until her strange dream changed the flow of our life completely.

10. Although I had become a proper postman then, and, apart from seven or eight people, all my co-workers were British, the early days at the Royal Mail were gloomy. I felt a longing for home like a persistent pain in my jaw that reminded me of a long gone toothache. I missed chatting away with the seductive, tall Russian girl and I wanted to be with my wife all the time. While watching English soaps, I felt safer with her. I struggled to gain control of my emotions and not let my mind cross the UK borders. First, I thought, it is something like unfamiliarity with a new environment, but the state I was in dragged on and on. Guys, there, were chatting far faster than the BBC, humming along to all the songs playing on the radio and sometimes saying something that I could not get however deep I dug into dictionaries. 'Get a grip', I told myself, and decided to set off on my journey of integration from the very office which, in fact, was a microcosm of society. Like them, I started drinking coffee every single morning, following the English Premier League, putting on shorts rather than

trousers though London's winds made me shiver to the bone. I memorised one or two songs which were most often played on the radio, and was ready to support England's national football team, in a probable sometime somewhere match versus the Iranian national football team.

5. We bought our case from an author who writes case stories for asylum seekers and makes a fortune out of it, but remains anonymousness. The end of the story was: if we go back to Iran we will be executed. We would be hanged in front of the eyes of spectators who had come down just for the occasion, hanged from a huge crane in a town square in Tehran, our limbs fluttering skyward. The story, though abstract, was convincing. Our application successfully went through and we were recognised as refugees. Shortly after we were entitled to welfare support, the NHS and the social service and we also got an integration loan which helped us to get housing, a job or education. Integration is a noble word that means combine, unity and togetherness and its genealogy goes back to Latin.

Though the money is not enough for a deposit or university fees, the good faith of governors for trying to insert us into society is commendable.

7. My first payslip shows I was not on benefit for long and soon became a bartender in a hotel close to Junction 4, M1, the post code was: NW7 3HU. That, indeed, was taking the first steps toward integration. A three floor hotel where most of the guests were businessmen or people who come down to London and stay over there for a couple of days or so. Before long, faces became regular and you got used to calling them by their first name. All I seemed to do was greet them, serve them, and get a few tips. If I'd had the chance to get to know them, I would have learned a few English phrases or something about English culture. But you were always cut off by either TV or somebody else's order or them flirting with birds, in the middle of the conversation.

11. We were seven or eight postmen on a temporary contract and every single day we were getting closer to the end of our contract. In such a situation, in any company, in any corner of the world, people will fight tooth and nail to keep their job to the extent of duelling to the death like eighteenth-century lovers so that the one who stays alive keeps the job.

This then was more or less our case. There were widespread rumours that our office was planning to cut all but one or two temporary positions. The recession was not far off. After a short while, following two auspicious incidents, we were diminished to six. One of us was flattering and charming and buttered managers up so very much that little by little he turned into a grey-blue cat with a vague trace of a crown logo on his forehead. He still wandered about the office, not knowing that he had dropped out of the race. And the other was shot dead one night. No wonder. Such things occur in a recession.

2. There were so many similarities between my ex and my wife. And sometimes I imagine that my current spouse is a mental substitute for the deceased ex, or even worse maybe, a slight guilty conscience was the cause of my duplicate love. Though slightly different in appearance, both shut themselves off from anything going on in Iran and did not want to set foot anywhere on Iran's soil. Neither walked barefoot on the ground, they always have something on, be it shoes, sandals, socks or whatever. This was because my ex used to be a flight attendant and my wife with the aid of yoga and meditation levitated several feet above the ground. Except, she, unlike my ex, was not so much in love with Paris that she would stubbornly apply twenty four times for a visa, like a prisoner constantly digging an escape tunnel with a spoon. After my ex committed suicide, to not let my wife's melancholy last long and not let her body turn to ashes drizzling softly down like rain, we applied for a UK visa and we were granted it…

8. The hotel's staff were foreigners and except one British girl of Egyptian origin, all the rest had strong accents. In the very early days the Egyptian girl with the British accent and I began to get on very badly, and I came to hang out with a tall Russian girl whose English was better than all the others except the Egyptian girl's. She would be the angel to help me survive and change the flow of my life. A typical Russian female, tall and blonde, with a body that confirms all the stereotypes. Once, I happened to see her topless in the changing room while the door was ajar. We grew quite fond of each other but it was all just chatting away like friends and greeting each other with kisses on the cheek or maybe just practising our English.

On one of those misty London days, while we were walking along together towards the bus stop and she kept moaning about the hotel manager, I grabbed the chance to use the phrase I'd learnt last night, jumping in with 'Get a grip!'

She didn't get me and I, disappointed, lectured, while she was sobbing, on the meaning of that phrase which I had glanced at the other night. It was right there that I came to understand that I was not on the right path to integration, even if my mate was a tall and beautiful Russian girl in a changing room.

13. There were not too many years left to get a British passport. It is not very British to take refuge in the occult, in divination or the tarot. Yet I resorted to an old hag whose wrinkles were far deeper than the inequality gap, and whose predecessors dated back to Buddha's grandsons and Indian fortune-tellers to utter incantations on me. She wrote a prayer and told my father to tell me how it should be read. I had to read the prayer ninety-nine times before the sunrise and not go to sleep until it turned dark again. So I got to sleep after sunset for a couple of hours and got up to finish off the long prayer before sunrise. As the old hag predicted just two days after the moon passed through the sign of Scorpio I was offered that historical contract which was like the nineteenth-century treaties between Persia and the British Empire.

I took the contract.

A treaty consists of twenty-nine terms. By this treaty they acknowledged me as a full time permanent Royal Mail employee plus pension and other benefits along with a Wish Form attached to nominate people to whom I bequeath a lump sum benefit if I die in service before the age of 75.

And under the contractual obligation my job was to be a red cast iron cylindrical pillar box type B which required me to start my duties at

Spring Close,
Bells Hill, High Barnet,
Greater London
EN5 2UR

In full time occupation. Right next to Cantelowes care home, opposite the cemetery.

POEMS

Ghassan Hassan

Untitled

1

Hill top green cliff seaside beach.
Daisy flower silent speech.
All the power matters reach.
Dividing space existence breach.
Sense and meaning endless teach.
Circles are the only shape.
Nothing really is at peace.

2

reality
a cross
between duality
do you understand all the laws that surround you?
and all the repercussions of the actions that define you?
or do you understand them like when nature gives you a sign
and you puzzle life away trying to get to a design
or have you humbled down so low
that you don't need to understand
and it's better safe than sorry under any circumstance
or have you reached the point
where you'll give it another go
cos if you get down to that point my dear
then there's nowhere left to go
and you might as well throw in the bloody towel
and start growing an afro
cos I've done had it up to here you know

and all of this just goes to show
once you've seen it then you know

3
I only have one memory
and its not even mine
I walked down that road
ignored the sign
I really didn't know though
What I would find
Numbers and lines
Numbers and lines
Numbers and lines made me lose my mind

*****

Medina Whiteman

Back Where The Paths Begin

Some men love the idea of Islam
for its manliness and its femininity
the gendered garb
strokable beards
scarves like petals round a woman's face
feet marching with a purpose
heart stirred with beauty
but then
the allure of being manlier
kicks a kink in their path
and the lamp shining
on a womanhood bashfully admired
disappears behind a brick wall.
The frowns deepen
the march becomes military

the segregation obligatory
no touching hands – don't break
my wudu' – and the beards are now
not thoughtfully stroked but
firmly put in their place.

Chivalry is confused with chauvinism,
gallantry with greed.
Man ascends to the position
he feels is owed to him,
a towering throne from which to judge
how well the womenfolk
are keeping their earlobes covered
lest the animal within him wakes
and he grows so comfortable there
it seems this seat of power was
made purposely for him.

Barbed wire goes up to warn off girls
who might think they
could grow learned and give advice
and every passing decade sees
fewer of them sneaking through the palisade
until the lookouts start confirming
the old ones' belief:
they just don't do intelligence like us.

Meanwhile sunlight dashes
fleet-foot over beardless faces
laughing in private, weeping in private
knowing in private, loving in private
cracking almonds, brewing tea
holding a lost one in their arms
stroking her hair while she finds herself

seeking in dreams and the unseen

for guides whose hands
they are forbidden from kissing
and all this round the crook in the path
where the lamp still flickers
and the watchtower sentries
have forgotten the path begins.

Hidden Under The Things They Grasped

They carried a plague on their fingers
when they went to seek gold and sell guns
took a ruler and pen to a map
birthed nations by caesarean
sliced human terrain in hot places where
their germs settled into the hot skin
and they returned thinking
their hands were clean
only the sores on their palms were
hidden under the things they grasped
They took back their queen and flag but
the disease was marrow-deep
fed by fictions of our happiness
ads for things they cannot possess
because they are working in the factories that make them
films with white heroes and brown villains
until some took the bait offered
by canapé waitresses at arms fairs
grinning bankers offering loans to pay for it all
and one surgically created side
was pitted against another
so the wound never heals
And the sickness we gave them never left us
the pockmarks on our diseased body
are hollows in the wet sand
along the outline of our nation on the map

And we decry their assault on our fortress
calling their desperation
greed
€1,500 to board a lethally overcrowded boat
invasion
the desire for a safe home and enough food
threat
And while the borders grow metal spikes
develop a rash of guard dogs
ossify into concrete walls
a man and his wife
hold hands each night
and try to leap onto a train
travelling fast underwater
until they reach the promised land
or die

REVIEWS

OBSTINATE SOVEREIGNTY

S Parvez Manzoor

In a moment of despair, Dick Howard regrets the inability of modern theory to provide a cogent account of, what he perceives as, the 'world (dis)order that began with the fall of the Berlin Wall in 1989', and wonders whether 'this incapability (is) a sign of the impotence of Western political thought'. If so, he reasons in *The Primacy of the Political*, why not abandon the ideological moorings of this hallowed tradition and renounce its foundational premises altogether; why not seek guidance and enlightenment elsewhere rather than trusting 'the West to the exclusion of the rest'? Indeed, 'why reconstruct what should properly be deconstructed, if not destroyed once and for all?' For this critic, it is beside the point whether political theory has now been replaced by political economy, or whether 'the critical spirit of modernity', as insisted by some must be contained by a conservative respect for the limits of human action'. The question that haunts him is: 'Is the Western tradition of political thought deservedly dead? Was it built on the domination of others and even of nature itself?' Whatever the merits of such self-doubt, or of the perplexity that even 'if a modern theoretical discourse that was not permeated by the hubris of mastery was conceivable', the issues of power and domination would always be paramount in any account of modernity. All appraisals of the West, indigenous or alien, must therefore focus on the moral landmarks of its historical project, the exploitation of (non-Western) man and the subjugation of (non-human) nature.

If this be deemed a legitimate line of inquiry in the West, which still possesses all the vestiges of political and intellectual authority, how come that the only worthwhile calling for a Muslim public intellectual is to be pretentiously deferential to the authority of the classical heritage and have no intellectual and moral encounter with the seminal thought of the last five centuries that, unfortunately for us, has arisen outside 'the abode of

Islam'. The dire outcome of the self-referential, self-authenticating public discourse of our times is that Muslim dialogue with history has almost ceased to exist. All that we have is a castigation of the incumbent political order and an intellectual and moral posturing that produces endless *ressentiment* but no viable ideas. Our putatively Islamic thought is nothing more than a reiteration of its foundational principles. Unfortunately, triumphalist racist ideologies, which now have a vociferous presence in academia, also perpetuate the myth of 'the Islamic specificity', an ontological propensity for fanaticism, violence and inhumanity. None of this is conducive to the promotion of a mutually enlightening conversation across civilisational boundaries or helpful in the pursuit of an interdisciplinary vision of the human reality.

The academy, however, it appears, is not willing to underwrite 'the clash of civilisations' thesis as the basis of postmodern politics, as it cannot sustain the capitalist utopia of a single globalised market. Political economy is not market economy (the state controlling the market vs. the market running the state), and instead of a pluralist order of territorial states kept in check by the deterrent of power/terror and legally consolidated by the claims of sovereignty, the market demands a single, interdependent and interconnected, network of global powers and hierarchies, the empire. Not surprisingly, the academy that once relished erecting disciplinary walls and protective enclosures around 'primitive cultures' and 'pagan religions', that insulated the West from the Orient and the 'civilised' from the 'barbarians', that posited a moral, political and technical divide between tradition and modernity, is in search of a new master theory that both comprehends the globalised order of our day and makes it more palatable. Modernity, it is argued, is no longer solid and heavy but liquid and light. And so, we may add, are the discourses of power and knowledge. Islam and West are neither two incompatible, transcendence-affirming vs. transcendence-denying metaphysical worldviews, nor two clashing civilisations, religious vs. secular, but partake of a single human reality whose moral unity cannot be ruptured by the triumphalist ideologies of power and salvation. Any judicious reading of the manifestly disparate texts presented here would suggest that contemporary political thought, secular as well as Islamist, presented as postmodern theory or medieval history, does not deserve to be

Works Discussed in the Review

María Pía Lara, *The Disclosure of Politics*, Columbia University Press, New York, 2013.

Ronald Beiner, *Civil Religion: A Dialogue in the History of Political Philosophy*, Cambridge University Press, Cambridge, 2011.

Panu Minkkinen, *Sovereignty, Knowledge, Law*, Routledge, New York, 2011.

Randi Rashkover and Martin Kavka (eds), *Judaism, Liberalism and Political Theology*, Indiana University Press, Bloomington, 2014.

Graham Hamill and Julia Reinhard Lupton (eds), *Political Theology and Early Modernity*, University of Chicago Press, Chicago, 2012.

Works cited

Dick Howard, *The Primacy of the Political*, Columbia University Press, New York, 2010.

Giorgio Agamben, *State of Exception*, University of Chicago Press, Chicago, 2005.

Ernst Kontorowicz, *The King's Two Bodies. A Study in Medieval Political Theology*, Princeton University Press, Princeton, 1957.

Walter Ullman, *The Carolingian Renaissance and the Idea of Kingship*, Routledge, London, 1969

Talal Asad, *Genealogies of Religion: Discipline and Reasons of Power in Christianity and Islam*, Johns Hopkins University Press, Baltimore, 1993.

Erik Petersen, *Theological Tractates*, Stanford University Press, Redford City, CA, 2011.

Carl Schmitt, *Political Theology II: The Myth of the Closure of any Political Theology*, Polity Press, Oxford, 2008.

Reinhart Koselleck, *Critique and Crisis*, MIT Press, Boston, 2000 (reprint).

confined to two separate mental worlds. Reading these works in conjunction not only opens fresh vistas but also affords an opportunity for the discovery of an 'Islamic option' in the intellectual currents of our time. The life of the mind knows of no logical or ideological apartheid.

The secularisation thesis, it is becoming increasingly fashionable to assert, has been refuted by the very forces of history whose demise it predicted with such schadenfreude and awaited with such relish. Our concern here, however, is with the intellectual challenges to secular liberal theory that have arisen from within the Western tradition itself and whose foremost articulator was none other than the German legal scholar and political scientist with Nazi leanings, Carl Schmitt. Schmitt was first to offer a polemical definition of secularisation as the transference of religious idiom to the realm of the political. 'All significant concepts of the modern state', he roared, 'are secularised theological concepts.' Even more cataclysmic has been the impact of his claim that 'sovereign is he who decides on the exception.' It is fair to say that since Schmitt initiated the modern debate on political theology, the discourse of political theory has never been the same. All the theoretical works discussed here respond to Schmitt's intellectual challenges explicitly, while the historical studies are implicitly mindful of the discourse of political theology.

Sovereignty, for moderns, is the *locus classicus* of the state, the *sine qua non* of political life. It is the starting-point for all political theorisation. More precisely, it is encountered in modern thought as a juridical question in relation to the sovereign state, a political question in relation to sovereign power, and a metaphysical question in relation to sovereign knowledge. As a general intellectual concept, however, sovereignty predates its modern secular interpretations. It cuts across the diverse realms of theology, politics and psychology: God, State and Self have all been ascribed the attribute of sovereignty in human history. That the concept of state sovereignty, which transforms the essentially moral claims of God's trans-political and trans-existential authority, and the freedom of human conscience that comes with it, into a positivist juridical order causes much distress among monotheists is no secret. What must also be underlined is the fact that even 'modernity's moral conscience' finds this legal positivism abhorrent. Or, as a modern critic expresses it, 'As a form of political representation, sovereignty in its contemporary practice is always idolatrous, that is to say it is a form of representation that interferes with rather than facilitates or expresses popular power.' In short, both religious and secular conscience finds the problem of political sovereignty morally intractable.

The foremost challenge of Schmitt's insights on sovereignty was/is to legal theory, as noted by Giorgio Agamben, one of Schmitt's more philosophically incisive interpreters. Agamben notes that despite widespread commentary and analysis, 'there is no theory of the state of exception in public law.' Agamben's own work, particularly *State of Exception*, aimed at filling this gap. In his incisive *Sovereignty, Knowledge and Law*, Panu Minkkinen argues that the aspirations of constitutional theory to capture sovereignty within the framework of modern science 'can only be materialised through a series of contradictions that require setting state sovereignty against the sovereignty of an emerging juridical science, a conundrum of a "contradiction" that Immanuel Kant attempted to evade by postulating sovereignty "inscrutable"'. (Minkkinen's first chapter provides a very perceptive account of the constitutional theory of Hans Kelsen, Schmitt's ideological opponent and architect of German legal positivism). One contradiction in any positivist science of law is that 'the overall idea of absolute power that is inherent in the common notion of sovereignty is incompatible with the idea of a modern *Rechtsstaat*'. Schmitt's decisionism and Kelsen's legal positivism cannot be reconciled in a constitutional state. The tension between the legal and the political readings of sovereignty remains unresolved. These dissimilar approaches to the constitution of sovereignty are clearly noticeable in the case of modern European states. While in the French tradition, sovereignty is understood as popular sovereignty, the German tradition understands it almost exclusively as an attribute of the state.

In historical terms, the sovereign state that emerged in Europe as a result of the protracted conflict between church and state as it is generally known, testifies to the link between Christian eschatology and the practice of politics. In fact, according to a modern scholar, the 'turmoil over how the transcendent God's earthly embodiment transformed earthly rule and governance is one of the most striking features of Western history.' The dialectic of Church and State, it has been long recognised, poses an almost insoluble problem for Christian conscience. Or, expressed more cautiously, it is asserted that 'there are no absolute relationships of church and state, of religion and politics, and perhaps no ideal ones either'. The state being the outcome of the Original Sin is at best a necessary evil, and politics, to the extent that it incarnates the sheer struggle for power, 'is bound, in Christian terms, to be the realm of the devil by definition.'

According to Walter Ullman, one of the most renowned authorities on medieval political theory, as Europe become more Christianised, a more traditional form of monarchy based on blood and ancestry was usurped and superseded by a new form of 'theocratic' and 'ecclesiological' monarchy based on grace and anointment. This is very instructive as Ullman reads it as an incursion of the political by the ecclesiastical, not a process of secularisation but that of sacralisation. It is this sacralisation that turned the Frankish people into a 'Christian body', with the consequence that the notion of power and authority was transformed from something specific and local, based on dynastic solidarity, to a transcendental and universalist principle of rule.

The idea that sovereignty is connected to Christian doctrine has been long recognised by scholars including the outspoken critics of messianic politics and apocalyptic religion. Secularism too, it is often claimed, is an (illegitimate) offspring of Christianity. Certainly, it is impossible for a Muslim not to take notice of the theological moorings of sovereignty that are Christian not only theologically but also historically. Secularism as doctrine, it has also been claimed, cannot be disentangled from the cardinal Christian dogma of Incarnation. The secular notion of the state, further, devolves straightforwardly from the theological vision of the incarnated God. That transcendent God dwells in an (immanent) human body and human form easily lends itself to being turned into a political theory: the King's two bodies, as theorised by Ernst Kontorowicz, German-American historian of medieval political history, are Christian.

The Christian dimensions of political theology, not the general concept but the discourse initiated by Carl Schmitt, were further underlined by an exchange that took place between Erik Peterson and Carl Schmitt. Erik Peterson's *Monotheism as a Political Problem* appeared in its original German in 1935, two years before Hitler's accession to power. It is a short book, deliberately allusive, coding his criticism of Carl Schmitt in Latin quotations from Augustine. Carl Schmitt himself is mentioned only in the book's final footnote. Peterson was prompted to write this tractate because the fusion of politics and theology was the staple of the emergent Catholic *Reichstheologie*. In Weimar, Catholics began propagating the idea that Christ had come to establish a sacred earthly empire, *sacrum imperium*, and that the conversion of Constantine inaugurated the true 'Christian Aion'. Germany, these Catholic theologians argued, had inherited the mantle of *sacrum imperium* as the Holy Roman Empire (*Reich*). Germany's only hope for salvation after the humiliation of Versailles lay in the rejection of the model of the modern liberal state and return to its Christian past. In 1933, they even pinned their hopes on Hitler as God's chosen instrument for the creation of the new Christian world empire. Peterson's ostensibly philological monograph masks a political statement. His is a claim for the incompatibility, if not the impossibility, of the triune Christian God to become a model for the new Holy Emperor. Monotheism, by which he meant Judaism, devolves into a monarchical political order while the Christian trinitarianism forecloses the possibility of 'divine monarchy' altogether. This was a firm rejection of Schmitt's political theology on purely theological grounds. Schmitt later issues his rejoinder, which is now available in English translation. The discourse of political theology however acquires greater clarity and focus when we encounter it through the prism of Judaism.

Whatever the political orientations of modern Jews, there certainly exist a stereotype of a deep alliance between Jews and Liberalism, that Judaism, or Jewry, in the modern period has firmly aligned itself with the secular liberal state. Yet, is the Jewish support for the liberal state entirely secular and for tactical reasons, or is there a potential conflict between Judaism as a religion and the liberal state? Such a reflection, which provides the rationale for the highly stimulating collection of crisp and intellectually gratifying essays, *Judaism, Liberalism, and Political Theology*, is of immense interest to a Muslim reader. Not only does it provide a welcome counterweight to the monopoly of the essentially Trinitarian perspectives in the discourse of political theology, or in the intellectual and spiritual worlds of its interlocutors, but it also has the merit of providing a very accessible summary of the philosophical debates that have followed in the wake of Schmitt's claims. Given the fact that Jews are insiders to the Western academia and intimately familiar with intra-Western debates, the critical perspectives provided by them are a boon for the Muslim reader, not to speak of the intellectually gratifying spirit that pervades throughout this volume. The editors have done their work remarkably well supplying faithful summaries of the contributors' labours, while the contributors themselves have shown exemplary diligence and intellectual clarity.

The critique of liberalism found in political theology, it is contended, overlaps awkwardly with the tradition of Jewish thought. In the 'hidden dialogue' between Carl Schmitt and Leo Strauss, the editors find a convenient starting-point. Both, they claim, shared two of the central stances of political theology: a suspicion of Enlightenment liberalism's promise to extirpate political disagreement and inaugurate an era of perpetual peace, and a belief in the theological nature of the political realm. They also notice that 'the rhetoric of "political theology" at its inception is also a rhetoric about Judaism' (Just as, it is, at its heyday about Islam!). Strauss's response, which later crystallised in a general thesis about the 'theological-political problem', and the intellectual honesty demanded the recognition of the tension between the claims of reason and that of revelation, and not proclaim the victory of one or the other, or offer any facile models of reconciliation. Ultimately, it is argued, Strauss's critique of Schmitt amounted to a 'Jewish riposte' to Schmitt's 'tendency to succumb to a Christian interpretation of the world.' Behind Strauss's conviction about the intellectual bankruptcy of contemporary philosophy, his radical doubt about modern rationalism and his recognition of its spiritual and moral crisis, lurks the giant of medieval Jewish philosophy, Moses Maimonides and his Islamic predecessors. That Strauss himself studied Muslim philosophers, and through them discovered his 'mentor' Maimonides; that one major academic enterprise for the study of medieval Islamic philosophy by Professor Muhsin Mahdi and his students has been directly influenced by Strauss's ideas; that Strauss's indictment of modernity for its 'theological-political' shortcomings fully coheres with the Islamic judgement in this regard, count, I believe, more than adequate reasons for the Muslim interest in the work of Leo Strauss.

Needless to say that Schmitt is criticised for his failure to reflect and examine the role of Judaism within political theology. Strauss's political theology, within the discourse of Jewish political thought, helps to illuminate the consequence of political theology for the Jewish critique of liberalism. Strauss shows that Schmitt failed to apprehend fully 'the irresolvable conflict between the authority of revelation and the authority of reason.' Strauss's critique also reveals aspects of political theology 'that warrant an encounter with Jewish conceptions of monotheism and Jewish assessments of the relationship between revelation and reason.' Further, Strauss was able to identify liberalism's 'nullification of both theological authority and philosophical freedom' as stemming from Catholic scholasticism. Contrasting Maimonides's *Guide* with Aquinas's *Summa*, where the latter simply opens his statement by wondering 'whether the sacred doctrine is required besides the philosophic disciplines', Strauss justly points out that 'one cannot even imagine Maimonides opening the *Guide*, or any other work, with the question as to whether the *Halakha* is required besides philosophic disciplines.... Maimonides, just as Averroes, needed much more urgently a legal justification of philosophy, i.e. a discussion in legal terms of the question whether the Divine Law permits or forbids or commands the study of philosophy, than a philosophical justification of the Divine Law or of its study.' Strauss's conclusion is that Aquinas's subjection of revelation to reason and Maimonides's contrary respect for the absolute authority of revelatory law mirror the difference between revealed theology and revealed law. Revealed theology identifies the contents of revelation with those of reason, and thereby reducing the authority of revelation to that of the limited status of human reason. Catholic theology then sets the stage for the liberal Enlightenment's valorisation of reason. 'Such an elevated portrait of reason morphs into moral nihilism and political failure.'

If secular thought perceives political theology as an ideological adversary, it finds the discourse of 'civil religion' as an ideological ally. Civil religion is quite simply 'the appropriation of religion by politics for its own purposes.' Or, stated equally candidly: 'Civil religion is the empowerment of religion not for the sake of religion, but for the sake of enhanced citizenship – of making members of the political community better citizens.' For Ronald Beiner, the civil religion question is 'a gateway to political philosophy', hence his book, *Civil Religion*, is subtitled 'a dialogue in the history of political philosophy'. He starts his intellectual voyage by marvelling at the fact that great thinkers tend to be full of surprises, and that the guiding lights of the secular tradition display ambivalent feelings towards religion. Machiavelli, for instance, celebrates Francis of Assisi,

Hobbes extols the practice of Christian martyrdom, Rousseau, 'the great champion of republican freedom', praises the politics of Islam, and Nietzsche, the father of the infamous scream 'God is dead' is, 'according to the political structure of his argument, an emphatic theist.' Political philosophy's relationship with religion, indeed with theocracy, cannot be described as one based on unambiguous spite and animosity.

In this historical survey of the leading thinkers of Western political philosophy, starting from Rousseau and ending with Heidegger, Beiner seeks 'to unpack some of the complexities, riddles, ironies, tensions, and paradoxes in their views about religion.' To the socially and politically forever burning question 'what should define the relationship between politics and religion?', Beiner lists three available possibilities: (1) the idea that politics and religion should be kept separate (liberalism), (2) the idea that politics and religion should be joined together but governed by the supremacy of religion (theocracy); and (3) the idea that politics and religion should be joined together but governed by the supremacy of politics (civil religion). It is not obvious that the first and the third answers have much in common, but 'on deeper examination', Beiner believes, there is 'a latent alliance between the third and the first possibilities.' Civil religion, in other words, can be made to work in tandem with liberalism.

As for what we can learn from the theorists of civil religion, his answer is: we can learn from Machiavelli, Hobbes and Rousseau that the state as a locus of political authority must be wary of claims to authority emanating from religion. Or, as Hobbes put it, 'men cannot serve two masters'; the contest of two conflicting authorities must be eliminated. It does not follow however, Beiner insists, that one should go the civil-religion route, to 'go so far as to appropriate religion, to make it a direct tool of political power.' Religion, Beiner is fully aware, 'is a perilous device in the realm of politics, and putting it to work for directly political purposes seems an extreme response to the predicament' of the theo-political problem. He feels that 'one can take seriously the civil-religion statement of the problem without embracing the civil-religion solution.' Spinoza, however, presents more of a dilemma for political thought: on the one hand, he holds that politics and morality need religion, the civil-religion side of his thought; on the other, he also believes that politics needs to be liberated from religion, the liberal side of his philosophy. Nevertheless, there's no denying that each theorist of civil-religion did not merely utilise civil religion for politico-moral purposes 'but also sought to liberate human beings from the yoke of religion.' If so, the obvious conclusion is that civil religion is 'an inherently unstable and contradictory mode of political thought.' In the end, all the insights of civil-religion tradition are not really liberating and uplifting. For, as Rousseau pointed out, civil religion is a hopeless project', which leads Beiner to wonder, 'if civil religion is a hopeless project, then it may well be that civic republicanism is a hopeless project.' Leaving aside the fact that the whole discourse of civil-religion is not only historically and conceptually dependent on Western experience but that the two meta-categories 'religion' and 'politics' have limited purchase in the global market of ideas in our day, we may simply note the perplexity, if not the inadequacy, of the modernist discourse to provide guidance in postmodern times.

The argument that the Western model of Christianity need not be posited as a normative universal category of 'religion' has been forcefully presented by Talal Asad. The secular, it is also being claimed, has been replaced, in historic terms at least, by the 'post-secular'. Jürgen Habermas, for instance, has spoken of the necessity of embracing moral institutions of faith in order to regenerate a declining secular consciousness, or 'a modernisation spinning out of control'. Beyond these polemical encounters, there is a deep-rooted concern about the foundational claim of secularism that reaches to the heart of the religious-secular schism, namely the autonomy of politics. Both *The Disclosure of Politics* and *Political Theology and Early Modernity* present a vigorous defence of the claim that the modern, secular understanding of politics as the realm of freedom and action, is in the face of ongoing re-enchantment of the world worth defending.

Many political theorists, blinded by the startling disclosures of political theology, are busy deriding the derivative and unoriginal insights of the secularist discourse. Indeed, according to Maria Pia Lara, 'politics seems to be losing grounds, and the so-called Weberian disenchantment has vanished.' For others, as Dick Howard argues in *The Primacy of the Political*, anti-politics seems to be replacing politics. Retracing the key terms of the modern debate about the increasing focus on religion in political theology, Lara insists, the secular concepts of politics represents a sea change in our conceptual world. German theorists – Löwith, Blumenberg, Arendt, Kosseleck, Habermas et al – had already identified secularisation as an

ambiguous concept because of its articulation of temporality. It was the
novel perception of 'time' that completely transformed the social and
political vocabularies of modernity. Time as eternity, as aeon, gave way to
time as saeculum, the world we know and live in. The German debate on
the autonomy of politics became associated with the process of conceptual
change, and the way our notion of time was altered, specifically in relation
to politics. In Lara's opinion, the present debate has seriously exaggerated
the interdependence of religion and politics, minimising the importance
of the conceptual paradigm shift in modernity – essentially a reissue of the
German intellectual historian Hans Blumenberg's argument in *The
Legitimacy of the Modern Age*.

The method adopted in this conceptual history that specifically
concentrates on political and historical concepts through a genealogical
account of their emergence and their possible disclosure of new political
dimensions owes a lot to another German historian, Reinhart Kosselleck.
It further highlights Blumenberg's argument, crucial to which was his
description about how modernity made possible new kinds of fields of
action – like art and science – when actors regarded themselves as self-
referential subjects. Or, how the altered perceptions of temporality were
responsible for the emergence of the newer forms of subjectivities.
Blumenberg also allowed us to envision the space of the social imaginary
and of culture as vital sources for politics. To this debate, Hannah Ardent
made her own contribution by making a significant effort to define the
meaning of worldliness (the secular) as the capacity to construct an
innovative theory of politics. Habermas, on his part, introduced the
distinctive notion of the public sphere and the practice of public debate as
the central process wherein democracy and justice are constructed by
social and political actors. Kosselleck's study on *Critique and Crisis*, a
historical account uncovering how absolutism planted the seed of the
Enlightenment's thought, reveals that 'the struggles of politics to survive
without religious semantics made it possible for new actors (civil society)
to define themselves through political justice as they actualised a horizontal
(rather than vertical) structure of social relations.' The disclosure of politics
then takes on a Heideggerian meaning; it defines the capacity of a concept
to open up a previously unseen area of interaction between social and

political actors. You may almost say that through it, the truth comes to be known and it reveals itself as politics.

Political Theology and Early Modernity also presents variations on the same theme but with a difference. It has a definite historical focus and examines the role played by sixteenth- and seventeenth-century literature and thought in modern conceptions of political theology. It explores texts by Shakespeare, Machiavelli, Milton, and others that have served as points of departure for such thinkers as Schmitt, Strauss, Benjamin, and Arendt. But the variety and richness of the contributions is very impressive and the editors' synopsis and introduction is a model of clarity. It also has its ideological commitment. The editors admit to using the concept in a polemical meaning, in which politics and theology, understood as contest rather than alliance, delineate the schism around which early modernity is constituted. Given this perspective, political theology seems to unlock the occasion in which personal sovereignty transforms into its opposite: as citizenship, the *corpus mysticum*, the multitude, or civil society. Thus in the historic setting of early modernity, political theology is neither a set of themes nor a particular form of government but, rather a scene of recurring conflict, and 'the impossibility of the state to totalise politics.' Unlike other traditions where political theology functioned as a kind of civil-religion, political theology in early modern Europe has the status of a founding event, a sea change in the mental world of the times, or a paradigm shift on the ideological plane. Hence, 'whether taken up critically or creatively, political theology confronts its readers as crisis and not content, as recurrent question rather than established doxa.' There is also a commitment by the contributors to recapture, *pace* Schmitt, 'democratic promises of Spinoza borne by his iconoclastic re-reading of Scripture.'

The refutation of Carl Schmitt, and along with it any restitution of religious perspective in modern political philosophy is what *Political Theology and Early Modernity* seeks, albeit diligently and suggestively. By its own admission, 'political theology recovers the specificity of literature from the potentially neutralising force of culture by taking seriously Renaissance literature's definitive disclosure of political making as what is at stake in key moments of revelation and scripture.' The editors inform us, such moments include 'the signature of circumcision, the violence of sacrifice, the dream of a corpus mysticum, the challenge of neighbourly love, the unions and disunions of marriage, the dialectic of idolatry and iconoclasm, and the inextricable bond between enlightenment and terror.' There is also sustained dialogue with Strauss, and his question, 'can there be a version of political philosophy that is based on reason and not revelation?' resonates through the whole volume.

The arguments and debate continue.

THE CULTURALIST TENDENCY

Talat Ahmed

The US policy on Iraq and the 'war on terror' is in tatters. For over a decade the most advanced, sophisticated and lethal military machine the world has ever known wreaked death and destruction on the people of Iraq. The dictator Saddam Hussein was gone, the Islamist leader Osama Bin-Laden had been caught and killed, Al-Qaeda soldiers routed and Iraq was undergoing a transition to Western democracy where all citizens would be respected. Western intervention had made the world safe. And suddenly out of nowhere, a new generation of jihadists have emerged – the Islamic State of Iraq and Syria (ISIS) – on the ashes and debris of a failed Syrian revolt to overthrow Assad and a US occupation and imposed political elite in Iraq. The Islamic State of Iraq and Syria (ISIS) is now public enemy number one as were Al-Qaeda and the Taliban before it. Barack Obama has vowed 'to degrade and destroy' ISIS, a group described as 'monsters' by David Cameron who later went on to say that destroying the extremist ideology they represent was the struggle of our generation.

In this climate, the publication of Arun Kundnani's *The Muslims Are Coming* is particularly welcome. It challenges the widespread notion amongst policy makers and government agencies that there is a causal link between Islamist ideology and committing violent terrorist acts. As well as reminding the reader how impressionistic, lazy and superficial such commentary is, Kundnani charts how the discourse of 'radicalisation' has come to dominate Western thinking about Islamism and Islam, a discourse shared by heads of states, government officials, policy makers, academics and journalists.

Arun Kundnani, *The Muslims Are Coming: Islamophobia, Extremism and the Domestic War on Terror*, Verso, London, 2014.

The book takes apart the radicalisation models that dominate the 'thinking' of the authorities in Western states. Radicalisation theorists provide what policy makers demand – an easy and digestible set of simple explanations for what are complex problems. A plethora of think tanks and university departments devoted to 'Terrorism Studies' and 'War Studies' had been set up in the wake of 9/11 to attract government funding for national security research. The task was simple: to identify those indicators that 'made' a terrorist. The approach is predicated on the belief that certain factors can be isolated which can lead some individuals towards Islamism. These factors include: the growing of a beard, wearing certain clothing and so on.

Kundnani provides a detailed survey of the scholarship that has provided intellectual credibility to discourses on 'terrorism' studies in the US. One such academic is Walter Laqueur, a 'seasoned Washington insider' whose pedigree includes being Israel's representative in the 1950s to the CIA-funded Congress for Cultural Freedom. Kundnani notes how Laqueur's explanation for the attack on the twin towers lies in 'a religious commandment – jihad and the establishment of sharia' and this is due to 'a cultural-psychological predisposition'. His ilk view Europe as the 'most vulnerable battlefield'; as the 'main base of terrorist support groups'. American political think tanks and academics based in Defence/War Studies and Terrorist Studies departments work in tangent with officials from the White House, Pentagon and the spooks in the CIA and US corporations such as the Foundation for the Defence of Democracies (FDD).

The FDD published a 'study' in 2009 based on data obtained from statements from detained and imprisoned individuals, trial transcripts and newspaper reports. On the basis of this information they proceed to identify clusters of indicators with the most occurrence to suggest a shared trajectory of radicalisation. These indicators include behavioural changes such as the adoption of a legalistic interpretation of Islam; trusting an ideologically rigid religious authority; believing Islam and the West to be irreconcilable; perceiving other religious attitudes as deviant; attempting to impose religious beliefs on others and expressing radical political views. The first five are seen to derive from 'religious' ideology and so Kundnani states that there are glaring problems with this type of study. In purporting to be a study about psychological and theological factors it is curious how it does not include a control group of 'non-terrorists' to assess and compare whether religious manifestation is in any way associated with terror acts, while relying upon trial transcripts and newspaper reports is highly problematic.

The last indicator of political radicalisation scores the highest but rather than examine the factors that might lead to this radicalisation, the authors read religious zealotry into every attribute. The FDD is one of several neoconservative pressure groups established in the wake of 9/11. This particular study was funded by the Lynde and Harry Bradley Foundation, who donated more than $1.2 million to the Project for the New American Century. Other theories locate radicalisation in friendship and kinship ties and so Marc Sageman argues that the most striking feature of a jihadist profile is that 'joining the global Islamist terrorism social movement was based to a great degree on friendship and kinship'. So a group of friends, family members either decide to collectively join a terrorist outfit or they join a childhood friend who is already a terrorist. Either way, social bonds come before ideological commitment. In this scholarship dangerous religious ideas and identities are activated by group dynamics that transform individuals into terrorists.

Kundnani is critical of these psychological theories that seek to pathologise Muslim behaviour. Even the more liberal wing of the US response to radicalisation is predicated on highly dubious thinking. They may talk in terms of the use of 'soft power' as opposed to the gung-ho lunacy of the 'bomb and bomb until annihilation' position, but this implies the managing of radicalisation in terms of 'neutralising' it. Sageman's work and that of others on social networks has been most influential in guiding the policies of law enforcement and intelligence agencies.

The New York Police Department developed its strategy based on theoretical formulations of Sagemen and identified four stages to the radicalisation process: pre-radicalisation; self-identification; indoctrination and jihadisation. And each of these has a set of indicators that allow for predictions to be made about future terrorist risks. So stage two of self-identification includes giving up cigarettes, drinking, gambling and urban hip-hop gangster clothes; wearing traditional Islamic clothing and growing a beard. Even though the study admits that this behaviour is 'subtle and not criminal' it nevertheless maintains that to identify individuals at risk requires intelligence gathering on such targets. Kundnani points out this entails the use of recruited informants referred to as 'mosque crawlers' and undercover officers known as 'rakers' to spy upon would-be terrorists. And what they are trying to detect is any 'hostility to the United States'. A former informant has exposed how the NYPD use a strategy called 'create and capture' which entails initiating conversations about jihad and violence and then capturing the response and sending it to the police intelligence Unit. Informant activities include collection of names attending mosques or study groups on Islam but also sending undercover operatives to student protests against Israel's attack on Gaza in January 2009. This student informant was rewarded with a thousand dollars a month for his efforts!

The British Government's Prevent strategy has been deployed in a similar vein. Greater Manchester Police have set up an anti-extremist project called Channel, which is part of the Prevent Violent Extremism programme. This is predicated on profiling young people thought to be at risk of radicalisation. It entails high levels of surveillance that seeks to incorporate police officers, teachers, youth workers, health workers, and social workers. Under this strategy would-be radicals would be identified and then offered counselling, mentoring and religious instruction to counter the effects of radicalisation. In some cases individuals were moved and re-housed to prevent them from 'bad' influences. One individual, Jameel, identified as at risk, was visited by police at his aunt's house and asked about his political activity, which included attending anti-war meetings, Love Music Hate Racism and Unite Against Fascism events. Kundnani notes how between 2007-2010 this resulted in 1,120 individuals being identified as potential radicals. Out of this, 290 were under 16, fifty-five were under 12 and over 90 per cent were Muslim. And by 2012 almost 2,500 people were identified by the Channel project as possible risks. Jameel's assessment of such intrusions are most revealing: he states the police officers, who albeit friendly, were operating with vague concepts that were 'not an attempt to curb terrorism [but] an attempt at de-politicisation, spreading fear, and making people actually feel unsafe around their neighbours.' Herein lays the real motive behind this approach: viewing dissent as extremism and therefore equal to terrorism. These initiatives are based on the same psychological and theological theories of their US counterparts. In other words, there is no attempt to consider what is happening at a deeper level of politics. To consider political motives such as anger at continuous wars and Western interference in the Middle East would be to entertain the possibility that what is at fault is Western state policy and corporate and military interests. And this cannot be permitted.

Initially the British (Labour) government welcomed the formation of the Muslim Council of Britain (MCB) in 1997 as a moderate and non-political umbrella organisation. However, it began to lose state patronage after the 2003 invasion of Iraq as MCB voiced strong criticism of British policy. They were not alone. Kundnani provides an example from the Bolton Council of Mosques which has been generously endowed with Prevent money and works in tandem with police authorities. In March 2010, when the English Defence League (EDL) planned a demonstration in the town, representatives of the Mosque Council agreed with the police to issue a call to discourage Muslims from entering the city centre that day. As Kundnani concludes, the real enemy for the police that day was not the racism and extremism of the EDL, but the fear that their presence would provoke 'radicalisation' amongst Muslim youth, and the right of Muslims to protest 'was dispensed with'.

In Britain, Kundnani tracks the growth of a 'reformist' approach to tackling 'radicalisation', one which prides itself on championing the supposed liberal values of 'good, decent, law abiding' Muslims as opposed to extremists who have distorted Islam. They also assume that by data collection, intelligence gathering and counter knowledge they can identify and neutralise those considered 'at risk', while demanding Muslims 'integrate' and demonstrate that they share 'British' values and stand against 'extremism'. The Quilliam Foundation for example was set up in April 2008 by Ed Husain and Maajid Nawaz, both former members of Hizb ut-Tahrir. Along with Husain's 2007 book, *The Islamist*, this Foundation quickly became pivotal to the state and official narrative of terrorism that rooted radicalisation in the politicisation of Islam as opposed to issues such as the Iraq war. A key activity of these think tanks and those that lead them has been to generate lists of Muslims at 'risk' of potential radicalisation and encourage the policy of persuading professionals in the state sector to report to the state. What emerges is a frightening picture of organisations operating in a completely unaccountable manner and individuals left with little redress or protection.

Kundnani makes the point forcefully that the bar for Muslims to be accepted into the mainstream is raised so high that it makes a mockery of so called Western values of tolerance, equality and democratic rights. Muslims are effectively told they can only be accepted so long as they give up the right to behave as other citizens and remain aloof from political participation, do not express opinions contrary to government policy and above all surrender their right to express and practice their faith like any other citizen.

One key merit of this book is how Kundnani demonstrates that counter-intelligence, the use of informants, surveillance, entrapment, character assassination are part and parcel of a long established strategy by the state. He makes several comparisons with the McCarthyism of the late 1940s and 1950s, and the title of the book *The Muslims are Coming* is deliberately reminiscent of the great 1966 film 'The Russians are Coming, the Russians are Coming', satirising the McCarthyite paranoia that swept the US in the 1950s. This was a period in which former radicals became turncoats and were more than willing to testify against former comrades and friends, or become informants. Kundnani notes that by 1970 the NYPD had collected dossiers on 1.2 million New Yorkers, which it shared with private investigators, academics and prospective employers.

The term 'Cold War liberalism' was coined to characterise liberals who shared a broad social democratic world view but believed that American security lay in strident and militarised anti-communism abroad and suppression of 'communist' tendencies at home. Just as communism was public enemy number one for the post-war era, Islam and Islamism has come to replace communism in the post 1992 period with the collapse of the Soviet Union. The goal now was the suppression of radical tendencies at home.

The book also focuses on the 'culturalist' right, who reject and are suspicious of community partnerships, and of working with groups like the Quilliam Foundation. For them there is no such entity as a 'moderate Muslim' and they view every Muslim as a suspicious 'enemy within'. Any rapport with moderate community leaders is seen as pandering to the enemies of the West. For these neo-conservatives, Islam itself is the problem and is held as incompatible with Western values and culture. The fear of Europe in particular becoming the transmission belt for 'Eurabia' is the fantastical nightmare of hard-line conservatives and based on old fashioned racism and xenophobia. Kundnani defines culturalists as those who believe 'jihadist violence is rooted in Islamic texts, teachings and interpretations that constitute sharia'. They see Islam as a theocratic, totalitarian political ideology; as a fifth column infiltrating American schools, universities financial institutions, the armed forces and the political establishment. They tend to gloss over the fact that if anyone preaches literal interpretations of texts it is the fundamentalist Christian right. The irrationality of a position that on the one hand Muslims refuse to integrate but on the other they are burrowing their way deep into the fabric of American society is breath-taking. This is the hallmark of previous racist and Nazi organisations who blame immigrants for taking jobs whilst simultaneously living on welfare and being work shy. The chief purpose of this for Kundnani is that it applies pressure on liberals to abandon any defence of civil liberties. The framing of Muslims as the chief problem for Western society has developed in layers as older stereotypes have been utilised and built upon to crystallise narratives of terrorism as Islamic. Politicians have accepted the narrative of multiculturalism being the problem as making too many concessions to minorities.

In the culturalist view Islam is completely incompatible with Western values and all Muslims are the problem. The publication of Melanie Phillips's *Londonistan* demonstrates what the right perceives to be the critical issue confronting Europe – the dangers of a Muslim presence that is viewed as pernicious and perilous for civilisation. According to public figures, once positioned on the left and progressive camps such as Salman Rushdie, Melanie Phillips, Christopher Hitchens and Martin Amis, Britain is full of ghettoised Muslim communities that are insular and fundamentalist in their outlook. Their high fertility rates threaten to change the very fabric of British society and turn it into 'Londonistan'. Kundnani notes how American perceptions of Europe generally and Britain specifically, are shaped by such distorted stereotypes.

Where all this leads can be seen when Kundnani describes the state violence of Guantanamo Bay and the torture chambers of extra-rendition – the horrific recent detainment, abuse and constant surveillance of Moazzam Begg is but one very public example of this. The counter-productive nature of these strategies is clear - it breeds suspicion and resentment as communities begin to see each other as suspects and traitors. All manner of things become justified in the name of defending Western civilisation, and the baying of the right is all too visible in the US itself. In 2010 plans were leaked for the building of a Muslim community centre in Manhattan. The right went berserk with a right wing talk show host declaring on national TV 'I hope the mosque isn't built, and if it is, I hope it's blown up and I mean that'. This had repercussions in other areas. In Houston, the wealthy, upper middle class enclave of Katy is home to the oil and gas corporations. A large number of highly skilled, corporate professionals have been recruited from overseas as residents and many of these are Muslims from South Asia, the Middle East and even the UK. Planning permission had been given for a Mosque and community centre in Katy. But it led to animosity and outbursts. Pig racing competitions were organised near the mosque site, beer bottles were left in the mosque driveway and 'Islam is evil' was daubed on walls near the site. These words remained there for two years! An Arab-American primary school child needed surgery after his jaw was broken in a racist attack where he was taunted with the words 'terrorist' and 'Muslims go home'.

Kundnani rightly suggests that the far-right and fascist parties have benefited from the 'culturalist' and 'reformist' discourse on radicalisation and the war on terror. Rather than creating greater understanding and tolerance, the political terrain has been further pushed to the right over questions on immigration. In the UK it is UKIP that has benefited, creating an even larger space for racist ideas to grow. The official narrative of Islamophobia is the oxygen that fascists breed in. Kundnani correctly identifies the BNP and EDL as Nazis. He points to the connections between Islamophobes, right wingers, fascists and right wing Zionists. He notes Vlaams Blok, a Belgium neo-fascist group, has formed links with the Israeli right. Their leader, Filip Dewinter, visits Israel regularly and believes that Europe's 20-30 million Muslims are a Trojan horse. Geert Wilders of the Dutch Freedom Party, had called for a ban on the Qur'an and when he visits Israel, demands the annexation of the entire West Bank and forcing Palestinians further off their land.

Kundnani points to interconnections between US right wing bloggers and commentators such as Pamela Geller and Robert Spencer, founders of the Freedom Defense Initiative and Stop Islamization of America. These groups were labelled hate groups by UK government officials, who barred Geller's entry into the UK in 2013. Their co-authored book *The Post-American Presidency: The Obama Administration's War on America* in 2010 is indicative of the hatred they hold for Obama's 'liberalism'. Another right-wing extremist is Bat Ye'or whose *Eurabia: the Euro-Arab Axis* makes the outlandish claim that European politicians want to facilitate Muslim immigration into Europe to subjugate Europe and turn the continent into an Arab colony – Eurabia! This theme unites the likes of Melanie Phillips and Niall Ferguson with the Vlaams Blok, the Freedom Party, the Front National in France and the EDL. The whole sharia conspiracy of the Islamicisation of Europe is akin to the Jewish conspiracy nonsense of the twentieth century.

The politics of demonising Muslims and viewing Islam as an alien ideology has been with us at least since 9/11, but its antecedents go back much further to narratives of foreigners with an apparently alien culture, and values apparently inimical to 'Western' ones. Whereas one hundred years ago we had the so-called 'Jewish conspiracy' of the *Protocols of Zion* so too we now have the lunacy of a Muslim conspiracy to take over Europe. Cultural markers associated with 'Muslimness' such as forms of dress, rituals and language are turned into racial signifiers. In this way Islamophobia is analogous to anti-Semitism and is inseparable from the wider and longer history of racism.

The book explores the differences between US and British experiences. The US system of multiculturalism as ethnic and national identity of Italian American or Arab American or Pakistani Americans leads to differences in terms of movements against racism and so such a movement of solidarity is lacking amongst Arab and Muslim Americans. This is chiefly due to differences in class and ethnic make-up. Most Arabs were seen as white in terms of 'assimilation and social fluidity,' but as one activist noted, '9/11 took away their social white card'. There are class and ethnic differences between the US and Britain in terms of Muslim communities. In Britain the composition of Muslims is largely working class of South Asian origin. This is in part due to the pattern of migration and settlement in the post war period with people coming from former colonies to settle in Britain and take up employment in mostly manual work in the NHS, London transport, the textile mills of north England and in factories. The US experience is one of a more heterogeneous presence and drawn from the Middle East and Africa, South East Asia as well as South Asia. Muslims have been predominantly professional and middle class. The different approaches taken to multi-culturalism also help to explain divergences — the history of anti-racism and struggles against racism in Britain are quite distinctive in comparison to the US.

This is an immensely valuable book that charts in detail the systematic ways in which the state has prosecuted its counter-terrorist strategy, identifying the shift in Islamophobia from an external threat to becoming an internal problem for a West focused on Muslims within America and Europe. It provides a strong theoretical critique of culturalist and reformist paradigms that have underpinned strategies of counter-terrorism. Kundnani makes a compelling case for how Obama's liberalism has normalised the war on terror, and Obama's presidency has rescued a discredited, counter-productive foreign policy and given a new lease of life to the war on terror. 'Neoconservatives invented the terror war, but Obama liberalism normalised it', he says.

I would highly recommend it to all those who wish to counter Islamophobia today.

INAPT RENDERING

Naima Khan

Imagine a world where *wudu* is sexy. Not the soothing, somewhat impractical habit we know and love, but real come hither performance of ritual ablution. I can guess what you're thinking but it turns out such a feat is indeed possible and they managed to depict it in the recent National Theatre production of *Dara*, a play exploring the conflict between two of the Mughal empire's defining leaders: Shah Jahan's sons Dara Shikoh and his brother Aurangzeb.

Wudu here is imported into the life of Hindu dancing girl Hira Bai, by her Muslim master. While pouring water up her nose, Prince Aurangzeb's favourite sassy slave girl takes on a coquettish air, enlivening his measured palace existence and mitigating his tense relationship with his father. To Aurangzeb's dismay, Hira's positivity is lost forever when she dies young and he becomes a dogmatic, despotic ruler in her absence. Intent on controlling his family's vast and varied empire through conservative Islam, he locks himself in an ideological power struggle with his Sufi-inclined brother, Dara.

Dara, at Lyttelton Theatre, National Theatre, South Bank, London, 20 January – 4 April 2015

Originally written in Urdu by multilingual Pakistani writer Shahid Nadeem in 2010, this adaptation by Tanya Ronder was commissioned by departing artistic director of the National Theatre, Nicholas Hytner. It covers the years 1659-1707 during which time Aurangzeb held power. Does the choice to adapt a play by a fluent English-speaking playwright, rather than commission him to translate it concern you too? Let's talk about it later. Suffice to say this adaptation could have been an exploratory

philosophical freewheeler of a play. Instead, Bonder squeezes its themes
into a family saga, binds it in an unconvincing love story and seals it with
uncomfortably reductive notions of Islam that come to a head in a crowd-
pleasing court room scene.

For director Nadia Fall, who has worked with National Theatre for over
ten years, Dara is her biggest production to date. Her previous work
includes the 2013 Bush Theatre production of Ayad Akhtar's Pulitzer Prize-
winning Disgraced, which follows Amir, an atheist lawyer living in New
York battling with his career prospects, his Muslim background and his
loyalties. Like Dara, Akhtar's play was hailed for its consideration of
contemporary headline themes, specifically the discussion on Islamophobia
and the identity of Muslim Americans. But while Dara is rooted in its
historical setting, it is similarly en vogue in its desire to pit Aurangzeb's
emotionally fuelled enforceable Islam against Dara's rationally conceived
liberal interpretation. It's another theatrical search for the ever elusive
moderate Muslim, and it seems the spiritually enlightened Dara model is
what we should all be aiming for.

Critics across the board have lauded the show's production values and on
that point, they're hard to argue with. The show's beautifully constructed
set by designer Katrina Lindsay is staggering in its grandeur and her eye for
opulent costumes with intricate layering and embroidery is remarkable.
The music, performed by a live Qawwali band, is comfortingly
atmospheric and Neil Austin's lighting design expertly illuminates Shah
Jahan's palace, hollows Dara's prison cell and takes us into Aurangzeb's
troubled hallucinations. But while the production is alluring to the eye, it
is entirely frustrating to any mind that wants to consider the moral
ambiguity that makes up most faith systems, particularly those that are
used in the creation of empires. On the surface, small things irritate
immediately, like the Anglicised pronunciations of basic Arabic terms. In a
production of this magnitude, which unashamedly pats itself on the back
for reaching out to British Asian audiences, it's hard to believe they
couldn't get a dialect coach to double-check every one on stage can get
'Ramadhan' out convincingly. I admit I'm still torn about whether this is
just quibbling or if my instincts that this is something that should be treated
with care are valid. Maybe it only matters to a few people but the depiction
of Muslims saying words and phrases like 'Bismillah' and 'Lailahaillalah'

with Lawrence of Arabia-esque distance from such everyday phrases is jarring. These are yet more mainstream depictions of my history that make me feel invisible.

The performances only add to this. Dara, played with regal assuredness by a bearded Zubin Varla, has a presence that seems modelled on filmic depictions of King Richard the Lionheart, while his brother Aurangzeb, a brilliantly unlikeable baddy played by Sargon Yelda, takes after envious Prince John. Unintentional though it may be, the manifestation of these characters on stage smacks of Western royals storming around foreign lands. The Mughals have historically been used to justify the later British rule in the region as they too arrived uninvited and set up camp for centuries. When, after meeting a spiritual leader who explains life in a few handy metaphors, Dara begins sharing his newfound spiritual understanding, it feels like European proselytising even if, like me, you agree with almost everything he says. While his philosophies are technically Eastern and centuries old, under Fall's direction they are delivered in a recognisably Anglicised way.

Ronder's script doesn't help. She presents us almost immediately with the hackneyed old image of a Muslim drinking alcohol to exemplify all that is contradictory and confusing in the practices of Islam and the behaviour of its followers. In 2015, it feels patronising and repetitive when the drinking challenge is posed not only to Dara's younger brother Murad in a functional move used to explain that his grandfather, Jehangir, too had a relaxed take on religious observance; but also to Aurangzeb by Hira in a test of his love for her. For South Asian audiences, especially majority Muslim audiences such as the ones Nadeem's original would have been performed to, the knowledge that many Muslims drink is nothing new, nor is it that contradictory. For some it's a vice albeit a serious one, for others, it's become an accepted, if secretive, norm. In Britain however, it's still a reliable old trope that the majority of audience members seem to accept. It's time we called for a more sophisticated depiction of the relationship between faith and conviction.

Add to this the excessive discussion – mostly by men – on the questionable necessity of hijab and one begins to suspect this adaptation exists solely to explain the National's centre-left take on multiculturalism. It may have been necessary for the prophet's wives, says Dara, but it is tied to a time and a culture that doesn't exist anymore, he insists, Awkwardly, he uses the word 'hijab' which wasn't common term in Dara's time nor a common practice in his father's vast empire which would have included Persian, East Asian and South Asian interpretations of the head covering. None of which would have looked anything like the contemporary Arabised hijab worn by myself and countless others in Britain today. Like much of the discussion on Islamic practices in Ronder's adaptation, talk of hijab here is unhelpfully oversimplified. Nothing of individual agency or political relevance or the combination of religion and patriarchy is addressed. For a British audience to gain something beyond an introduction to the subject, I'd argue these aspects are essential to the theme. Without proper consideration of them, I'm tempted to use the O-word. But I'll hold off for now.

I hesitate to completely pan the show because the family element is handled with complexity although it is overused in many ways. In flashback scenes, we see Aurangzeb's relationship with his father break down spectacularly when Shah Jahan chooses to believe an apple-conjuring Fakir over his son. Scantily clad, and eschewing all mainstream notions of what it is to be a Muslim, the Fakir turns up at the palace and reluctantly reveals, at Shah Jahan's insistence, that Aurangzeb will eventually facilitate his father's downfall. In a fit of rage Shah Jahan almost drowns his son and Aurangzeb is considered a suspicious adversary from that moment on. What that does to his notions of power, loyalty and supremacy are key to the familial ties explored in his relationship with Dara.

Similarly, Dara's sister Jahanara (Nathalie Armin) has a curious co-dependent relationship with Shah Jahan who is simultaneously abusive and loving towards her. Her sister Roshanara (Anneika Rose) is a sprightly, engaging rebel whose sense of self-determination is miles ahead of Jahanara's.

Each is loyal to one brother and their understanding of themselves as Muslim women and social leaders is cleverly teased out. But in this wordy play, we don't get a full picture of Aurangzeb's working mind. He isn't really allowed to show himself as a strategist, employing Islam to preserve the family power that Dara appears to take for granted. Instead his fear of Dara's inclusive, optimistic Islam is explained as a deep-seated emotional trauma from his childhood coupled with a broken heart.

The play also skirts over the abuse of religion to satisfy ego, of which both Aurangzeb and the more popular Dara could be accused. Rather, the text focuses on an overly defined good Islam vs. bad Islam showdown in the key court room scene where Dara must defend himself against charges of apostasy. Dara believes all spirituality, including Islam, is useful to the soul and the land but also that it should not be forced into something tribal. He sees it as a path to understanding intangible divinity and the solid earth around him. His Islam is far beyond a set of enforceable rules. He makes his poetic case to a group of bumbling mullahs who appear to be imported from modern day Iran and a prosecutor whose infantile arguments are intentionally laughable. So when Dara asks 'Who cares which door you open to come into the light?' they mock him but are noticeably dumbfounded.

Dara's discovery and expression of a less distinctly visible Islam, one that's more palatable to British audiences in these dark times, could be interrogated to great theatrical effect. But alas, here it is padded out with lacklustre fables about a dehydrated king giving up his kingdom for a sip of water. Watching this kindergarten explanation unfold in a court of lumbering religious traditionalists, is what convinces me the O-word is called for here. What else could a Western view of stupid, yes-men clerics and optimistic objectors be but Orientalist? The idea that Aurangzeb cannot think for himself and remains cocooned in his past is Orientalist. The image of Dara gaining relevance only in his rebellion is Orientalist. The excessive, male-dominated discussion on hijab and the fascination with Muslims who drink is Orientalist. Sexy *wudu* is definitely Orientalist! And it makes me wonder whether this production of *Dara* isn't one of the most successful examples of twenty-first century cultural imperialism in contemporary British theatre.

With this in mind, I feel we should question the need for a British writer to pen a new version of a play by a fluent English-speaking playwright like Shahid Nadeem. Given what a great opportunity the development of this production has been, it feels more relevant to ask what a Pakistani playwright would like to convey to a British audience about our intrinsically linked history, than to ask a white British playwright what she would like to convey to British audiences about a figure like Dara. In a recent panel discussion called 'The Global and the Local in the Arts:

Translating Pakistan's Vibrant Cultures,' this idea of cultural imperialism was posed by an audience member to Nadeem himself. 'The best thing' he replied 'would maybe to stage the play in the original Urdu with subtitles.' I wonder if National Theatre would consider such an impossible task. At what point can we stop expressing our gratitude to mainstream powerhouses for engaging with 'international' theatre on a basic level and start demanding that they play their part in its evolution?

AMERICAN HERO IN POSTNORMAL TIMES

C Scott Jordan

Once you've seen one American war-in-the-Middle-East movie, you've seen them all. That's what I thought. But the controversy surrounding *American Sniper* somehow persuaded me to pay a visit to my local multiplex. As the lights dimmed and I positioned my popcorn, something unexpected played out on the massive screen. We open with your cliché American troop caravan moving through a generic Middle Eastern 'urban warzone'. As the story played out, my mind fell into the sniper's scope as a dazzling, yet tragic metaphor materialised.

American Sniper is loosely based on the book by the same name that gives us the story of the late Navy SEAL, Chis Kyle – a man who became famous for killing people. When I think of other such Americans, I think of Timothy McVeigh or Charles Manson, yet this man has been made into an iconic celebrity. An American hero. By his own account, he is your average American, born in Texas, simplistic, and a good friend. He came from your typical *Leave It To Beaver* style family and dreamed of being a cowboy. This should be troubling to American ears. After having seen the film, I forced myself to plough through 'The Autobiography of the Most Lethal Sniper in US History'. It is 377 pages of remorseless arrogance with a soupçon of love letters to his departed fellow American troops. The film gives us the development of a character, the book, from its first sentences reveals a monstrous product of the American mind. There is no development, the damage is done. The training is complete, his humanity stripped, and I am amazed at how good a distance shot he was when I doubt this individual had the ability to see beyond a mirror what else exists in this world. It's really quite sad, because perhaps at one time this individual could feel empathy without callousness. His volunteering after his tours of duty, that gives him the impression of being a real hero, is only a minor end note to the book and appears more as a distraction or something other to do than war. War and killing were his only problem-solving mechanisms. Tragically, he meets his end at the hands of another twisted mental product of contemporary America. The vicious cycle goes on. Clint Eastwood's film takes this tragic American alloy and turns his story into a surreal metaphor that dares to teach us a lesson that Kyle could not express in his own words – thanks, to the structure of his manufactured mind.

American Sniper, directed by Clint Eastwood, Village Roadshow Entertainment Group: Los Angeles, 2014.

Much of the film has the all too familiar feel of your prototypical dystopian post-9/11 American war flick. A background, not to down play its significance, story developed that even gave one the feel of a Robert Ludlum cat-and-mouse suspense. The audience is also given a tasteful broad brush stroke approach to post-traumatic stress disorder (PTSD) and naïve youth's loss of innocence to modern warfare. I am not sure if it was the audio toggle between the real and the protagonist's internal soundtrack or, to the best of my knowledge, the first drone's-eye-view camera shot, but as the reel rolled on, a deep significance was revealed.

Bradley Cooper portrays Chris Kyle, our sniper. The film plays with the idea of Kyle's legacy. But its conclusion, he remains, at the very least, a metaphor for the good ole U. S. of A. A metaphor of what the United States has become since its rise to global dominance, leaving the audience with a choice as to the trajectory of the future course. We meet a young Kyle in an America long tarnished by recent history. His father has taken him for his first kill, a buck. A prodigy is born, as he sets his gun aside to bask in its glory, but his father is quick to scold him for he is never to leave his gun in the dirt. We see him save his younger brother from a bully as his father gives us the good old romanticised idea of a world where there are the meagre, the predators and then, a superior being, the guardian. He loves Texas, he loves guns, and he wants to be a cowboy. More importantly he has the classic American, preternatural sense of justice. Bullies must always be finished off. The father uses an interesting choice of words for his children's lesson. The metaphor used resembles countless other empty metaphors about wolves and sheep that draw on a fundamental world view disconnect from reality that exists in the radical realist American psyche. Then Kyle is given a higher calling, similar to America's call to protect the world. While America's need to be the globe's shield against evil perhaps predates the Monroe Doctrine, a heightened divine calling follows George W. Bush's presidency. In the film, Kyle watches a news report of the US Embassy bombings in Kenya in 1998 as though he is seeing his little brother beneath the bully's pummel. This minor shot elegantly captures this world flipping moment. A society so bent on a fundamentalist individualism suddenly feels for strangers only when connected to them by the word 'American'. This feeling is echoed later in the film as Kyle and his wife watch the horror of 9/11 play out on their television screen, an all too familiar memory for Americans who lived through that particular day.

The news voice's commentary spews forth chaotic fear and a deep uncertainty over the new enemy. This enemy is not as easily identified as our prior enemies. The Communist, The Japanese, The German, all with distinguishable characteristics easily caricatured, now are usurped by a shadow. The enemy is no longer a human who can be diminished through multiple rinses of nationalism and racism. The enemy is a spectre, almost inhuman. Thus, America must also lose its humanity. We watch Kyle's SEAL training, which is expected to be a stripping of humanity, but instead the training feels more like manual online training, a nuisance that we must all endure in order to get an extra hour of pay for the week. Then reality settles in.

Just as Kyle has it all, a perfect bride, a child on the way, the American dream, we learn shooting deer or paper targets is no preparation for killing living humans. The enemy is not simply military-age males. In fact, the enemy is an evil force that can possess children and women as well. Contradictions compound as the glorious duty of war turns into a historically ignorant euphemism for murder and assassination. America watches the world through a high-powered scope, and to be the shield the world needs, it must decide, through this false buffer, who lives and who dies. The tragedy begins as we find out a simple fact: Kyle is really good at what he does.

The defence of the greatest country on earth makes him a legend. Americans long to have a symbol to stand behind like Captain America, but punching Hitler on the nose is not enough, The enemy is brutal, savage, and merciless. War for Americans is not men against men, good versus evil, it is what remains of the sacred human verses Lucifer himself. This is how we justify our own savagery. They are waiting to kill when we least expect it and so we must be ever ready. There is the belief that the enemy is no longer human. Much like aliens in sci-fi flicks, they are simply beasts and killing them is no big deal. The other soldiers around him echo the themes of American exceptionalism, racism against the people of the Middle East, and an overall blood lust surrounds questions of good and evil, the nature of God, and the sanctity of life. All of this is a haze of white noise surrounding the cold omniscient scope's eye that Kyle becomes.

He is even faced with the Other in the form of an elusive enemy sniper. He is the American stereotype of today's terrorist. He is al-Qaeda, he is ISIS, he is the next Western public atrocity. He wears all black, is clean cut with a mix of ethereal youth and devilish sex appeal. Bouncing from roof top to roof top, this enemy sniper is a ninja with perfect accuracy and precision. He even wears a headband. He calls Kyle out and becomes the microcosm of evil as his and Kyle's game echo the War on Terror as if it were a one-time Pay Per View event that no one will want to miss.

The very term 'hero' is put to the pitch like a soccer ball, kicked back and forth, transformed before the audiences' eyes. Chris Kyle is our hero. He is not simply a man looking to overcome a challenge and grow from it. Kyle's war is multifaceted, complex. He has the internal challenge of maintaining his own sanity in the face of utter destruction. The challenge of maintaining his humanity and his family weigh on Kyle's shoulders as he must persevere through the chaotic character changes that mould him throughout the film. His duty is to kill anyone who tries to kill him or his brothers before they can accomplish their missions. We watch a simple boy from Texas become a complex man caught on the fault line between killing machine and superhero guardian. In this position, we are clearly shown contradictions in his values that pull Kyle into the deep uncertainty of what Ziauddin Sardar calls 'postnormal times'. The result is a self-detached, quixotic hero whom the audience is perpetually shifting between rooting for and hoping he fails so that he can simply go home and no one has to die.

Postnormal Times (PNT) is characterised by 3Cs: complexity, chaos and contradictions. We live in a world where complexity is the norm, characterised by a plethora of independent parts interacting with each other in a great many ways. Everything is connected to everything else in networks upon networks that generate positive feedback that amplify things in geometric proportions leading to chaos. We thus end up with many positions that are logically inconsistent and contradictory. The end products are uncertainties and ignorance. PNT cannot be saved by Superman flying faster than the bullet or by *The Matrix*'s Neo accepting his being the chosen one and defeating the Agents. The hero of postnormal times cannot simply defeat the bad guy or defuse the bomb, for PNT cannot be managed toward resolution. The postnormal hero is a navigator above all. This hero is challenged by the complexity of the world and our multiple selves, he is at the mercy of utter chaos, and subdued by countless contradictions. The postnormal hero is faced with taking our old conceptions, putting them to the test, and demanding that we re-educate ourselves or be doomed to fall at the hands of the true enemy – ourselves. He is not an antihero per se, but he is by no means something that can easily be made into an iconic action figure either.

The first of these heroes are almost certainly damned to become tragic heroes, for an unfamiliarity with postnormal times will prove a deadly challenge. I am not ruling out that the postnormal heroes will come in all shapes and sizes. Some will accept the complexity and contradictions of PNT, others will look to transcend it, and still others will be killed by it. The specific type I investigate here are characters faced with a growing complexity that presents greater chaotic challenges, which in turn bring out the contradictions within their very foundational values. These characters will be swallowed by the uncertainty surrounding them; and their options are limited to how they handle their own ignorance. Of course, authentic American characters are inherently assured. The choices they must now make is whether to remain stubborn to their old ways, or to take a new approach to their own ignorance.

And Kyle comes face to face with this choice. A scene gives us Kyle on a distant roof top providing support for his team on the ground. A faceless man with an RPG peels around the corner, his aim set on Kyle's men. BANG. The man is taken out. Easy, classic, our hero beats evil. Then, we see a native boy watching from a short distance, shocked, pensive. The boy drifts towards the dead, faceless man. He picks up the RPG. Kyle watches, beginning to pray out loud, please put it down. The perfect metaphor for America! We watch through a sniper's scope as history develops into the chaotic cradle to grave mess of killing and fear. Put it down. Kyle is faced with an impossible decision. Women and children must be spared at all costs. Americans, fighting for justice, must be kept from harm, at all costs. All bullies must be finished. The uncertainty and contradictions play out in a postnormal burst as the audience's heart rates rise.

After a multi-toured back and forth between Kyle and Mustafa, finally, Kyle has Mustafa in his scope, a shot over a mile away, an impossible shot. Kyle knows he can take it and finish his own war. The man who has killed several Americans can be taken out. Justice. Other soldiers call for him to stand down. If he takes the shot, he will give away their position and they will be swarmed. Kill this one man and Kyle ends his war, the war. Kill one to save a thousand, but in killing this one, you condemn all your men, the men you are sworn to protect faced with certain death. A sandstorm approaches. Kyle takes the shot and the sandstorm consumes the building where the American troops are positioned. Kyle sets his rifle to his side, in the dirt, and produces a radio phone. He calls his wife, sand zipping about in all directions. He pleads to his wife that he is ready to go home. He finds himself in a nearly literal postnormal event, and his attempts to control the convergence of complexity, chaos, and contradictions have landed him in an unmanageable pit of uncertainty. Only navigation will bring him out again. The old methods and the old mind-set will not work any longer. His mind is reverted back to a primitive childhood notion of needing security. The man who never wanted his tours to end, who only wanted to be with his brothers, killing the monsters, now wanted more than anything to go home. A long mental recovery awaits Chris Kyle beyond this deployment. The stories of our childhood that take us to such horrible places but always manage to have a happy ending are, after all, just fictional stories.

There is no awareness in *American Sniper* of the theory of postnormal times; it's the reality of postnormal times that is shaping the narrative of the film. And, of course, it provides no answers for how we are going to navigate postnormal times. Yet, quite unconsciously, it portrays the basic dilemmas, internal contradictions and deep ignorance of America in postnormal times.

As the credits rolled, showing documentary style footage, the comfortably packed theatre I sat in remained seated – still. Then the credits rolled against black and no soundtrack played. A phenomenon occurred where the theatre slowly and silently emptied. I only hope the metaphor was not too deep and that my fellow Americans in the theatre were persuaded to reflect on the ridiculous condition we find ourselves in. We still hold to the 'laws of Americana' Ziauddin Sardar and Merryl Wyn Davies ascribed to the American mind in the current era. 'Fear is essential,' 'War is necessary,' and 'Ignorance is bliss'. We live in an America where there are more guns than human beings (an estimated 350 million), campus shootings are the norm, and exporting war is an essential component of foreign policy. We idolise men who are really good at ending human life, and our politics are driven by what we fear: we want guns so no one shoots us, we oppose difference because we don't want it to rub off on us, we support foreign engagement to kill them before they kill us. America, the proverbial 'greatest country on Earth', is skewed by false beliefs in permanence, the innate superiority of its values, and an inability to adapt to a rapidly changing world.

Do not get me wrong, *American Sniper* is quite ridiculous if taken at face value; it is nothing more than another artist's view on modern war. But on a deeper examination, with all its faults, it gives us an American portrait in dire need of reflection and adjustment. A mirror is presented to the audience, revealing our half-cocked mind-set that is hurling us towards perpetual violence.

Racism, rash decision making, and an attempt to hide from trusting humanity is juxtaposed with a hope that we will stop living in the dark. America's continued war against shadows fuelled by deep uncertainty and a dedication to ignorance of the world beyond its borders is always going to spell tragedy for our postnormal hero. And, as the metaphor goes, for America herself.

ET CETERA

ON HAPPY MUSLIMS

Samia Rahman

> Because I'm happy
> Clap along if you feel like a room without a roof
> Because I'm happy
> Clap along if you feel like happiness is the truth
> Because I'm happy
> Clap along if you know what happiness is to you
> Because I'm happy
> Clap along if you feel like that's what you wanna do

Many years ago, I read what should have been a cheery, bite-size Q&A with the writer and academic Slavoj Zizek, on the *Guardian* website. Question: What makes you depressed? Answer: Seeing stupid people happy. I can think of many things that make me melancholy: war, illness, poverty, injustice, but the happiness of others, even those I may or may not admit to finding a little bit stupid, is certainly not one of them. What could Zizek have possibly meant? More recently, in a webchat on the same news site, his views on happiness were reprised. Is it important to be happy? How does one go about achieving this hallowed state? Zizek's retort was that humans flail about unsure of what it is we want. Happiness is a fantasy and the pursuit of dreams is what actually makes us happy, not the reality. 'Happiness is for opportunists. So I think that the only life of deep satisfaction is a life of eternal struggle… If you want to remain happy just remain stupid. Authentic masters are never happy, happiness is a category of slaves.' This cynical definition of an emotional state that many spend their lives seeking to attain made me chuckle, and also made me a little depressed, not unlike the contemptible notion of aspiration that is so lauded in contemporary society. Surely the balance between contentment and the drive to do better, be better, feel better, is the ultimate zenith?

I was reminded of Zizek when social media, the harbinger of illusory happiness, had one of its moments. It was April 2014 and I woke up one morning to a mini-explosion of joy on my Facebook timeline. Few British Muslims who are active on social networking platforms could have failed to notice the frenzy of activity known more accurately as 'going viral'. Reluctant to remain an impassive bystander I couldn't help but shuffle over and take a look. A music video on YouTube by a hitherto unknown group called The Honesty Policy. Great, I'll click on that...The robot dance definitely made me smile. Yep, I was feeling it... this was undeniably giving me a happy vibe. Watching The British Muslims Happy video was like a guess-who of the great and good of the British Muslim community dancing with abandon and devoid of censure. Shaykh Abdul Hakim Murad even made an appearance in a playful subversion of all our stereotypes of the scholarly Muslim's ability to have a bit of a laugh. His inclusion also added theological credibility that doubtless gave many Muslim viewers the green (read halal) light that they could relax and enjoy the show as it obviously had his blessing.

Initially there was euphoria. Everyone seemed swept along by the positivity. Here we had an uplifting, slick and charming take on the irritatingly catchy Pharell Williams song 'Happy'. There were more than a few voices lamenting why they didn't have a starring role as they definitely had all the moves. The vibe was infectious, everything about the video looked and felt good and watching it made everyone happy... Well, almost everyone. It wasn't long before the backlash erupted and, in echoes of Zizek, the very concept of Happy British Muslims was rabidly decried. The feelgood factor was overtaken by critics rushing to slam the video as unIslamic. Matters of jurisprudence relating to music, gender segregation and dancing were cited and the halal/haram debate rumbled on. Adam Deen, who featured in the video, wrote on his blog: 'to no one's surprise, Puritanical Muslim preachers have been outraged by the video (although to be fair, it really doesn't take much), expressing hard line verdicts to excite the Islamic sentiments of the ignorant.'

An unhappy theme of many discussions was the disproportionate scrutiny directed at the female participants. Always a fetishised arena, in this instance the positioning of women subsumed what little analysis there was on the representation of Muslims in general. Debates on how Muslim women should or should not be(have) are age-old and here was an example of deliberation that descended into the grossly misogynistic. Accusations of immodesty, lasciviousness and demeaning the sisterhood were bandied about along with shrill denunciation for usurping the Muslim female voice and bringing shame on the notion of *awrah*. In the same breath these female participants were dismissed as not speaking for anyone but themselves. One participant described feeling isolated and humiliated by the condemnation that frequently got personal. Degrading comments about the size and shape of some of those featured made uncomfortable reading while the hijab/non-hijabed were compared and chastised with vulgar moral equivalence. It cannot be denied that those who find themselves in the public domain must expect a level of dissection but for Muslim women it is impossible to occupy neutral territory. The objectification of women is rampant by both Muslims and non-Muslims alike, leading to the inevitable collusion with stereotypes that undermine any attempt to challenge assumptions. There seemed little acknowledgement that part of the human experience is to express and celebrate joy without being judged so harshly on the grounds of faith-bound gender norms. Deen touched on this double-standard, stating 'this quasi-Islamic reasoning can lead to reductio ad absurdum, whereby any innocuous act can be deemed Haram. And, it's precisely this type of obscure "Islamic reasoning" that results in women becoming invisible in society. What about women walking in public, hosting a TV programme or even driving? It's simply an abuse of Islamic teaching to universally prohibit acts which some have a fetish problem with. Once you strip away the layers of obfuscation, all you discover is a naked obsession with sex, women and control masquerading as religious devotion'.

A valid critique of the video relates to the credentials of the singer who inspired the parody – Pharrell Williams. His collaboration with tabloid favourite Robin Thicke on 'Blurred Lines' and that misogyny-oozing video is hardly an association to write home about. Yet, this video was not the first of its kind – groups of people dancing to this popular song were part of the cultural lexicon already but the Happy Muslim video generated considerable debate amongst Muslims. Courtesy of the dominant narrative, people are not used to watching Muslims dance around. They aren't used to them being happy. Yet, there is a wider issue concerning the positioning of Muslims in popular culture that is significant. The charge that the video promotes the aping of Western liberal culture by Muslims hankering to be accepted by a society that secretly despises them was vehemently articulated by Raana Bokhari of Lancaster University: 'what is refreshing about a group of Muslims who appear to be so reactive and apologetic for being Muslims, that they appear as if they are desperate to "show" they are happy?' In a tone not dissimilar to Zizek, she claims that the 'happiness' announced by the British Muslims in the video is one sanctioned by Western imperialism that dictates norms of behaviour and defines what happiness is, who should be happy and how they may acceptably express said happiness. How can Muslims prance around carefree while their brothers and sisters are being oppressed around the world? As the only tolerable Muslim is a moderate Muslim, a display of Western hegemony by dancing and singing to show acquiescence is the secret to being tolerated. 'There is a huge power discourse behind the production of the video if we deconstruct its various elements. Who is its target audience? British Muslims? I think not. Its purpose is perhaps to explain to non-Muslims that we are just like you: can laugh and dance (like you); sing (like you). My discomfort with this is – why do I have to be like you or anyone else?… is this neo-orientalism at work here? With the implication that the Muslim is still the "other" and must be sanitised and de-Islamicised to be acceptable? Is Islam in need of reform for Muslims to be acceptable in the West?' Sociologist Fauzia Ahmad, describes Bokhari's reaction as 'a political response that critiques the ways consistent negative stereotyping impacts on the psyche of Muslims – including those who are prominent – that in turn then causes them to seek to demonstrate their commonality with a dominant culture that still none-the-less, continues to subjugate, stereotype and demonise Muslims.'

The impassioned debate the video generated among intellectuals reflects the dynamism surrounding British Muslim identity politics. The Brookings Institution's H A Hellyer countered: 'this interpretation of post-colonial analysis, ironically, takes the same pole of power as its starting point – just in reverse. Whether one is trying to ingratiate oneself to a particular hegemony, or define oneself against that hegemony – the hegemony is still the centre of gravity in the universe.' I also find Bokhari's opprobrium simplistic. She makes sweeping assumptions about the socio-economic demographic of the participants, casting them all as middle-class, media-savvy, moderate Muslims. Many do indeed enjoy a certain profile and move in privileged circles with access, resources and agency that appear adrift from the alienated, disaffected and struggling who are far more likely to experience the harsh reality of Islamophobia and discrimination in twenty-first century Britain. The fact that the Honesty Policy claimed the video represents 'everyday Muslims' was perhaps a little naive. According to Hellyer this was also disputed by anti-Muslim sections of social media 'who insisted that for every "Happy Muslim" there were those who were sympathetic to extremism and radicalisation'. Yet the background of a significant number of participants is unknown. By speculating about the biodata of everyone in the video, Bokhari engineers a disconnect between those involved in the video and the rest of British Muslim society. By viewing the video through the prism of 'them and us' she fails to acknowledge the complexity of who is appropriating who and the power of engagement. Should communities not participate because this is a meme that is alien to a narrowly defined identity? Well, actually, no. British Muslims are well into the third generation, and if anything, the video illustrates that instead of hovering on the fringes, British Muslims are firmly positioning themselves in the mainstream of popular culture, on their own terms.

This phenomenon played out on social media, affording it an almost immediately democratising effect. There was no monopoly on power and those who were critical of it, conservative Muslims for example, only served to show that they themselves were well-versed in popular culture via that very medium. To be socially attuned enough to access the video and be outraged by it betrays that you are not speaking from a position of pure innocence. More optimistically, it challenges the lazy stereotype of hardline Muslims who do not engage with mainstream culture. In this age of digital attrition, social media is forming the frontline in the war against highly sophisticated and technologically adept extremist groups such as ISIS. The effort to win hearts and minds is not to be under-estimated.

The 'Happy' video was parodied by many countries, individuals and communities. Short films made by Muslims in the US, Germany, Singapore and wait for it... Gaza (are they even allowed to be happy?) emerged, yet the vitriol and flagellation was almost exclusive to the UK version. The Honesty Policy may have been seeking to convey a message about the diversity of British Muslim identity but this was conflated by critics, some of whom made an 'Unhappy Muslims' video in a display of pious angst. The Muslim communities are heterogeneous and multifarious so it should hardly be a surprise that responses to a video labelled 'British Muslim' should provoke such a spectrum of opinion. Unity within the Muslim communities has been a consistent red herring as Muslims in Britain are far from homogenous, in which case let there be respectful dissent and disharmony as from the vicissitudes there is borne creativity and growth. Journalist Remona Aly, who appeared in the video, concurs: 'It shouldn't be expected that everyone welcomes the video with open arms – we all have our own opinions, as Tim Winter [Abdul Hakim Murad] says: "Muslim unity comes not from the triumph of a single view, but from courteous respect for difference". However, some of the responses to the Happy video verged on unfair judgemental reactions. Since the makers of the Happy video retained anonymity, the participants were left even more open to direct abuse – on social media, blogs, and even reactionary YouTube videos. The "Unhappy Muslims" video assumed that the Muslims in the Happy video lacked morality and had no regard for the human suffering taking place in Iraq, Chechnya, etc. Those in the Unhappy video based their reductionist judgement of the Happy Muslims on a four-minute appearance'.

The anonymity of the creators of the Happy video is problematic for a variety of reasons. Today's call-out culture has rendered activists from all denominations and those with even a whiff of a public profile hyper-paranoid about a hidden agenda of those they may be seen with, share a platform with, and even happen to be photographed walking past. Among Muslim groups there is the indelible taint that comes with becoming involved, even fleetingly or tenuously, with an organisation that is suspected, never mind proven, to be funded by the government or some other objectionable entity. The polarisation between those for and against the counter-terrorism machine has created a groundswell of conspiracy theories buzzing around any and every new initiative. The consequence is a scramble to ensure one is hermetically sealed from possible exposure to designated toxic individuals. The opaque origins of The Honesty Policy led to murmurings that puppet masters were at work to promote an acceptable face of Islam. Their wearing of 'Anonymous' masks renders the project a tad political. Or should that read contrived? The group expressed the desire that actions should speak for themselves but the stance proved as distracting as the video itself. According to those who took part, the film crew were volunteers who had no direct contact or knowledge of the mastermind. The Honesty Policy went to great lengths to maintain their anonymity, as if protagonists in a fabulous spy thriller. Their aim to transcend cultural, sectarian and philosophical constraints seemingly backfired leaving the contributors somewhat exposed. The mystery surrounding the creators fuelled suspicion. According to their YouTube page, they are seeking to "empower the previously disempowered individual" presumably through this portrayal of a set of communities. They are anonymous because they say their names don't matter – the medium is the message – and that status shouldn't be part of the equation, even though it inevitably is when it features a troop of well-known media personalities. Even the song choice is a little anonymous. The year this video came out, the song *Happy* was everywhere. It was elevator music and supermarket music and radio music. It was inescapable. This matters: they could have picked any song but they chose this one and it is more than just a song about happiness. What remains is a song so overplayed it has lost all meaning. If you watch the video with the volume down, the message still comes across. This isn't a music video or a dance track – here we have a video with a song running through it and the perfect anonymous backdrop for these smiling faces. It doesn't matter what they are singing along to, it matters that they are there and are playing out their own stories.

Zizek's sorrow at the stupid-inducing allure of happiness is inspired by Nietzsche's 'Last Man'. These last men are wholly delighted with the superficial idyll of a life unchallenged and comfortable while utterly ignorant to its hollow reality. The British Muslims Happy video is a far cry from such cynicism. The Honesty Policy is not guilty of insincerity: their names do not matter but who they are does. Watching the video, I found myself searching for clues to their identity. This was the narrative of the dialogue that exists in my head and probably in the head of others watching the happy spectacle, perhaps even Zizek, if he has seen it. This is what the Honesty Policy miss in their anonymity — who they are is as important as who they are talking to. The video has to be more than a mirror in order to be part of the cultural conversation.

SHANON SHAH'S TOP TEN JIHADI JANES

There's an old riddle that is surprisingly current. If you haven't heard it before, allow yourself some time to answer before reading past the end of this paragraph: a father and son are in a terrible accident that kills the dad. The son is rushed to the hospital but just as he's about to be operated on, the surgeon says, 'I can't operate – that boy is my son!' Discuss.

Did you guess that the surgeon is the boy's mother? If yes, you're in an obvious minority. In research conducted as recently as 2014 at Boston University, only 15 per cent of schoolchildren and 14 per cent of psychology undergraduates said the surgeon was the mother – even self-described feminists.

What does this have to do with Jihadi Janes? Taking a cue from the surgeon-mother scenario, picture this: a suicide bomber straps on explosives, marches through a crowded marketplace but stops when a bearded man walks past, saying, 'I can't do this – that's my husband.' Would you have guessed that the hypothetical suicide bomber is a woman?

Women terrorists trigger particularly morbid fascination because it is men that we usually associate with power and aggression. In the Western mass media, with abundant stereotypes of Islam as exceptionally anti-women, the idea of Muslim women terrorists provokes even greater horror. Their monikers simultaneously recognise their chilling actions yet reduce their motivations to the influence of the men in their lives, usually their husbands. They are 'Black Widows', or the 'White Widow', or 'jihadi brides'.

So these are the myths that end up becoming common sense – Muslim men are radicalised by religion, women by romance. But surely we should investigate the concrete factors that attract men and women to various terrorist groups – within and beyond Islam – and the roles they actually play once they join? Only then can we find effective ways of overcoming terrorism.

The fact that so many men and women are engaged in the vile and indefensible killing of innocents in the name of Islam should be of urgent concern for Muslims and non-Muslims. But the solution lies neither in the Islamophobic parading of female jihadis as freaks nor in whitewashing violent jihadism as mere anti-imperialism.

With this in mind, we present our eclectic but admittedly limited list of Top Ten Jihadi Janes, in chronological order.

1. Judith

OK, a 'chronological' list is partly an excuse to start with a Biblical figure. Picture this: the hilltop town of Bethulia is besieged by Nebuchadnezzar's invading Assyrian army, led by Holofernes (meaning 'stinking in hell' so no, not the hero of this story). The townspeople despair, but a beautiful and respected widow, Judith (meaning 'the Jewess') announces her secret plan to the elders. She sneaks out at night, meets Holofernes, allows him to think he has seduced her and after he falls asleep in a drunken stupor, she beheads him. Hello? Can anybody say 'Jihadi Judith'? For juicier details, consult the Book of Judith in the Old Testament. Also, check out the story of Jihadi Jael in Judges 4:21, who hammers a tent peg through the Canaanite army commander Sisera's temple (as in the side of his head) to the ground. The verse concludes: 'So he died.' The Bible portrays Judith and Jael as heroes, but we include them as reminders of the complex inheritance and interpretations of violence in sacred texts.

2. Rose Dugdale (b. 1941–)

Born into a wealthy English family – her millionaire father was an underwriter at Lloyd's of London – Dugdale was ostensibly radicalised by the student riots of 1968 and joined the Irish Republican Army (IRA). In January 1974, with IRA member Eddie Gallagher, she hijacked a helicopter and used it to drop bombs – in milk churns – on a Royal Ulster Constabulary station. The bombs failed to detonate and Dugdale went on the run as Ireland and Britain's most wanted woman. Later that year, Dugdale and other IRA members staged a violent art heist, ransoming their nineteen stolen paintings for the release of jailed comrades. Dugdale was arrested and in June 1974 was sentenced to nine years in prison after pleading 'proudly and incorruptibly guilty'. She now leads a low-profile life in Dublin, but in a rare interview in 2012 she said she had no regrets and added: 'You mustn't forget it was very exciting times … the world looked as if it could change and was likely to be changed and, whoever you were, you could play a part in that.' Another example of a perception gap – Dugdale sees herself as a hero, but can the same be said of the wider British public?

3. Astrid Proll (b. 1947–)

In the 1970s, the West German government considered the Baader-Meinhof Gang – a far-left militant group eventually known as the Red Army Faction – a terrorist organisation. For over three decades, the Red Army Faction engaged in bombings, assassinations, kidnappings, bank robberies and shoot-outs with the police. In 1977, they provoked a national crisis dubbed the German Autumn. Proll was an early member, implicated in a bank robbery where she drove the getaway car for a fellow member. She was soon arrested and charged with attempted murder, but escaped to London. The attempted murder charge was eventually dropped. Proll did not re-join the Baader-Meinhof but found work as a picture editor in Britain. In a 2007 interview, Proll denied being ashamed of her past but objected to the Baader-Meinhof's increasingly violent tactics. Her example offers a glimpse into the multi-layered role of politics and personal values in an individual's terrorist and post-terrorist career.

4. Dhanu, a.k.a. Thenmozhi Rajaratnam (b. 1974? – 1991)

Thenmozhi Rajaratnam, also known as Dhanu or Gayatri, assassinated India's former Prime Minister, Rajiv Gandhi, in 1991. Her birth year has not been established, but it is widely thought she was a teenager and member of the Liberation Tigers of Tamil Eelam (LTTE) at the time. Gandhi had sparked the ire of Sri Lankan Tamil militants for an earlier decision, made while in power, to send peace-keeping troops to the island nation during its civil war. Gandhi was on his re-election campaign in

Sriperumbudur, Tamil Nadu, when Dhanu approached, greeted him and detonated her denim suicide belt containing six grenades, killing Gandhi, herself, and 14 others.

5.Wafa Idris (1975 – 2002)

On 27 January 2002, 28 year-old Wafa Idris became the first female suicide bomber in the Israeli-Palestinian conflict. The Red Crescent volunteer set off a bomb outside a shoe store in the centre of Jerusalem, killing herself and an 81-year-old man and injuring more than 100 others. Born in a refugee camp, Idris was 12 when the first intifada began in 1987; she distributed food during curfew hours and supported prisoners' families in various ways. After her death, Idris was hailed by much of the Arab mass media as a hero and a nationalist.

6. The BlackWidows

In October 2002, 40 separatist Chechen militants took 912 hostages at the Dubrovka Theatre in Moscow, where the popular musical *Nord-Ost* was playing. The three-day siege ended with Russian special forces pumping sleeping gas into the hall, then storming in and killing all the attackers. There was public outrage as some 130 hostages also died, apparently because of the effects of the gas. The siege also became infamous for the disturbing televised images of Chechen women dressed in black chadors, their waists and chests adorned with bombs. They became known as the Black Widows, suggesting that their recruitment into terrorism was primarily driven by the deaths of male relatives in separatist violence. The theatre siege marked the start of two years of further terrorism in Moscow, in which the Black Widows were prominently involved. They were implicated again in a series of suicide terror attacks beginning in 2010 with deadly bombings on the Moscow metro.

7. Lynndie England (b. 1982 –)

In 2004, a few disturbing pictures went viral, depicting naked prisoners piled on top of each other, others hooded and wired with electrodes.

Along with reports from Amnesty International, they provided evidence of the torture of detainees at the Abu Ghraib prison in Iraq, dating from the US-led invasion in 2003. Condemnations worldwide and in the US forced President George W Bush to downplay the abuses as isolated incidents. Eleven military personnel were convicted through courts-martial in 2005, including Lynndie England. Although other female soldiers were involved, England became the face of the scandal; the most notorious photo shows her holding a leash tied to the neck of a naked man crawling out of his cell. She served less than two years in prison and says she does not regret what she did. She claims she was unduly influenced by Charles Graner, her then-fiancé who was also an Abu Ghraib torturer. As an officer in the military of a sovereign state, England is technically not a Jihadi Jane. Yet her own telling of her descent into ideologically-driven violence echoes a running theme in debates about female jihadis, so succinctly captured by Lady Gaga – 'caught in a bad romance'.

8. Samantha Lewthwaite (b. 1983 –)

According to right-leaning tabloid the *Daily Mail*, Samantha Lewthwaite commands an army of 200 jihadi women whom she has trained to infiltrate governments and carry out suicide attacks on behalf of Somali terror group al-Shabaab. Among others, Lewthwaite has been linked to attacks on a shopping mall in Nairobi, Kenya, in 2013 and Garissa University in 2015. Lewthwaite was born in Buckinghamshire and converted to Islam as a teenager when she started attending the School of Oriental and African Studies in London. Within weeks Lewthwaite – dubbed the White Widow by the media – dropped out and married Germaine Lindsay, who would go on to become one of the four suicide bombers attacking the London Underground transport network on 7 July 2005. In 2008, Lewthwaite went to South Africa where she met and married her second husband, Fahmi Jamal Salim, introduced to her by radical preacher Sheikh Abudullah el-Faisal. She then acquired a fake ID, entered Kenya and things have been a mystery ever since. The 'White Widow' is not to be confused with 'Jihad Jane', a.k.a. the American Colleen LaRose who pleaded guilty to conspiracy to murder a Swedish cartoonist in 2009. Female jihadis are horrifying enough, but those that are white converts scare the bejesus out of many in the West – testament to related-but-unnamed fears of Muslim males as potential sexual monsters. The *Daily Mail* warned that 'thousands of British women on holiday in Turkey this summer [2015] were at risk' of being smitten by jihadi toy-boys and facilitating their entry to the UK.

9. Boko Haram's female suicide bombers

In April 2014, the Nigerian militant Islamist group Boko Haram sent shockwaves throughout the world when it abducted 276 female students from their secondary school in Chibok. Headline grabbing as it was, the Chibok incident was just one terrible case of Boko Haram's kidnappings of girls. Later in July, Boko Haram unleashed a spate of suicide attacks by women and girls, leading to speculation that the group was turning its schoolgirl abductees into combatants – this was eventually verified by Amnesty International. Boko Haram's use of female suicide bombers could be a sign of desperation or a calculated move to further intimidate the Nigerian government. Either way, it is a reminder of the multiple vulnerabilities of women and children caught up in violent conflict.

10. The Bethnal Green jihadi brides

In February 2015, Shamima Begum and Amira Abase, both 15, and Kadiza Sultana, 16, boarded a plane from London's Gatwick Airport for Turkey on their way to join the so-called Islamic State of Iraq and Syria (ISIS). Their unsuspecting and distraught families blamed the police for not warning them that one of the girls' friends had already flown to Syria in December 2014 to join ISIS. It is suspected that the girls were groomed by another jihadi bride – Aqsa Mahmood from Scotland – via Twitter. The trio's recruitment into ISIS lays bare the messy, interlocking factors in the making of a Jihadi Jane in the West, including multiple online networks of male and female jihadis criss-crossing national borders, misplaced youthful idealism and adventure-seeking, real or imagined grievances at home, a pre-existing spotlight on immigrants and Muslims fuelling stark feelings of 'us' versus 'them', the wider geopolitics of Islam, and missteps by intelligence and security agencies.

CITATIONS

Introduction: Postnormal Blues
by Ziauddin Sardar and Samia Rahman

Scott McCloud's *Understanding Comics: The Invisible Art* is published by William Morrow, New York (2001). On postnormal times, see Ziauddin Sardar, 'The Future of Arab Spring in Postnormal Times', *American Journal of Islamic Social Sciences* 30 (4) 125-136 (2013); and the special issue of *Futures* edited by Merryl Wyn Davies 43 (2) 136-227 (2011).

On Benjamin Netanyahu's allegations against the Mufti of Jerusalem, see Peter Beaumont, 'Netanyahu condemned for allegations over Holocaust', *Guardian* 22 October 2015; on the historical truth, and how this mythology has been perpetuated in American history texts, see Michael A Sells, 'Holocaust Abuse: The Case of Hajj Muhammad Amin al-Husayni', *Journal of Religious Ethics* 43: 4 723-759 (2015). For Homeland's Arabic slogans, see Elahe Izadi, 'Artists got "Homeland is racist" Arabic graffiti into the latest episode of "Homeland"', *Washington Post* 15 October 2015. Heba Amin's blog can be read at: www.hebaamin.com.

Adam Curtis's BBC documentary, *Bitter Lake*, can be viewed on YouTube or at: www.bbc.co.uk/iplayer/episode/p02gyz6b. And Joseph Harker's comments on the racist bus incident appeared in the *Guardian*, 16 October 2015, and can be found at: ww.theguardian.com/opinion/race issues

ISIS by Anne Alexander

Harleen Gambhir of the Institute for the Study of War rounds up ISIS's activities outside Iraq in May 2015: ISIS Global INTSUM, Institute for the Study of War, www.understandingwar.org/sites/default/files/ISIS%20 INTSUM_Final.pdf. The ISW also covered ISIS's loss of Derna on 24 June: Institute for the Study of War, 2015, 'ISIS loses Libyan stronghold', www.

understandingwar.org/backgrounder/isis-loses-libyan-stronghold. A perceptive article by Evan Fowler in December 2014 underlined the fragility of ISIS's grip on its Libyan territories: 'From Raqqa to Derna: exceptionalism in expansionism', *Jadaliyya* 4 December 2014, http:/www.jadaliyya.com/ pages/index/20182/from-raqqa-to-derna_exceptionalism-inexpansionism

For more detail on America's imperial disaster in Iraq, see Anne Alexander and Simon Assaf, 'Iraq: the rise of the resistance', *International Socialism Journal*, Winter 2005; Eric Herring and Glen Rangwala, *Iraq in Fragments: the Occupation and its Legacy* (C. Hurst & Co., London, 2006); Anne Alexander, 'ISIS and counter-revolution: towards a Marxist analysis', *International Socialism Journal*, Winter 2015. The downfall of Morsi and the contradictions of the Muslim Brotherhood following the 2011 revolution in Egypt are discussed in Anne Alexander and Mostafa Bassiouny, *Bread, Freedom, Social Justice: Workers and the Egyptian Revolution* (Zed, London, 2014). Aaron Zelin wrote about 'The Islamic State's model' on the Washington Post's blog on 28 January 2015 (www.washingtonpost.com/blogs/monkey-cage/wp/2015/01 /28/the-islamic-states-model/).

Aymenn Jawad's archive of Islamic State administrative documents can be found online here: www.aymennjawad.org/2015/01/archive-of-islamic-state-administrative-documents. To read the full text of the collective letter by MPs to David Cameron about the use of the name Daesh to refer to ISIS, go here: www.rehmanchishti.com/sites/www.rehmanchishti.com/files/25.6.15 _letter_to_bbc_re_daesh.pdf. Human Rights Watch's website published a report on sectarian 'cleansing' by Shi'a Islamist militias in the Amerli area of Iraq on 18 March 2015: 'After liberation came destruction: Iraqi militias and the aftermath of Amerli', and the aftermath of Amerli', www.hrw.org/ report/2015/03/18/after-liberation-came-destruction/iraqi-militias-and-aftermath-amerli

Time interviewed a 'Sunni businessman' in Syria who claimed that the Assad regime was pragmatic about dealing with ISIS on 26 February 2015, time. com/3719129/assad-isis-asset/ Ghayath Naisse discusses the role of former Ba'thist officers in ISIS in 'The 'Islamic State' and the counter-revolution', *International Socialism Journal* 147 (summer). Patrick Cockburn analyses the reason for recruitment to ISIS in the *London Review of Books* on 2 July 2015: 'Why join Islamic State?': www.lrb.co.uk/v37/n13/patrick-cockburn/ why-join-islamic-state

Hanna Batatu's superb history of the old social classes and revolutionary movements of Iraq (Princeton, 1978) deals with the Mosul rebellion and its aftermath.

Linda Robinson's testimony on behalf of Rand Corporation was published in June 2015: 'An assessment of the counter-ISIL campaign', RAND website, www.rand.org/pubs/testimonies/CT435.html

Extreme Weirding by John A. Sweeney

The works cited in this essay include: Pierre Berthon and Brian Donnellan, 'The Greening of IT: Paradox or Promise?' *The Journal of Strategic Information Systems* 20 (1): 3–5 (2011); Paul Crutzen and Christian Schwägerl. 'Living in the Anthropocene: Toward a New Global Ethos.' Environment360, January 2011; Gwynne Dyer, *Climate Wars: The Fight for Survival as the World Overheats* (Oxford: Oneworld Publications, 2011); Nature, 'Extreme Weather', *Nature* 489 (September): 335–36 (2012);

Susan Fiske, 'A Millennial Challenge: Extremism in Uncertain Times.' *Journal of Social Issues* 69 (3): 605–13 2013; Jay Golden, *Global Warming Effects on Extreme Weather*. House of Representatives, 2008; Colin Kelley, Shahrzad Mohtadi, Mark A. Cane, Richard Seager, and Yochanan Kushnir, 'Climate Change in the Fertile Crescent and Implications of the Recent Syrian Drought.' *Proceedings of the National Academy of Sciences* 112 (11): 3241–46 (2015); Bruno Latour, *We Have Never Been Modern,* Cambridge, Mass: Harvard University Press, 1993; Bill McKibben, *The End of Nature,* London: Bloomsbury, 2003; original 1989; Timothy Morton, 'This Biosphere Which Is Not One: Towards Weird Essentialism.' *Journal of the British Society for Phenomenology* 46 (2): 141–55 (2015); W J Steffen, P Grinevald, P. Crutzen, and J. McNeill, 'The Anthropocene: Conceptual and Historical Perspectives.' *Philosophical Transactions of the Royal Society A: Mathematical, Physical and Engineering Sciences* 369 (1938): 842–67 (2011); John Sweeney, 'Command-and-Control: Alternative Futures of in an Age of Global Weirding.' *Futures* 57 (March): 1–13 (2014); Andrew Revkin, *Global Warming: Understanding the Forecast* (New York: Abbeville Press, 1992); and Liao, S M, S. Anders and R. Rebecca, 'Human engineering and climate change' *Ethics, Policy & Environment* 15 (June (2)) (2012) 206–221.

On postnormal times, see Ziauddin Sardar, 'Welcome to Postnormal Times.' *Futures* 42 (5): 435–44 (2010) and 'Postnormal Times Revisited', *Futures* 67 (2) 26-39 (2015); and Ziauddin Sardar and John Sweeney, 'The Three Tomorrows of Postnormal Times', *Futures* (75 (2016) 1-13).

The Light of Muhammad by Raza Ali

In this wonderful digital age, hadith collections are widely available online. So the hadith I have quoted can all be accessed easily. This is where I found them, in order of appearance in the essay: (1) Bukhari 3747, sunnah.com/bukhari/62/94 (2) www.livingislam.org/fiqhi/fiqha_e30.html (Light of Muhammad)   (3) www.sunnah.org/msaec/articles/hadith_of_lawlaak.htm ('Were it not for Muhammad...'); (4) Nasa'i 5045, sunnah.com/nasai/48/6;   (5)Nasa'i 5072, sunnah.com/nasai/48/33; and (6) Nasa'i 1578, sunnah.com/nasai/19/23

A translation of Qasida Burdah is available at: www.deenislam.co.uk/burdah/burdah.htm

Paupers and Plutocrats in Early Islam
by Benedikt Koehler

For more on wealth distribution see Benedikt Koehler, *Early Islam and the Birth of Capitalism,* (Lexington Books, Lanham, MD, 2014). Two stimulating books on early Islam's approach to business and to charities are Mahmood Ibrahim's *Merchant Capital and Islam,* (University of Texas Press, Austin, 2011) and Yaacov Lev's *Charity, Endowments, and Charitable Institutions in Medieval Islam* (University Press of Florida, Gainesville, 2006).

Sociology and economics in Islam were set out in the fourteenth century in Ibn Khaldun's *Muqaddima. An Introduction to History,* (Routledge, London, 1967). A blog detailing why Ibn Khaldun's work matters to this day can be accessed at: www.capx.cocapx-essay-ibn-khaldun-islams-man-for-all-seasons

See also: Gene Heck's *Charlemagne, Muhammad, and the Arab Roots of Capitalism* (de Gruyter, Berlin, 2006), Maxime Rodinson's *Islam and Capitalism* (Saqi, London, 1978 and 2007), and A L Tibawi, *Pious Foundations in Jerusalem* (Islamic Centre, London, 1978).

In No Uncertain Terms by Gordon Blaine Steffey

Kelsey D. Atherton, 'ISIS's Rejection of Modernity is Hyper Modern: Some Thoughts from Shadi Hamid on Graeme Wood's "What ISIS Really Wants",' *Storify*, February 2015, storify.com/AthertonKD/isis-s-rejection-of-modernity-is-hyper-modern (accessed 14 September 2015).

Scott Atran, 'Here's What the Social Science Says about Countering Violent Extremism,' The Huffington Post, 25 April 2015, www.huffingtonpost.com/scott-atran/violent-extremism-social-science_b_7142604.html (Accessed 10 September 2015).

Peter Beinart, 'What does Obama Really Mean by "Violent Extremism"?';*The Atlantic*, 20 February 2015, www.theatlantic.com/international/archive/2015/02/obama-violent-extremism-radical-islam/385700/ (Accessed 10 September 2015).

J. M. Berger, 'Enough about Islam: Why Religion is Not the Most Useful Way to Understand ISIS,' Brookings Institution, 18 February 2015, www.brookings.edu/blogs/order-from-chaos/posts/2015/02/18-enough-about-islam-berger (Accessed 5 September 2015).

J. Scott Carpenter, Matthew Levitt, Steven Simon, Juan Zarate (2010). 'Fighting the Ideological Battle: The Missing Link in U.S. Strategy to Counter Violent Extremism,' The Washington Institute for Near East Policy, July 2010, www.washingtoninstitute.org/uploads/Documents/pubs/StrategicReport04.pdf (Accessed 1 September 2015).

Office of Civil Rights and Civil Liberties, 'Terminology to Define the Terrorists: Recommendations from American Muslims,' Department of Homeland Security, January 2008, www.dhs.gov/xlibrary/assets/dhs_crcl_terminology_08-1-08_accessible.pdf (Accessed 16 August 2015).

Matthew Duss, Yasmine Taeb, Ken Gude, and Ken Sofer, 'Fear, Inc. 2.0: The Islamophobia Network's Efforts to Manufacture Hate in America,' Center for American Progress, February 2015, cdn.americanprogress.org/wp-content/uploads/2015/02/FearInc-report2.11.pdf (Accessed 18 September 2015).

Steve Emerson, 'Obama's Policy Bans References to Islamic Extremism, Jihad,' *Newsmax*, May 2013, www.newsmax.com/Emerson/Obama-Islamic-Extremism-Jihad/2013/05/14/id/504527/ (Accessed 14 September 2015).

Shiraz Maher, 'The roots of radicalisation? It's identity, stupid,' *The Guardian*, 17 June 2015, www.theguardian.com/commentisfree/2015/jun/17/roots-radicalisation-identity-bradford-jihadist- causes (accessed 17 September 2015).

Andrew C. McCarthy, 'Don't blame the Charlie Hebdo Mass Murder on 'Extremism,'' *The National Review*, 7 January 2015, www.nationalreview.com/article/395876/dont-blame-charlie-hebdo-mass-murder-extremism-andrew-c-mccarthy (Accessed 31 August 2015).

'Minnesota Muslims Concerned about New "Stigmatizing, Divisive, and Ineffective" CVE Pilot Program,' 2015, files.ctctcdn.com/bd15115b001/d068ad69-9ad8-46a0-bdcd-b9d57454ed20.pdf (accessed 12 September 2015).

Muslim Advocates, 'Countering Violent Extremism,' 9 March 2015, www.muslimadvocates.org/cve-countering-violent-extremism/ (accessed 14 September 2015).

National Security Strategy, Office of the President of the United States, February 2015, www.whitehouse.gov/sites/default/files/docs/ 2015_national_security_strategy.pdf (accessed 20 August 2015).

National Security Strategy, Office of the President of the United States, May 2010, nssarchive.us/NSSR/2010.pdf (accessed 19 August 2015).

National Security Strategy, Office of the President of the United States, March 2006, nssarchive.us/NSSR/2006.pdf (accessed 18 August 2015).

Sean Piccoli, 'Terrorism Expert: West "Caving" to Muslim Intimidation,'*Newsmax*, 7 January 2015, www.newsmax.com/Newsmax-Tv/Steve-Emerson-Paris-attack-Charlie-Hebdo/2015/01/07/id/617080/ (accessed 31 August 2015).

Mark Potok, 'The Year in Hate and Extremism,' *The Southern Poverty Law Center*, 9 March 2015, https://www.splcenter.org/fighting-hate/intelligence-report/2015/year-hate-and-extremism-0 (accessed 12 September 2015).

Graeme Wood, 'What ISIS Really Wants,' *The Atlantic*, March 2015, www.theatlantic.com/magazine/archive/2015/03/what-isis-really-wants/384980/ (accessed 15 August 2015).

Graeme Wood '"What ISIS Really Wants": The Response,' *The Atlantic*, 24 February 2015, www.theatlantic.com/international/archive/2015/02/what-isis-really-wants-reader-response-atlantic/385710/ (accessed 2 September 2015).

Charlie Hebdo and Extremism in the Arts
by Samir Younés

Several studies and anthologies have recently been dedicated to this subject of mean thought, *la pensée méchante*, in France. Studies include Jérôme Duhamel, *Encyclopédie de la méchanceté et de la bêtise*, Paris, Acropole, 1987; Clément Rosset, *Le principe de cruauté*, Paris, Éditions de Minuit, 1988; Pierre Drachline, *Le grand livre de la méchanceté*, Cherche-midi, re-edited by J'ai lu, 2006; Jean, Cooren, *L'ordinaire de la cruauté*, Paris, Hermann, 2009; Lucien Faggion & Christophe Regina, eds., *Dictionnaire de la méchanceté*, Éditions Max Milo, 2012.

The statement of FNMF regarding legal proceedings against *Charlie Hebdo* can be found at:

www.lemonde.fr/europe/article/2006/02/10/le-cfcm-va-porter-plainte-contre-les-journaux-francais-ayant-publie-les-caricatures-de-mahomet_740246_3214.html

The televised debate between Tariq Ramadan and Charb can be viewed at: https://www.youtube.com/watch?v=4WnafcVXUYw

Sikh Extremism by Sunny Hundal

News reports and comments mentioned in the article can be found at the following sites:

www.theguardian.com/politics/2010/feb/11/bnp-nonwhites-members-sikh-join

www.pickledpolitics.com/archives/7240

www.bbc.co.uk/news/uk-england-nottinghamshire-24580970

www.pickledpolitics.com/archives/11633

www.theguardian.com/commentisfree/belief/2012/jul/03/edl-sikh-men-women

https://www.facebook.com/EDLSikhs

https://www.youtube.com/watch?v=e7mnijoDVu0

www.pickledpolitics.com/pictures/media/article_khilafat.jpg

www.pickledpolitics.com/archives/1194

www.independent.co.uk/news/asian-vs-asian-as-khalistan-row-strikes-uk-1259642.html

www.theguardian.com/society/2013/sep/10/abuse-asian-girls-missed-white-victims
www.thisiswiltshire.co.uk/news/9795689.Militants_try_to_halt_multi_racial_wedding/
www.bbc.co.uk/news/uk-21721519
www.bbc.co.uk/news/uk-england-birmingham-32426555
news.bbc.co.uk/1/hi/world/south_asia/7466916.stm
www.newindianexpress.com/magazine/Drug-epidemic-leaves-Punjab-in-dazed-stupor/2013/06/09/article1622895.ece
www.thefword.org.uk/2011/03/british_asian_w/
www.cosmopolitan.com/politics/news/a5708/honor-diaries-jasvinder_sanghera/
www.independent.co.uk/news/uk/crime/my-people-refuse-to-talk-about-honour-killings-1845103.html
www.thesikhencyclopedia.com/historical-events/sikh-struggle-against-mughal-empire-1708-1799/sikhs-relations-with-mughal-emperors

The New Atheists by Andrew Brown

Sam Harris' *The End of Faith: Religion, Terror and Future of Reason* is published by Free Press, New York, 2006. Tim Minchin's 'rally for reason' can be viewed, at: www.youtube.com/watch?v=zUPxqGYt5iw. The Charles Taylor quote is from an interview in the *New Statesman*: www.newstatesman.com/books/2012/02/interview-secularism-religion

Americn Hero in Postnormal Time by C Scott Jordan

Chris Ryle's book, *American Sniper: The Autobiography of the Most Lethal Sniper in U.S. History* is published Harper Collins Publishers, New York, 2012. The 'Laws of Americana' can be found in Ziauddin Sardar and Merryl Wyn Davies, *American Dream, Global Nightmare* (Cambridge: Icon Books Ltd., 2004) p 20-26.

On postnormal times, see Ziauddin Sardar, 'Welcome to Postnormal Times' Futures 42 (5): 435–44 (2010) and 'Postnormal Times Revisited', Futures 67 (2) 26-39 (2015); and Ziauddin Sardar and John Sweeney, 'The Three Tomorrows of Postnormal Times', *Futures* (75 (2016) 1-13).

Last Word: On Happy Muslims by Samia Rahman

Various comments on Happy Muslims video can be found at:
Raana Bokhari, To Be HappyMuslim# Or Not to Be: allegralaboratory.net/
to-be-happy-muslim-or-not-to-be-anthroislam/
Adam Deen, Happy Muslims, Angry Puritanical Muslims: adamdeen.
com/2014/04/18/happy-muslims-angry-puritanical-muslims/
H A Hellyer, To be A Happy Muslim or Not, That is the Question: english.
alarabiya.net/en/views/news/world/2014/04/21/To-be-a-Happy-British-
Muslim-or-not-that-is-the-question.html
Slavoj Zizek comments on happiness can be accessed at:
www.theguardian.com/lifeandstyle/2008/aug/09/slavoj.zizek
www.theguardian.com/books/live/2014/oct/06/slavoj-zizek-webchat-abs
olute-recoil

CONTRIBUTORS

Talat Ahmed is a lecturer in South Asian History at the University of Edinburgh ● **Anne Alexander** is an editor of *Middle East Solidarity* magazine and co-author of *Bread, Freedom, Social Justice: Workers and the Egyptian Revolution* ● **Raza Ali** runs a book club for London-based Muslims ● **Elma Berisha** is a translator and works for the Asian Institute of Finance, Kuala Lumpur, Malaysia ● **Andrew Brown** is a leader writer and editorial board Member at the *Guardian* and former editor for the Belief section of Comment is Free ● **Ivan Carromero Manzano**, who divides his time between Madrid and London, is a visual artist specialising in photography and the comic book form ● **Navid Hamzavi** is an award-wining Iranian writer; his debut collection of short stories, *Rag-and-Bone Man*, published in 2010, was severely censored by the Iranian Ministry of Cultural and Islamic Guidance ● **Ghassan Hassan** is a Palestinian poet ● **Sunny Hundal** is a journalist, commentator, founder of the political blog Liberal Conspiracy, and author of *India Dishonoured* ● **Rahul Jayaram,** who lectures at the Jindal School of Liberal Arts & Humanities, India, is hard at work on a book on the lives of Asian workers in the Gulf ● **C Scott Jordan** works at the Asian World Centre, Creighton University, Omaha, and is a Research Fellow at the Centre for Postnormal Policy and Futures Studies, East West University, Chicago ● **Naima Khan,** a writer and broadcaster, produces and presents Shamaj, a weekly panel discussion show for Betar Bangla Radio ● **Benedikt Koehler** is a historian and former banker and the author of *Early Islam and the Birth of Capitalism* ● **S Parvez Manzoor** is a Sweden-based Muslim writer and thinker ● **Farouk Peru** is a Malay academic and Qur'anic scholar based in London ● **Samia Rahman** is the deputy director of the Muslim Institute ● **Jerry Ravetz** is a renowned philosopher of science and co-founder of the theory of 'postnormal science' ● **Shanon Shah** is still happy that he now has a doctorate in the sociology of religion from King's College London ● **Gordon Blaine Steffey** holds the Barbara Boyle Lemon '57 and William J. Lemon chair in Religious Studies at Randolph College, Lynchburg, Virginia ● **John A Sweeney** is a futurist and deputy director, Centre for Postnormal Policy and Futures Studies, East West University, Chicago ● **Medina Whiteman** is a writer, musician and translator ● **Samir Younés** is Professor of Architecture at the University of Notre Dame.